Francis X. Walter, at home in Sewanee, Tennessee, 2007

FROM PREACHING TO MEDDLING

A White Minister in the Civil Rights Movement

FRANCIS X. WALTER

FOREWORD BY STEVE SUITTS

NewSouth Books

Montgomery

NewSouth Books
105 S. Court Street
Montgomery, AL 36104

Publisher's Cataloging-in-Publication Data

Names: Walter, Francis X., author.
Title: From preaching to meddling: A white minister in the civil rights movement /
Francis X. Walter ; foreword by Steve Suitts.
Description: Montgomery : NewSouth Books [2021]. | Includes bibliographical
references and index.
Identifiers: LCCN 2020948951 | ISBN 9781588383907 (hardcover) | ISBN
9781588383914 (ebook).
Subjects: Walter, Francis X., 1932– . | White civil rights workers—Alabama—
Biography. | Religious leaders—Civil rights movement—Biography. | Civil rights
movement—History—United States. | 20th century—History—United States. |
South—History—United States. | Alabama—History—United States. I. Title.

Design by Randall Williams

Printed in the United States of America by Sheridan

*The Black Belt, defined by its dark, rich soil, stretches across central
Alabama. It was the heart of the cotton belt. It was and is a place of great
beauty, of extreme wealth and grinding poverty, of pain and joy. Here we
take our stand, listening to the past, looking to the future.*

To my mother, Martha Marsh Walter, pianist, outboard motor racer, mother, wife, fighter of racism.

And to my wife, Faye, a wise woman who never stops loving once she starts.

Contents

Foreword

BY STEVE SUITTS

Francis Walter was my first boss more than fifty years ago when he was director of the Selma Inter-Religious Project, an organization that began as one white Southern man's mission of faith and became an interracial, multipronged catalyst for ending white supremacy in the Black Belt of the Deep South. My job interview ended with Francis stating, "I'll be glad to hire you, but we don't have any money to pay you a salary." It was an offer I luckily could not refuse.

Looking back, I am startled by the fact that Francis was my boss for no more than thirteen months before he resigned and moved from Tuscaloosa to Birmingham to accept a pastorate. The impact Francis had as a person and as a leader on me—and on others who worked with him—has been so enduring that I find it hard to accept that our days working together out of an old boardinghouse represent little more than a year of my life.

It is not that Francis has a larger-than-life Southern personality. I have had those friends, too. Quite the opposite, as this memoir illuminates, it is Francis's humility, his gentle, if subversive, humor, and his disarming honesty about himself and others that has made a permanent impression on those who have come to know him.

I knew very little about Francis's life before the 1960s and Selma Project, and, as a twenty-two-year-old, I was not actively interested in his past when we worked together. I should have been—as these pages prove. The stories of

Francis's life before the Selma Project are rich and fascinating, whether about his immediate and extended family members, some of whom have helped to give the word "character" a special Southern meaning, or about his awakening into the wider world as he grew up around Alabama's Mobile Bay, went off to Sewanee (today, the University of the South), and tried to become a good Episcopal priest navigating how to avoid condoning the racism and white supremacy that most of his extended family and most of his Southern congregants believed were their God-given right.

His recollections are at times funny, baffling, and heart-saddening, but always relentlessly honest. Francis writes in a gentle, intimate style that encourages us readers to believe that he has written these recollections only for us and Memoria, his semi-reliable muse. In fact, they comprise the many dimensions of a white boy growing up and coming of age in the heat of Alabama racism amid a confluence of interracial and inter-ethnic diversity.

I was surprised to discover that Francis's family does not fit neatly into the traditional white South's social hierarchy. They were on hard times when he arrived in this world, but, as he grew up, they included a bevy of elderly women whose heritage provided the family some claim and access to Mobile's higher white society. His life as a boy and young man around Mobile Bay was not in many ways anything like the rest of Alabama, except, of course, on matters of race.

Race and racism were the central organizing themes of both the world in which Francis emerged and his own journey through it. His abiding Christian faith and his many years as pastor evidently caused him to question his own motives and actions at several junctures in his life—at moments to find almost as much fault in his own shortcomings as with those who held segregation dear. But, there is never a doubt in his actions and thoughts of rejecting the wrongs of the South's system of white supremacy. It was not for him a question of what to believe. It was a lifetime of questions about how to live out what he believed. You will find few who tell this story so honestly, so well.

This memoir includes the dramatic events and experiences in Alabama that moved him as a Southern white minister from pastoring (and pestering) segregationists, including Alabama's own Episcopal Bishop, to agitating for and supporting black and white community leaders in the work of challenging segregation and economic injustice. These events also were some of the defining moments of the civil rights movement of the 1960s. But, Francis never—from the first pages to the last—attempts to overstate his role and his place. No, he seems truly unaware in his telling of how significant his example was, then and later, for young white Alabamians who wanted to find a constructive role in deconstructing racism and making the South better for all people.

Francis's mischievous muse helped him write a profound, personal tale, revealing so much of himself and the interracial but separate South of his day, In so doing, this memoir is one of the best, enduring examples of a Southerner whose conscience and actions remain a meaningful guide to anyone of any race or ethnicity wishing to combine soul-honest reflection and intentional action for change today. This book is both an understanding of and undertaking in the collective journey toward realizing a South and nation that Dr. Martin Luther King Jr. and Congressman John Lewis always envisioned as "the beloved community." It is a journey worth your joining.

Steve Suitts is an adjunct at the Institute for Liberal Arts of Emory University and author of Hugo Black of Alabama. *Steve began his career as a staff member of the Selma Project, then was founding director of the Alabama Civil Liberties Union, executive director of the Southern Regional Council, and vice president of the Southern Education Foundation. In recent years he has been chief strategist for Better Schools Better Jobs, a Mississippi-based education advocacy project of the New Venture Fund.*

FROM PREACHING TO MEDDLING

Invocation

Memoria, help!

Undependable friend, yet to go off with you is bliss. This is why I tell your stories, even when my hearers look at their watches.

About this memoir: stop hiding things from me! Then pulling them out when I'm without pen and paper.

Another thing—stop improving, making me a little sun around which the past revolves; the man who gave a perfect put-down fifty years ago, the one who saw the lie. Who nursed a thing to bear fruit. The one who got it done.

You know my faults. You know the small white-man part I played in the movement of thousands.

1. Four Times with Dr. King

When people hear I was in the racial justice struggles of more than a half century ago—if they have any interest—they will often ask three questions:

"Did you ever meet Dr. King?"

"Were you ever in jail?"

"Did you ever get shot at/beat up?"

The short answers to those questions are that I was with Dr. King, close up, four times. I was jailed once; it was up North and only for about an hour. It hardly counts, but I will tell it anyway. I was never shot or beat up but I believe I was close to being shot at by a white man called "One-Eyed Jack."

The second time I was with Dr. King was a month after I started representing religious groups in Selma after the voting rights march. The meeting was an SCLC (Southern Christian Leadership Conference) planning session held November 5, 1965, in Atlanta. There I began my alphabet-soup learning process. Present were Dr. King, Ralph Abernathy, Andrew Young, and others of SCLC; an ESCRU (Episcopal Society for Cultural and Racial Unity) staffer, the Reverend Henri Stines; John Lewis and another member of SNCC (Student Nonviolent Coordinating Committee). The Reverend Bruce Hanson of the NCCC (National Council of Churches of Christ) flew down from New York. Bruce was the reason for my having the job that got me to this meeting toting a new set of letters: SIP (Selma Inter-Religious Project).

The meeting was dominated by Chuck Morgan, author of *A Time to Speak* and lately chased out of Birmingham's legal fraternity. He then joined the ACLU's southern office in Atlanta. Chuck gave cautionary examples of subtle and not so subtle man-traps awaiting us in the Southern administration of justice.

The third time I met with King and his lieutenants was at SCLC headquarters in Atlanta. King was at the table, hunched, silent, almost asleep from exhaustion. The dynamic was for one part of his divided staff to prevail over the other on whether to have a march. The issue was how to address the murder of Jimmie Lee Jackson in Marion, Alabama, by an Alabama state trooper. They were not easy on King. Hosea Williams pushed for the march on grounds of what was right and needed; Andrew Young was against it, on grounds that the logistics were impossible to meet. On went the pressure on their leader until, with a gesture or a weary word, Dr. King ended it. We wouldn't.

When was this meeting? For references I have my journal; the *Liturgical Desk Calendar, Episcopal* (I saved them from 1961 to 2010); pocket calendars; the *SIP Newsletter* (1965–72); and the work of historians. But all are silent on the date.

I did not try to speak to Dr. King at the end of the meeting. First, out of consideration of his exhaustion, then out of my own peculiar aversion to greeting celebrated people. But I'd heard years before that he knew who I was. How was that? Carl Braden, that long-haul fighter for racial justice, told me in 1960 of chatting with King about me, wishing to note a fresh supportive white face in Alabama. King was mystified—"Francis Walter for integration!"

His startled reaction was because the only man I ever knew to share my name was the virulent, race-baiting U.S. congressman and chair of the House Un-American Activities Committee in the 1950s. He represented Pennsylvania in the U.S. House of Representatives and sponsored the McCarran–Walter Act of 1952. No, Carl told Dr. King, there was another, younger, better Francis Walter, a minister now in Eufaula, Alabama.

There was a much earlier proximity to King. That would be the first meeting. At Christmas of 1954 I was home in Mobile from the School of Theology at the University of the South in Sewanee, Tennessee. This young black pastor I'd heard of had accepted the invitation of the Mobile black community to give the Emancipation Day address on New Year's Day 1955. King was then early in his ministry in Montgomery. He had accepted the call to Dexter Avenue Baptist Church in April 1954, reserving the right to travel to Boston from time to time to finish his doctoral dissertation. May 17, 1954, the Supreme Court handed down the judgment in *Brown v. Board of Education*. On September 5, 1954, King preached his first sermon at Dexter as pastor. In it he proposed restructuring the church to turn it to service and to put him firmly in control of all levers of power. The notion staggered entrenched church leaders; like it or not, they had selected a powerful and extraordinary man as their pastor. In *Parting the Waters*, author Taylor Branch quotes from a letter sent to King by his father, a minister in Atlanta: "... you are becoming very popular ... you must be very much in prayer. Persons like yourself are the ones the devil turns all his forces aloose to destroy." The letter is dated December 2, 1954.

When King appeared as the Emancipation Day orator on January 1, 1955, he was twenty-five years old; I was twenty-three. Two months and a day later, a black high school student, Claudette Colvin, refused to give up her seat to a white person on a Montgomery municipal bus and was arrested. Nine months after that, Rosa Parks was arrested under almost the same circumstances. Given Colvin's brassy and profane responses to the police, and her young age, the committee representing the black community chose not to use her spontaneous action to challenge the segregated seating ordinance. King was on that committee, putting into practice the forces of justice and love he delineated in his Emancipation Day address in Mobile. Rosa Parks's later case was, of course, different, was handled differently, and history was changed.

But all that was still in King's and our future when I found myself seated on a stage inches behind him as he spoke on January 1, 1955. It was on this wise, as St. Luke might put it: My sister Patricia, then fifteen, was home so I asked if she'd like to go. She agreed. I called my older cousin-in-law, Dick Wells. Dick was my great-aunt Ida Bolivia's eldest daughter's husband. We categorized him as bright and charming but a Yankee from New York. He was the only adult white person in Mobile I knew who might agree to go. I figured my sister had not a clue, but I wanted her to start thinking about our racial structures. Two down. Now I had the courage to ask my girlfriend, Mary Anne McPherson. Not courage because of it being a black event, but simply because I was a coward at asking for dates—if this could be called a date. Mary Anne said yes.

We four arrived at the International Longshoreman's Union Hall on New Year's Day. Years later, one of Mobile's black city council members confirmed the date and location for me; he reported the hall was still standing. In fact, it is now on the National Register of Historic Places. When I told him we were there that 1955 day, he yelped, "Get out!" At the entrance we saw two things: the hall was packed, and we were the only white people. Blocked by the crush, we stood outside the entrance along with others trying to get in. Not for long. We were bulldozed up the center aisle by ushers and found ourselves on the stage in four chairs seated directly behind the speaker's podium. Whites experienced these gifts of hospitality over and over in black churches and mass meetings in movement days. I would be flushed with gratitude and shame, accepting this welcome. Shame for the icy toleration or outright rejection when the color of hosts and guests was swapped, gratitude for the welcome because of my color.

The fourth time I saw Dr. King was in Atlanta, in a coffin in a poor farmer's wagon pulled by two mules. How hard it had been, a close thing, for his adjutants to locate mules and a wagon far beyond Atlanta's sprawl. How fitting for them to honor, to remember in this way, the rural poor in their thousands, so invisible to great Atlanta, yet the vanguard of the agape army. The day before the funeral procession, I passed through Alberta, in Wilcox County, Alabama, home of the Freedom Quilting Bee Cooperative (FQB), to pick up Mr. Eugene Witherspoon. He carried with him a king-size Double Star quilt for Mrs. King

*Estelle and Ernest
Witherspoon, Freedom
Quilting Bee stalwarts.*

from members of the Bee. The stars were as varied and brilliant as Joseph's coat. The fabrics came from New York, North Carolina, Georgia, from white people and black people. Mr. Witherspoon's older brother, Nero, joined us as we proceeded to Atlanta. My desk calendar tells me this was April 8, 1968.

Mr. Witherspoon was the husband of Estelle Witherspoon, the manager of the FQB. He was a respected movement leader in a county where previous to the movement not one black person had been registered to vote, though the black population was far larger than the white. The Black Belt counties of Alabama, so named for their dark rich soil suited for growing cotton, had been the center of slavery; after emancipation, the counties' population has remained 70 to 80 percent black to this day.

Mr. Witherspoon's brother's name puzzled me when we first met. Then I recalled from books read to me as a child that some owners of enslaved Africans, proud of their smattering of Latin, would give their chattel names like Nero, Caesar, Pompey, or Cicero as a joke. Nero Witherspoon was of the wrong generation to have been enslaved, so he was surely named after a beloved forebear. I should have known about such names right off; after all, Uncle Remus was the namesake of a founder of Rome. I cringe to think of the scene at the font when Episcopalian masters would give answer to "Name this Child." Did the priest smirk as he said, "Nero, I baptize thee in the name of the Father, and of the Son, and of the Holy Ghost. Amen."

Traffic in Atlanta miraculously opened up, allowing us to slip close to the processional route. We stood on a little rise, looking down. Mourners in the march passed in silence and passed and passed and passed. Then out of that silence came the sound of iron-banded wheels rattling and the creak of harness, and we saw Dr. King's lieutenants circling the wagon with their hands on the rickety sideboards as I had once seen them around him at a table. Then the Kennedys, Robert and Edward, enveloped by their retinue of high-intelligence, high-efficiency, fast-talking young white men. I had known them close up when black Alabama farmers and I lobbied Washington to fund an Office of Economic Opportunity application for a Black Belt farmers' cooperative. Back then it had amused me when we went from the Kennedy offices to that of Senator Lister Hill of Alabama. Kennedy's: intense listening, up-close faces, telephone numbers traded like stock sales. Then off to Senator Lister Hill who favored in his offices one or two middle-aged white belles in flowered dresses (so Memoria says), possibly not so high on IQ but oozing grace and welcome to our weary band of first-time lobbyists. After the dispensation of enough charm to pacify a bobcat, a lady called Senator Hill out of his inner chamber. I was standing just outside in the hall. The black delegation was ahead, filling the room. Hill craned his neck over the black entourage to nervously address me directly, "What do you all want?"

"Ask them," I said.

And he wasn't even one of the all-bad Southern senators.

Later, I went to Greensboro to a memorial service. I had not wanted to say anything but found myself standing again in the pulpit from which I had, three years earlier, struggled to speak of the murder of Jonathan Daniels. Hate had forced us together again to celebrate and memorialize Love. After the preacher was introduced, a man came to the pulpit and stood. With many, I expected he was the speaker. But then he began to sing King's favorite, the hymn "Precious Lord." I was seated directly behind him as I had been behind King once, such a short time before. His voice was high and it soared. It made the church, packed and now very hot in our Southern spring, seem bigger, higher, cooler. Able to receive now our grief, tension, love, guilt, and wonder. The man's back quivered before me. I thought how his muscles must be working. Our tears could come now. There was release like breath held too long but something was given too. The voice and the flowing out allowed a flowing in. Since I am a Christian, I named it the Spirit of God. The effect was to know, to be able to take, as if it were a material object: Love. The Love then was everything that is, bigger than hate or death, a force that binds, casts out fear, that sharpens, does not diminish, one's sense of tragedy, injustice, and hypocrisy, that gives courage, not ease. Our souls infused with Love stand, turn on these demons, and see them diminished and without power.

2. *Boss Hague Pols Teach Seminar*

"Were you ever in jail?" they ask. I must backtrack to answer.

Maybe jail time should have followed for my pastoral crimes. But that wasn't what got me in a cell. We had a "Summer Intern Program" at Grace Church in Jersey City, New Jersey, to which I had become the chaplain. It was partly a learn-by-doing workshop for community organizing. Young adults and teens were selected from the parish and the country. The parish kids were picked from our high school youth group; the outsiders, generally not poor, boarded with parishioners. Maybe we totaled fifteen when I directed the program in 1963. The program was to be both learning and direct action.

One delightful seminar used old pols from the Boss Hague Machine, who gleefully explained how to run an efficient, non-murderous, corrupt political machine. The Hague Machine even had its own, small, pet opposition party—on the payroll. The guys told us it wouldn't look right for there to be no opposition, election after election. They were sad that discipline was starting to slip under Boss Kenny. It showed that even then the Kenny machine was losing out to the Italians.

And yes, the machine proved to our satisfaction that it did deliver decent social services—except to those who tried to buck it.

The pols glowed as they explained how, in their prime, they had the city organized: first by precinct, then by blocks, then by single blocks, then tenements, then each family in a tenement. From a hierarchy of informers, they knew who needed coal, a job, welfare, a doctor bill paid, an arrest fixed. They also knew who wouldn't be getting any of these services. One old man was proud of how the Hague Machine got out the vote. An intern asked if he brought voters to the polls by blocks. Our lecturer thought that was funny, "No. Family by family. They were marched in by party workers at exactly the time stated. To the minute. Nice and smooth."

"Why did people cooperate?" someone asked.

"Scared," the old pols said. "We'd look at their signatures when they registered to vote, and then when they came to vote their names would be all shaky." If they got a tip that a few malcontents were headed to the polling station, say at 2:30, one solution was to tangle the levers in the booths with rubber bands.

"You'd be surprised," they told us, "how many people will come out of a booth like that before anybody complains."

Up a ways from Grace was St. John's, also following an inner-city model of ministry. It, too, had an intern program. Its rector, Father Bob Castle (later to make it to minor stardom in the 1992 movie *Cousin Bobby*, directed by his relative, Jonathan Demme), suggested we have a joint venture. Bob was more of a civic crusader than I, but the scheme was a righteous one, easy to buy into.

This was the issue: A chunk of the city had been condemned for urban renewal. People were moved out; then nothing happened. There sat derelict buildings, broken glass and mattresses carpeting the streets, no security. The city stalled on redevelopment. The property had become the haunt of vandals, drug addicts, and—our concern—bored kids.

St. John's had tried letters, meetings; nothing worked. Phase two was to load a truck with filth from the site and dump it on the plaza in front of City Hall. We couldn't get up the nerve to dump it *in* City Hall; we should have. The two intern groups notified the press—maybe the mayor, I can't recall—why and when we would do it. We divided the interns into demonstrators and observers. Castle and I chose to be demonstrator/dumpers. The observers were to jot notes, watch for police harassment, and be ready to testify in court.

Somebody asked the young CBS newsman Mike Wallace to come over from New York, and he did! The local media were invited, and we had mimeographed handouts prepared. No one even thought to bring a camera. Lord! What we could have done with cell phone cameras and Twitter!

The filth was flawlessly dumped near the City Hall steps. Mike Wallace was doing his job reporting; the cops doing theirs arresting. I was sorry the cops were so polite. One little mistake occurred that proves it is impossible to control the media. The trash was near a statue commemorating soldiers of some conflict. The *Jersey City Journal* wrote how we intended to dishonor our boys who had served, and so on.

We were loaded up, booked, fingerprinted, and locked in a cell with impassive professionalism. The Bishop of Newark, Leland Stark, was notified, and lawyer Raymond Brown appeared to bail us out. Ray and his family were members of Grace Church, and Ray had the distinction of being the president of the city's NAACP chapter.

Bob knew imprisonment would be brief, so right off he led us in songs sung by the sit-in and Freedom Rider folks. We sang loudly, but no one shut us up or even walked by the cell. It had a touch of the silly. Not a scratch on anyone, knew we'd be out soon, not even a frown on a cop's face, no mob outside. Yet we sang and meant it. Sang in solidarity with those who had truly suffered or died. I hope we were singing with them, not because we thought we were like them. Either way, though, it is such things that build a movement.

My reaction was based on privilege, thinking myself above those cops, those Italian and Irish venal pols. I was a polite Southerner, of northern European stock, educated, and soft-spoken. Not that I thought this; it was in my bones. So I didn't see that some of us were scared. I wasn't. The strawberry blond from Grapevine, Texas, whose father was a priest wasn't. The big black guy from North Carolina, who told us he was a Freedom Rider, wasn't. The well-off white Quaker interns weren't. More than not scared, I was contemptuous. The mayor and his minions were beneath me. Well, that's my default position for anyone in authority. It dawned on me later that I was born on the day after the Winter Solstice, the sun overcoming the darkness. It was fun to tell family the sun did it for me. So what was jail?

For more immediate help, we had Bishop Leland Stark and Suffragan Bishop George Rath on our side, a hell-raising black lawyer, and across the Hudson, a seminary rooting for us. Have I made clear my assumption that I was from a privileged WASP nest and was to some degree flying around doing good without much comprehension of the deepest needs of the people to whom I was assigned?

Forgive me, Lord; I know you have. But I didn't respond to the fear in my Grace Church black kids who were arrested. They knew they'd pay with redoubled harassment out on the street. After the trial, when we all hit the street, I recall how the police started hassling the Grace Church kids. I do recall how scared they looked, dumped out in front of the courthouse. I saw, but I didn't see. I don't recall ever seeking any of them out to talk about it.

The trial was weeks later. Entering the court, Ray told us we had been assigned to Jersey City's crazy judge: a man of Italian stock given to screaming angry paranoid riffs from the bench. Look for fireworks, Ray warned. Until the trial we didn't know the charges—littering. I suspect Ray and the city attorney made a deal. Ray told us to plead guilty to littering and pay a small fine with the understanding our convictions would disappear from the record after folks forgot about it. I've not checked to see if this happened so I still get a tiny rebellious thrill if I put "No" in a box asking if I've ever been convicted of anything.

The lesson I took away from the jail cell was that the privilege we white folks carry around may hide itself from us or get stamped down, but it never goes away and is completely obvious to people of color.

The crazy Italian judge yelled out examples of the enduring yet limited store of arguments used to keep people down. He focused his rage on the redheaded Texan, the big, gentle Carolina Freedom Rider (his name was Herman Harris), and me, the Alabama priest. He blistered us. He yelled that the colored people of Jersey City were valued citizens, all happy and peaceful. They appreciated having segregated George Washington Carver Housing to live in (trash and the wasteland of gutted buildings was not mentioned). These colored kids standing before him were the hapless dupes of us subversives. As he performed, the city attorney and Ray laid low.

Sample reconstructed rant: "I know what you're doing! Our city is full of happy, law-abiding colored people. They're happy! But you, you OUTSIDE SOUTHERN AGITATORS! You come up here and get our colored people all worked up!" All the words may not be right except OUTSIDE SOUTHERN AGITATORS! Who could forget that?

I was standing in the dock, enjoying my label, until I was dimly aware of our Grace Church kids. They were hang-dog scared, a dangerous state to be in when being cool was their main means of survival. Would they make it home or to school tomorrow without bad things happening to them?

3. *Did You Ever Get Shot at or Beat up? Part II*

In August 1965, I was in Selma to meet with Jonathan Daniels, a seminarian from the Episcopal Theological School in Cambridge, Massachusetts. The plan was for Jonathan to brief me before returning to Cambridge. I was to take over some of the things he was doing. In one way I was replacing him, but with the backing of an interfaith group and the promise of a salary. The briefing did not happen. On August 20, 1965, Jonathan was murdered, and a young Roman Catholic priest, Richard Morrisroe, was horribly wounded. The meeting was to have been the day before, August 19.

But on August 15, Jon and other peaceful demonstrators were arrested in Fort Deposit, Lowndes County, Alabama, then jailed. Because of the arrest, I was met in Selma instead by the Reverend Henri Stines, the associate director of the Episcopal Society for Cultural and Racial Unity. This unofficial group, ESCRU, was a prick to the lethargic forces of racial change in the Episcopal Church—"Prick," a goad, as in the King James Version of Acts 9:15 where Jesus says to Paul, "It is hard for thee to kick against the pricks."

On August 19, Father Stines and I visited Jonathan and his companions in jail at Hayneville, the Lowndes county seat. Jon refused the bail money

ESCRU telegraphed from its Atlanta office. Unless all could be bailed out, he would not be bailed out. We returned to the SNCC office in Selma where efforts to raise the bail money were in play but failed.

The next day, August 20, 1965, county officials unexpectedly released the prisoners. Within an hour Jonathan was dead, and Father Morrisroe was near death. Ruby Sales, a young black woman, shielded by Jonathan's body, had been spared. I had told myself I was going to Selma to decide about a job. After talking with Jon, I'd leave Selma and take a day or two to decide. Actually, I already knew I'd accept. But plans changed. I remained in Selma to act as a liaison between the local black movement leaders and ESCRU officially, and unofficially for the national Episcopal Church, or more accurately, that part of the church that saw Jon as a witness for the unity of Christ's Body.

The movement now had another martyr to mourn. In Selma a national memorial was taking shape that would be held at Brown Chapel AME Church, but there were to be similar services in every movement church in the Alabama Black Belt. My wife, Betty, drove down to join me. We hunkered down with a telephone in a room in the black-owned Torch Motel—behind the Methodist Children's Home in Selma.

One wrenching task was calling Episcopal priests in the surrounding Black Belt to give the date, time, and place of the main memorial service in Selma and then specifically to ask them to come. I knew all of them from growing up in the diocese. The Reverend John Morris, the founder and director of ESCRU, asked me to do it. One of the reasons was to give them no excuse to plead ignorance. Then ESCRU could expose their absence to the press, for we had little faith they would attend.

If this was disingenuous, we believed it was also an occasion of grace for them, a "crisis" in the sense of the original Greek: a moment of discernment. I tried to make the calls factual, even-tempered, and businesslike.

For half a century I've lived with my confused feelings during those calls: righteous vindictiveness, anger, sorrow, compassion for them, and shame at myself. I enjoyed sticking it to them, being the agent of a moral crisis. I believed that if they came, some might have to resign their cures. For some, even if they didn't come, it might awaken and wound their consciences. They were pastors to the birthplaces of slavery and Jim Crow. What had they done about it?

Segregation was the practice in Alabama and in white Episcopal churches. It was a sin against the oneness of the Body of Christ. Each Sunday we voiced our belief in the Church as One, Holy, Catholic, and Apostolic. Jon gave his life for that Oneness, as his posthumous writings show. Knowing that justified me.

Another part of me was strong to say: who was I to create a moral crisis for these men? The racist sins of my church were eating me up. But did I have the right to judge them by my zeal? I did force them to choose and have nursed a guilty feeling ever since. Writing about it now has unexpectedly given me an insight. Instead of masking my feelings and judgments, I could have admitted my anger at them and also my compassion riding just under the anger. Whadda ya know, you can do both.

Such as:

Look, I'm angry. I'm angry at myself. I'm angry at you. I'm angry at the diocese for the part we have played in the murder of Jonathan. But I also care about you. This call forces you—I hope it forces you—into a bind. I'm doing this but I feel bad about it. What right do I have? I'm sorry, but I'm doing it anyway. Please forgive me. Please pray for me. I promise to pray for you.

Something like that and I'd have rested easier all these years.

It was a privilege, having just arrived, to be invited to meetings at Brown Chapel to plan the black community's response. I was moved by the yearning of the local black leaders to use the attack on the two white ministers as a way to unite white and black Selma through an act of common mourning. What better, they thought, than to hold the service at St. Paul's Episcopal Church in white Selma, the place where Jon regularly worshipped? Jon's seminary dean, John Coburn, was coming, as was his bishop, the Right Reverend Charles F. Hall of New Hampshire. The planning group was sure that St. Paul's would agree; this was based on the often mistaken idea: "If this can't bring us together, nothing can."

I was asked to contact the rector, the Reverend Frank Mathews, which I did from my motel telephone. I had known Frank for years. Fresh from the planning meeting, I was infected by this invitation to unity by the black leaders. Frank was shocked that I would float such an idea. He used a bizarre comparison to the effect that surely I knew what a conservative congregation he led, worse than all the other white mainline downtown churches. He had pushed and pushed for air conditioning in St. Paul's like the other churches were getting and couldn't get it done until every other church around him had it. I forgave him the comparison, given the stress we were both under. I recall he also asked if I didn't know there were police sharpshooters on the roofs of downtown buildings close to the church—one of many rumors. He later told Charles Eagles, the author of *Outside Agitator: Jon Daniels and the Civil Rights Movement in Alabama,* "Tensions were at the breaking point . . . etc."

We will never know whether a joint service at St. Paul's would have calmed those supposed tensions. We do know that when the memorial was held at Brown Chapel, neither Frank nor either of Alabama's bishops attended. As far as I know, only two lay members of the entire Episcopal diocese of Alabama were present: William E. Hood, a close friend of mine, and Mattilene Lawrence, whom I was blessed to have years later as a member of St. Andrew's Church in Birmingham while I was rector.

When I reported the refusal of St. Paul's to the planning group at Brown Chapel, it was seconded by Wilson Baker, Selma's public safety director. Baker and I were the only whites at the meeting. I was surprised at the respect shown Baker by those whose goals he had so often thwarted. His opposition was often graphic: black citizens bottled up in "their" part of Selma, who often formed a line of demonstrators facing Baker and his police. However, Baker was "good cop" to the histrionic sheriff of Dallas County, Jim Clark. They disliked (hated?) each other. Baker's strategy was to cool things off, the sheriff's to heat things up. We all recall the film clips of Clark assaulting a woman waiting in line to register to vote at the county courthouse. Less seen today are the images of Sheriff Clark's mounted posse parading about Selma with massed Confederate battle flags.

The respect in that room for Baker came partly from his being intelligent, morally haunted, and always striving to use the least means to gain his ends—ends which still were directly opposed to those of the movement. Taylor Branch, in *At Canaan's Edge,* quotes a strung-out Baker speaking to journalists, just after announcing to a host of local and outsider movement supporters the murder of the Reverend James Reeb: "I'm a segregationist, but if I was a nigger I'd be doing just what they're doing."

The deep and almost pathetic black appreciation of Baker simply came from this: he met them on their turf, he sat down with them, he used courtesy titles, he listened, he gave reasons for his positions, and he was not angry or patronizing.

But, as we all know, it was Sheriff Clark, not Commissioner Baker, whose hateful intransigence ended up getting thousands registered to vote, opened the front doors of health and welfare departments, opened schools, county extension services, libraries, hospitals, and banks, and got blacks elected—even as Alabama sheriffs.

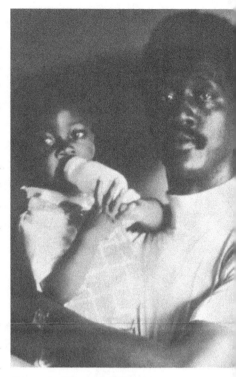

ESCRU director John Morris and I wanted to have representatives of the national Episcopal Church at every "mass meeting" memorial held for Jon in the Black Belt. It became obvious that this would have to involve me and other ESCRU staff. The Reverend Kim Driesbach, an associate director, joined me in Selma. I nominated myself to speak at St. Matthew's AME Church in Greensboro; Kim rode with me and I dropped him off

Thomas Gilmore of Greene County, here holding his son, was one of several blacks elected as county sheriffs after passage of the 1965 Voting Rights Act.

along the way to speak at Zion Methodist in Marion. In lieu of my conspicuous '50s model Mercedes 190D, I was driving my father-in-law's car, which Betty had driven down to Selma from Florence, Alabama. After dropping off Kim and driving alone in the dark to Greensboro, I thought not of the consequences to me of being shot, but that I would leave blood all over my father-in-law's upholstery. Then he would find out I was using his car for "civil rights."

It was quite dark when I found St. Matthew's on Morse Street. Because of all the cars already in front of the church, I parked on a cross street. As I walked up an incline, vestments slung over my shoulder, I noticed a brightly lit parsonage next door to the church. It looked to be an antebellum house—a raised or Creole cottage as we'd call it in Mobile, with its deep front porch, wide central hall, a solid door with side and upper lights, and some fresh bullet holes near the door. Obviously, it had once been a white church, now in a black neighborhood. A few black guys on the porch called down, "Come on in here, Rev"—as in "rev up your motor."

The central hall was lit and there were a lot more men inside. When one is out of one's world, anything can look odd but one imagines it's probably normal in this other place. So I didn't consider why so many adult black males were milling about in a preacher's house. I headed for a room off the central hall to vest. "Rev, put your robes on in here. We don't want you to get shot through a winder."

Six years before this, in my first church in Eufaula, Alabama, I'd signaled that I'd like to meet some local black ministers. Same thing happened, except no bullet holes. Same beautiful old raised cottage in "the colored part of town," same lit central hall and darkened rooms to left and right. In that meeting I was invited by my black hosts to sit in the central hall lit by one bulb, while the four rooms around us remained dark and shuttered. A classic floor plan, great for conspiring.

The guys in the Greensboro parsonage told me that lately there'd been some shooting into the preacher's house, so caution was due. Then I noticed the shotguns leaning along the walls. After the service was over and people dispersed, I returned to the parsonage to get my gear off and say goodbye to as jovial and self-possessed a bunch of black guys as I'd ever seen.

The cross street where my father-in-law's car was parked was at the bottom of a little hill, no street lights. There was a car parked nearby that I didn't remember being there earlier. Its windows were down against the hot August night. As I passed it I heard that reptilian murmur used so effectively by mean, sorry, white Southern males. It was not a threat, only a description: "You God-damned son-of-a-bitch." I went slowly back up Morse Street to the parsonage and reported what had happened. The guys thought it was hilarious, "Thass ole One-Eyed Jack, Rev. He's the one shot up the preacher's porch."

This was my first encounter with the Deacons for Defense and

Justice—Greensboro unit. The Deacons were prepared to die for Dr. King but had modified his nonviolent theories. The Deacons were not interested in recognition in or out of movement circles. They were interested in rural blacks' safety while meeting and organizing, and this they ensured by standing guard out in the shadows at many a meeting.

A little huddle, then, "You gonna follow us out of town, Rev. When we get out on the road, you see any headlights behind you, blink your lights. We'll drop back and cover you. If nothing happens we'll pull on around and lead again. We've called Marion. The Marion brothers will swap off with us when you pick up the other preacher. They'll get you back to Selma. Lately the Klan's been on the highways at night."

As we set out, I recognized Ben "Sunshine" Owens, a great and well-known hero of the movement, never far from Dr. King's side. Owens was the architect and manager of SCLC's Southern Voter Rights Campaign. What was he doing in Greensboro? He and the Deacons were in a dusty station wagon leading me out of town. As I settled in behind them on State Highway 14, I thought I saw two shotgun barrels angling up from the lowered rear window. No. It was the handle of a lawnmower blending in with the gun barrels that I did see when a bump flicked my headlights up into the station wagon. I've not forgotten that image. I found it endearing to be protected by men too casual to remove a lawnmower from their station wagon before setting out on a potentially dangerous mission.

At Zion Methodist in Marion, I met up with Kim and the relief Deacons team, we all shook hands, and I said goodbye to the Greensboro escort. Kim and I were delivered to Selma very late, but safe.

Ben Owens, 1968, in Selma as MLK speaks at Tabernacle Baptist. (Photo by Jim Peppler)

So the short answer to that third question, "Were you ever shot at (beat up)," would be NO. But to have written "NO" and been done with it would not have pulled One-Eyed Jack from the shadows or helped me enjoy State Road 14 again and ride with Sunshine Owens and the confident Deacons. Sunshine Owens was the organizational genius who operated the Voter Rights Campaign across the South, giving the franchise to thousands for the first time.

4. *Roots: Mobile and Mon Louis Island*

The Great Depression was grinding along, and my parents as a result were living with my grandfather, Franz Xaver "Pop" Walter, on Bayou Street in Mobile when I was born on December 22, 1932, a decent ten months after their marriage. My grandmother, Annie Luenberg Walter, had died shortly before my birth. Just after my birth, Pop lost his business, Walter Produce. So it was me, my parents, and Pop who, to survive financially, moved from Bayou Street to a rental house on Park Avenue off Spring Hill Avenue. Park Avenue had nothing of New York about it but referred to a pleasant open space of live oaks, azaleas, and camellias across from our house.

This was 1933 and no money. Daddy was part owner of a waterfront machine shop, but nothing was coming in. Pop had nickel-and-dime work as Mobile's last on-foot drummer. He had to be on foot because he never learned to drive. My father was driving Walter Produce trucks by age twelve, but he told me he couldn't teach Pop to drive because the hardheaded old German believed one should steer by aiming at distant objects and barrel on, ignoring the rest of the world. When he died in 1945, he was still walking, taking orders from a couple of waning downtown grocery stores—a kind former competitor, Warley Produce, had hired him.

My mother recalled telephoning Daddy at work to say that our water had been cut off. She was crying. She had no water for my formula. (I was born during a mean-spirited, clinical era that discouraged breastfeeding and dictated inflexible times for precisely calibrated bottles.) His shop on Commerce Street, Mobile Cylinder Grinding Company, was frequented by waterfront sages who provided advice, rumors, and opinions. He told her what Commerce Street was saying, "Fill the kid up till he runs over."

Mommee took the advice, but now there was no water. All over Mobile, the Water Works was shutting off meters for nonpayment. All over Mobile, people were heading to their meters with wrenches while compassionate Water Works men looked the other way. Daddy said he needn't come home; for her to walk out to the street with a wrench and turn the water back on.

Knowing them, I think he put it this gentle way to relieve her of shame: *Everybody's doing it. You can do it. We are like everybody else.* If so, it worked; they both became ardent New Dealers.

It was my mother's idea that it would be easier to make it if we moved where we could grow food. She found something even better, a place on Mobile Bay in a Creole community called Mon Louis Island. She argued that my father could commute eighteen miles to bring a little money home. The Creole men of Mon Louis fished and shrimped, so Daddy could barter his outboard and inboard motor repair skills to keep us in fish, crabs, and shrimp. Pop could garden and keep chickens.

All that happened.

They found what we called "The Camp" facing the bay just south of the Cut Off, where East Fowl River enters the bay. The property was acquired with a trade of my late grandmother Annie's "cut flower garden," which lay many blocks west of Bayou Street—Annie and her maid, Rebecca, would bring armloads of flowers home on the trolley. The owner of the bay property agreed to swap parcels of land. We moved in 1936. I was going on four.

Growing up there, the World's Fair could not have delighted me more than "The Camp": a log-strewn beach only steps out the front door, two tall kumquat trees on either side of the front gallery steps, an outhouse full of busy spiders, a shed of old and active wren nests. Inside, the mysterious kerosene-fueled kitchen stove with can-shaped burners one lifted up and down to regulate the heat. The stove brought the excitement of a massive kerosene truck right down our wooded driveway. Across its back, the truck had a row of nickel-plated spigots, and one called out to me one day. While the kerosene man and my mother were talking, I pulled the handle down. A flood of kerosene. I was not spanked but chastised; the memory is burned in. Fortunately, the truck didn't burn. The ice truck, too, livened our days, coming to replenish the icebox. Wasn't too many years ago I capitulated to the term "refrigerator," saying goodbye to "icebox." Icebox drips have been written of before, but so what: there is nothing as delightful as lying under a house, among the ant lion traps dotting the dust, anticipating each cold drip from the icebox drain to splash one's face.

My father, Francis Walter, right, showing off a cavalla (crevalle jack) caught off Mobile Bay in the late 1930s.

A while ago, science solved the mystery of predicting when a crab will shuck its shell. For a few precious hours after the molt, the crab ups its cash value—what, a hundredfold? It becomes a soft-shell crab fit for a coat of cracker meal and a lovely fry in butter.

But before science stepped in, my mother had a clever and doomed idea. The first thing she did was typical of intellectuals who need to ramp up before doing something hands-on. There is a line in a P. D. James mystery, *The Skull Beneath the Skin,* about a brass doorplate: "a fitting advertisement of irrational hope and ill-advised enterprise." Similarly, my mother went to print. I still have one of her books of receipt forms. "Walters' Crab Farm" it reads.

She and Daddy fenced in a crab pasture in the shallows fronting our house. They dumped in abundant hardshell crabs and waited for them to molt. The plan was to wade around daily to pick up the soft-shells. It took only a couple of squalls to destroy the corral. Our kind Creole neighbors said nothing.

Other ventures were more successful. Daddy set up a generator so we had electric lights. He ran a wire across the Summerlins' cornfield, a neighborly gift of electricity. This may have been a barter exchange for the labor of the Summerlin young men who helped him pile-drive down a well point. I well remember that job: a pine tree tripod, a pulley at its top, a rope, one end of which was attached to a great block of creosote wood scavenged from the beach, Daddy, Freddie, and Marshall pulling on the other end, the block slamming onto the pipe. The electric pump for the well was powered by the generator.

When we moved down to Mon Louis Island, my father asked how we were going to relate to this third race (Creoles): invite them into our house, sit on their galleries if asked? My mother told him we were the intruders in their community. We would treat them like ourselves. (She may have said "like white people.") So the electricity across the cornfield; Daddy fixing motors and never mentioning money; a washtub of mullet arriving on our back step; the freedom to fish from Joe Summerlin's wharf on Fowl River.

Daddy's electricity sharing brought down on him the wrath of the Alabama Power Company. It said it would sic the law on us. My folks said, "Do it." Nothing happened. Soon power poles ran on down to our end of the island. I suspect Roosevelt's Rural Electrification Administration had a hand in that.

Daddy's creativity was not all practical. He built an airboat. The hull was a Creole skiff with some sort of inboard engine and a big, handsome, mahogany propeller over the stern. Unlike such boats today, there was no metal cage around the prop. Daddy's approach to machinery was that you should have sense enough not to put your head or hands where they could get chopped off.

Before I came along, Daddy enjoyed airplane days. He flew surplus Jennys. He told me he once flew one close alongside one of America's great dirigibles, either the *Shenandoah* or the *Los Angeles,* and exchanged waves with a cook cooling off in an open doorway of its hull.

I long admired the propeller stored in the Commerce Street machine shop. He told me he got it from the Curtiss Flying Boat NC4 when it stopped in Mobile during a victory lap along the Gulf Coast in 1919. It had hopped, skipped, and jumped from the United States to Plymouth, England, May 8–31, 1919. The prop disappeared. I wish I had that beautiful object today. We shed memory and things the way we shed dead skin cells as we walk through life. Oh, well, we can't keep it all—dead skin or mahogany propellers.

Daddy plumbed the house and added a septic tank and bathroom, the door for which he found washed up on the beach. For our part, Pop and I used Joe Summerlin's wharf to catch eels to feed to the chickens. Pop told me if we were back in Germany we'd be eating them.

There is no wood as parched as the gray pine planks of an old wharf that has been baking in a Gulf Coast sun. One day Pop and I sat in that sun and still air, watching resin ooze out of the boards. Up rushed a cool wind from underneath a thunderhead. We sat in the sunshine, watching as widely spaced raindrops printed dark, silver-dollar-size circles rushing up the wharf toward us. I could have run between them. Then it was gone, sun again, calm, dark circles evaporating.

Besides seafood and eel-fortified eggs, we ate waterfowl and fried chicken. Daddy said he could walk any time out of the screened-in gallery and, with luck, shoot a duck or poule d'eau—North American coots, on arriving at the Gulf Coast, assume the more elegant name poule d'eau (pronounced *pooldoo*). They are slate-gray birds the size of small ducks, with chicken-like white bills. These birds do not have webbed feet; instead, they have toes equipped with flaps, which act as paddles. The Creoles taught us how to cook poule d'eau:

SMOTHERED POULE D'EAU
Two or three poule d'eau
Cup or so of white flour
Half cup butter, half cup olive oil
Five or so big onions
Salt and pepper

Skin, do not pluck, the birds. Remove excess fat. Most will come off with the skins. Remove head, neck, scaly feet, and entrails. Cut into pieces like chicken. Split the breasts. Remove birdshot. Dredge in flour, salt, and pepper. Cook slowly in skillet with butter or oil until brown, turning once. When the pieces are golden brown, cover with thick-cut slices of onion, add some water. Cook on low heat until onions are quite soft and thick gravy has developed. Check for sufficient water. Salt and pepper to taste. It is hard to cook the birds and onions too long. Serve over rice.

Cornbread, collards, or turnip greens complement this dish. A hot cup of pot likker goes well with the meal in winter.

White people on the Coast wouldn't eat a poule d'eau or croakers or gafftops'l catfish either; they considered these meats beneath them—"coloreds' food." Gafftops'l catfish, also called sail cats, have dorsal and pectoral fins with hard, sharp, venomous spines. This is the only saltwater catfish I knew of that Creoles ate. The large fin on its top looks like the gaff topsail of a sailing vessel. Today at Kroger, frozen croaker are pricey, if you can find them, and white folks buy them.

Mon Louis Island's early colonial history can be gleaned from two books, Peter Hamilton's *Colonial Mobile* and Jay Higginbotham's *Old Mobile*. Summarizing from them:

Nicholas Baudin arrived upriver in Old Mobile on February 11, 1708. By the spring, he had settled himself on Mon Louis Island down the Bay. Today we wouldn't call it an island but part of the western shore of Mobile Bay. Drive south toward Dauphin Island Bridge and you'll cross East Fowl River. The source of East Fowl River is an inland bog where once flowered pitcher plants, bachelor's buttons, and sundews; it is also the source of West Fowl River, which runs in the opposite direction to empty into the Mississippi Sound. Our Creole neighbors told us that in that marsh you could hop from Mon Louis to the mainland. If the definition of an island is land circumscribed by water, no matter it be a trickle, then to the rational French it was an island. So it remains today, if in name only.

Nicholas's death notice in Mobile's *Catholic Parish Register* tells us he was a

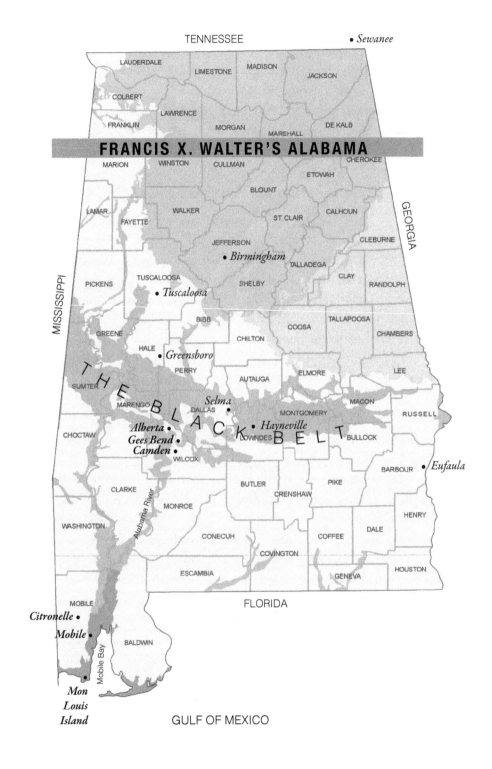

native of Mon Louis in the archbishopric of Tours-en-Tourain. People refuse to process this fact and continue to invent meanings for the name "Mon Louis." "My dear Louie" can lead to romantic fantasies.

On November 12, 1710, Nicholas traveled up the Bay and the Mobile River to Old Mobile to receive his "concession" to the island. Now we glimpse a guy with a wit. He signs as "Nicholas Baudin, Sieur de Miragouine," awarding himself a title and his island a barony. "Miragouine" and all its other inventive spellings was local French for mosquito. Sir Mosquito, the Mosquito Knight. Anyone on the Gulf Coast, stepping away from air conditioning, would cede him the title.

The Baudins kept their fiefdom on down the line: France, Spain, Britain, and on to confirmation by the United States in 1829, ten years after Alabama joined the Union. In 1746, a year after the death of Nicholas, the *Parish Register* records two Baudin slaves as being "of his succession," that is, his descendants. The Mobiliens, an ancient tribe of the Original People, were also present on Mon Louis. They helped repulse a raid on the island by the Spanish in 1719. In 1796, Charles La Lande, "a free man of color," is mentioned in the *Register*.

Just before turning into our driveway, we would pass the house of our neighbors, the La Landes. The Baudins had a valued steward, Maximilien Colin, whom Peter Hamilton describes as "... a colored Creole who lived at Jack's Bluff above the pecan-surrounded house of the Baudins." Mr. Hamilton mentions the pecans because the grove was still standing when he published *Colonial Mobile* in 1897. We read him calling M. Colin "a colored Creole" because then the word still bore traces of its original meaning: the firstborn of immigrants.

Just before the gate of our nearest neighbors, the Summerlins, a road led off to what Mobilians called incorrectly "the Spanish shipyard." In my childhood boats were still hauled up the ways by a mule-powered capstan, and a Collins still owned and operated it.

Southwest Alabama's Creoles, few in number, struggled to be recognized by the powers as a third race. While living on Mon Louis Island, we learned of the social engineering necessary to this struggle.

Our neighbors were handsome examples of what we of the Gulf Coast all would have looked like had history taken a jog to favor French settlers, the Original People, and Africans. The English walled themselves up along the Atlantic while the French were paddling pirogues between Montreal and Mobile. The first French on our soil were not called settlers but *coureurs de bois* (literally, wood runners). And course they did. Administrators in France feared these far-rangers would dissolve into the Original People instead of nesting into colonies like they should, extracting goods to France. Early French settlements had no walls. In the early days of Mobile, little food was grown. When supply ships lagged, Governor Bienville shipped his soldiers off to live on cornmeal mush, venison, fish, clams, oysters, squash, and beans among the hospitable tribes. The soldiers taught the gavotte; the Original People demonstrated foot-stomping rhythms. Babies resulted from marriages by Native or Christian rites—or not. When the English first, then the French, imported Africans, and especially when those enslaved people escaped to live with the Original People, their blood was added. Thus the Creoles.

A Creole community called Chastang lies today twenty-five miles north of Mobile. Many of its citizens are named Chastang, descendants of Dr. John (Jean Baptiste) Chastang of France and his brother, who were granted land there in 1756. Dr. Chastang lived, appropriately, on Chastang's Bluff. No one on the Mobile River could miss the bluff, surmounted by a large log house.

In 1951, when I was nineteen, my friends and I camped at times on Jose Creb Bayou downstream from Chastang's Bluff, visiting Chief Tallawah, the hermit of the Mobile/Tensaw swamp. One place to rent a boat to get to Chief's was Chastang's Landing at the foot of Chastang's Bluff. At a time of unusually low water, I clambered down to the river just below the house (since burned). People who live in bluff houses shouldn't throw stones or trash over the side. But they do. I was not disappointed. Broken crockery, the butt ends of green wine bottles frosted by age, fragments of brick, and bits of rust littered the exposed bank. I pulled a coin-silver teaspoon from the mud. It was black with tarnish, but when polished I could see the tip of the handle was broken off. Someone had carefully rounded off and smoothed the broken stub. The bowl had little dents—bite marks—on what could be called its right side, as seen when one was holding the spoon straight out with one's right hand. Much later it occurred to me that the bite marks were on the wrong side of the bowl if someone were feeding herself. But if she were feeding someone else—a teething baby—the bite marks would be on the side of the spoon going sideways into the child's mouth. A Chastang baby spoon!

John Chastang, after settling into his riverine plantation, fell in love with one of his brother's enslaved Africans, Louison; he bought her, freed her, and, it is reported, married her sacramentally and legally. The administrators of the Chastang Family website have kindly allowed me to use its information if I acknowledge the source. What a family! Today they spread across the globe doing creative work. Some of Dr. John and Louison's sons served in the Confederate Army, and I learned they were at the Battle of Fort Blakeley with my great-grandfather, Jake, and his brother.

No one shot into the log house, no one snubbed Louison at church, and no one refused to speak to them. As for the spoon—an airy web of speculation. But there is nothing imaginary about the Chastangs, Dubrocas, D'Olives, Durettes, Baudins, and Collinses. The spoon that John and Louison's baby might have teethed on stood to me as a sign of racial peace and harmony.

After the "Americans" came and the Original People were deported or died of European diseases, the Creoles found it harder to preserve their third-race category. All the whites I knew called them "Cajuns." If you had ears to hear, they'd gently tell you they were not descended from the Arcadians of Newfoundland who had fled British sovereignty. When we arrived on the island, we were told they were descended from French and Indian stock; it was not politic back then to add African. Today Creole descendants are proud of their composite origins. But while we were living there (1936–39), some of our Creole neighbors occasionally low-rated black folk. A mild term was "American people" on down to "coons" or "rattlesnakes." It was a way to make a distinction.

Our neighbors the Summerlins, Joe and Rosa, had three sons: Freddie, Marshall, and Son. Joe told my father they all went together to Anniston, Alabama, to be inducted into the Army at the outbreak of World War II. The young men entered some big hangar-like structure, looking around. "Where do we go?" one asked. Freddie said, "I don't know about you all, but I'm gonna get in line with those white boys." The alternative, of course, was the line of blacks. Son, the youngest and most nervous, said he was going with Freddie. Marshall—if I'm keeping them straight—being darker, went in resignation to the black line. A sergeant came up to Son, standing behind his elder brother Freddie, and yelled, "Why the hell you standin' in the white line! Git over there whirr yew beelong," and escorted him to his fate. "But he's my brother," he said, waving at Freddie.

Amazingly, *Gulf Stream* by Marie Stanley, a 1930 novel set in Mobile in World War I years, tells a similar tale and deals with the social complexities of white, black, and Creole interactions, especially when white boys got the others pregnant. Stanley calls Mon Louis Island "'Mille Fleur' . . . with its tragic pretense, its twisted longings."

I had Creole playmates of every hue, painlessly learning diversity from a courteous people who out of their shrinking niche in the racial grid often had little good to say about the more persecuted race. Did I think my playmates were different? Yes. It was the smell. They smelled clean. Their mothers boiled the wash in backyard kettles using Octagon soap, Mrs. Stewart's Bluing, and cakes of Argo starch. Then came the sad irons heated on a wood-burning kitchen stove, adding that almost-scorched starch smell and a touch of wood smoke. I'd like to get a whiff of Mrs. Stewart's Bluing to see what it might have contributed. I once stumbled across a descendant of the family that made the stuff but he gave me a queer look and said he'd never sniffed it.

The Walters didn't smell that kind of clean; we didn't have a kettle outside. Perhaps my mother's mother, whom I called Bobbin, washed our clothes in Mobile, running the laundry back and forth in her Dodge. No, I think we had the old Maytag even then, one wringer white, one black. I got my hand caught in those rollers one time.

The only place I know of in the 1930s where blacks had legal access to the Bay for recreation was "Faustina's Beach," next door to our place. A few sheds were on the acreage and enough electricity had been cabled in from somewhere to operate a string of lights and a jukebox. Things would crank up on weekends. Joe, the island patriarch, came over to our house with his sons if he suspected my father would be late coming home on a Friday night. They eased onto our kitchen steps with shotguns. Whether my folks approved or not I don't know. Joe clearly wanted to protect me, my baby sister, and mother "from sich as that," with a nod toward Faustina's. But the only thing that ever came over to our place from Faustina's was the sound of 78-rpm records.

The first place I could go all by myself was Joe and Rosa's. Mommee would walk me to our gate, then stand in the dirt road until I reached the Summerlins' cattle guard across the road. Joe had built a four-square house after the 1916 hurricane. Around three sides was a gracious gallery, shady, screened-in, where for all but a few months the family did its living. I went because Joe told me stories. We would sit on a swing under a water oak that shaded the house. There he showed me how to roll a cigarette. A couple of weeks ago, one of Sewanee's grand dames told me she was taught to roll a Prince Albert when, as a little girl, she too sat under the spell of an old tale-teller.

Joe told two kinds of stories—true ones and glorious lies. One series of lies was about his "flappers," which were never quite on view. Joe had conceived of swim fins long before Jacques Cousteau dreamed of them. His were of such power that he had to "ease on out to the Bay" from Fowl River, or he would slosh all the water out of the river. When my sister Patsy was born in 1937, she entered the tales. The flappers allowed Joe to swim on his back all the way to Middle Bay Light, even tow a skiff tied to his toe. I would either fish from the skiff or from his stomach until we'd thrown enough fish in the skiff to satisfy ourselves. This was before Miss Patsy. After Miss Patsy, she was in the skiff tending a charcoal burner, cleaning, mealing, and frying white trout. She'd hand us fried fish sandwiches. "Mind she don't drop hot grease on my stomach," he'd say.

Other tales were true. Rough water, riptides, "Lord, talk 'bout backin' up goin' to praying!" Prohibition days. Mobile Bay exploits, nighttime trans-shipping of booze from big boats to smaller ones. Hiding cases of Scotch, bourbon, and Canadian Club in the marsh, outwitting the sheriff. The "little Indian" who made "shinny" at the Cut Off. The 1916 hurricane. Breaking up church pews to make coffins for the drowned, finding the mutilated body of his best friend under a mound of driftwood.

There were darker stories. Chasing unwanted black people off his wharf, sending buckshot their way as the car hit the cattle guard. What fun that was.

Strange the crevasses racial superiority sinks into—hiding until perhaps years later it is flushed out. Reminds me how not too many years ago you could murder somebody. Make an awful bloody mess, but with enough bleach, hot water, and elbow grease, no one could tell what you'd done. But then along comes new equipment and new chemicals. Now the floorboards light up like a Christmas tree. The blood was there all along.

All those years of friendship, all my mother's assurances that we treated our Creole neighbors without the old signals of being their betters. Will we white folks ever stop seeing through a glass darkly? Showing rare emotion, Joe once told me, "I got white relatives een Mobile; I can name 'em. I could walk een the Battle House (Hotel) today, rent me a room, go right up."

In 1954, I came home early for Thanksgiving from seminary at the University of the South, Sewanee, Tennessee. That had been my first time away from home. While I was away, our parish, St. Paul's, had acquired a reel-to-reel tape recorder, then a novelty. My father borrowed it, and most of our family set out for Mon Louis Island to visit the Summerlins and record Joe reprising his stories. My mother was not along; she had died the Sunday before Thanksgiving. The dean had given me an extended time off. In the car were my father; my sister Patsy, then eighteen; my great-aunt Minnie, eighty-nine; and me, twenty-four. My mother's mother, Bobbin, was not with us. "When the wheels turn," she sniffed, "Minnie is ready," she'd say of her elder sister. A grudge she held for some long-forgotten reason. My grandmother was a stick-in-the-mud and stayed at home.

Joe was pleased to reprise his best tales but only after all of us got over the strangeness of hearing our voices come out of a box.

During the visit, I heard a new thing: Joe teased me about the Summerlin nickname for me when I was five, "Bozo." I've fought having a nickname all my life, and this news produced the thrill of a fate escaped. What if Bozo had gotten out of the Summerlin house? It also stung a little to hear the context of Bozo. Joe recalled, "We'd say, 'Bozo, eef you'll stop talkin' for five minutes, we'll geeve you a nickel.'" He laughed, "You deedn git it neither." Well, if I'd been the sort to get the nickel, I wouldn't be writing this long memoir. We sat in their small living room. It was too chilly to be on the gallery. The reels turned. Our voices have wandered like ghosts from the seven-inch reels to cassettes to CDs to cyberspace. All the speakers are dead but me.

Not long ago, I was listening to the voices and heard what I'd not heard before. Joe and Rosa called my father and great-aunt "Mr. Walter" and "Miss Minnie." They called my sister "Miss Patsy," but that didn't count because we'd all called her Miss Patsy from birth. Since I'd hung around the Summerlins as a little boy, I escaped an honorific, and they called me "Little Francis" on the recording. My father and I, Patsy, and Arminnie called them "Joe" and "Rosa." I did it because as a kid that was what I heard my folks call them. How strange it would have been in 1954 if I had tried to honor the scales of racism then falling from my eyes by calling them "Mr. and Mrs. Summerlin." From their perspective, would that have pleased them or made them wonder what had happened to me up there in Tennessee?

Mon Louis was paradise. The bay was so shallow I could flounder around in it unchaperoned. Once I caught a piglet on the beach and sat with it under a cedar tree counting the fleas on its pink belly then ran to my mother to report they were bigger and of another color than the fleas on Tippie, our dog.

My parents were fans of the funnies. On Friday the New York papers and the Chicago *Tribune* of the previous Sunday would arrive in Mobile. The print part went in the trash and my parents stayed in bed Saturday morning to read "Buck Rogers," "The Katzenjammer Kids," "The Gumps," "The Boarding House," etc. Later my mother would read them to me at the beach on a platform up that same cedar tree overlooking the bay.

---

5. *A Creole Look-Ahead Correction*

Before leaving the Island and thoughts about Mobile's Creoles, I'll skip ahead to 1965 to a corrective about an earlier assumption. It occurred at a turning point in the Alabama civil rights movement, when the Student Nonviolent

Coordinating Committee veered from a role subsidiary to Dr. King's Southern Christian Leadership Conference by making a political choice the SCLC would not support. The gist of a critical meeting then and its effects I will treat later. I will record an encounter at that meeting that gave me a new insight about me, Creoles, and race. It happened on October 9, 1965, at a meeting of south Alabama activists at the Tuskegee Boy Scout Camp—Tuskegee because the camp was for black Boy Scouts, so as an integrated group we were welcome to use it. Present were representatives of SNCC, who had called the meeting, the SCLC, and the Mobile Improvement Association. I was there to represent the Episcopal Society for Cultural and Racial Unity (ESCRU) and the Selma Inter-Religious Project (SIP). I was then the only employee of the new SIP, which represented various religious groups: Jewish, Roman Catholic, Protestant, Unitarian. There may have been other movement groups present at this meeting.

At that time SNCC was moving rapidly toward the decision to get rid of its white members; the term Black Power was aborning. King's nonviolence, tinged with the Gospel, its heritage running from Tolstoy to Gandhi to King, was being subjected to a merciless critique by Stokely Carmichael. SNCC also knew with rational clarity that allowing whites in SNCC to organize poor rural blacks was counterproductive, a position for which I had much sympathy. Because they were fleshing this out at the meeting, it was not fun for me to hobnob with SNCC folk. Jerking me around—sometimes with a bad conscience—was helping them practice their new insights. My discomfort propelled me to an older woman, in dress and deportment like my mother, but not of her color and not a bit "SNCC-y" looking. I said hello. My goodness! We were both from Mobile; she still lived there. We got to talking.

It was passing strange for me to establish connections with Mrs. Dorothy Parker Williams as if we were two white people. To establish connections between two strangers by chatting until they discover a person they both know is to "bobo." (This has also been described widely as the "six degrees of separation.") At that time, I didn't know how black Southerners boboed. This is how white Southerners "boboed":

"You from ____? So am I [or my mother, uncle, sister. . . is from there]. I thought you'd know ____ because . . ." You do! So you must be kin to ____.

My father was ____'s best friend in high school. Was your grandfather ____?"

No one could "bobo" better than our populist, progressive Governor "Big Jim" Folsom. I saw him in action during a bizarre episode when he and I were judges for the University of Alabama Homecoming Queen Beauty Pageant in 1969. At that time, he was blind in one eye from a stroke or alcohol—("No! Poisoned!" he said)—and if some little girl from Lawrence County, Alabama, came trembling before us, Big Jim, like the Ancient Mariner, would fix her with his one good eye and not let her, or us, go until he had dredged up a connection from his bank of

My great-grandfather, Dr. J. G. Michael, owner of the Hygeia Hotel in Citronelle, Alabama, in the early 1900s with Polly Hopkins, the parrot.

political "bobo" lore. "Honey, you said you were a ____, didn't you? Didn't your grandfather own the old ____ place out by ____ Creek?" On and on until finally, "I know your people!" And then we could proceed.

Back then "boboing" across racial lines didn't work that well; too many pits to fall into. But with Mrs. Williams and me, it clicked. I told her we had lived on Mon Louis Island for a while. She told me she was a Creole. We got right down. She told me her husband's grandfather, Billy Wilson, had been chief cook at the Hygeia Hotel in Citronelle. The Hygeia was owned by my great-grandfather, Dr. Jacob Michael, once a Confederate Army surgeon. She said Mr. Wilson held my great-grandfather in high regard. That was balm to me after the drubbings I'd been absorbing from SNCC. But here are my journal entries from October 9, 1965:

> Arrived at Tuskegee Boy Scout Camp at 9:20. . . . Yesterday the Alabama Bureau of Investigation came, took pictures and refused to leave when asked . . .
>
> Mrs. Dorothy Parker Williams . . . is a Creole. She is directly Kin to the LeLandes [sic] and the Durettes, knows [my] Daddy, [and] is cousin of [the] Summerlins.
>
> More amazingly, her husband is the grandson of Billy and Henrietta Wilson. Billy Wilson, she told me, was the chief cook at the Hygeia Hotel. She recalls Mr. Wilson well and the high estimation in which he held my great-grandfather, Dr. J. G. Michael.
>
> That a Creole is in the Movement is stunning. Creoles are confirmed racists. [I'm ashamed to have written that in 1965. It wasn't true.] Yet for some of them the mildest expression for Negroes is American People. The usual is Rattlesnakes.
>
> Instead of correcting me, Mrs. Williams told me a story:
>
> When she was a kid in school on the Island, a new family moved down. This was always a problem to be resolved. Were they Creole or black? Since race is a demonic abstraction in tow to our white-run culture, that isn't easy. But many in the community believed it had to be decided to protect their little "not black" niche in Gulf Coast Society.
>
> It was decided the newcomers were black. The couple had a school-age child. The Creole parents agreed if the child showed up at their one-room school, the pupils would be removed by the parents.
>
> Mrs. Williams' father became angry. He laid into the other parents. "You don't want to remember, do you? We welcomed, accepted any escaped slave who could swim Fowl River. You know the story of our cobbler. He'd make a pair of shoes for any escapee from bondage. 'Here. You don't owe me. But now you are free. Now you can work and earn your own living. Pay me for the next pair.'"
>
> Then her daddy told them his girl would be in school when the child came. He expected every other child to be there as well. And they were.

Most of the time I can delete or reconfigure my assumptions. I did that time.

6. *To Spring Hill and School*

Driving home one evening from Mobile in 1939, my mother told me we were going to live somewhere else so I could start school. I started to cry.

We moved to Spring Hill. It was then outside the Mobile city limits but only seven miles from downtown. At two hundred feet above sea level, the town site was a big hill to south Alabamians. Daddy said in his youth the test of a car was if it could get up the hill in third. From the earliest days, it was a retreat for the well-off to escape the heat of summer and yellow fever. It really did have springs welling from its lower levels.

Later my folks told me that the one-room, one-teacher Mon Louis school was out for me because they didn't think I'd get much of an education there. They also believed, true or not, that Mobile County ran tripartite segregation. Since I was white I couldn't go there, and had I been black I couldn't have, either. (A few years ago I visited a much-altered Mon Louis and took note that the little schoolhouse was now a cute gift shop. I decided it was owned by white interlopers to the Island. Why would I have thought that, when the owners could have been some well-off Creoles? Ah, the tentacles of racism.)

We moved so that I could enter first grade at Spring Hill Elementary School in September 1939. We moved our stuff in stages. I have a Technicolor recollection of my father at Mon Louis stepping, unsmiling, out of the car the evening of September 1, 1939. My grandfather, my mother, and I are standing in the backyard. He's not smiling. He says, "Hitler has invaded Poland." The geopolitics was over my head, but the dark mood of the grown-ups fixed the memory. Daddy could be drafted. Surely Pop was thinking of his German family. Now the letters would stop, as they had during the First War. He would revisit the tension felt by Mobile's German community in 1918, when the men gathered at the Federal Building to pledge their allegiance. One of his last letters received from Germany in 1939 enclosed a studio photograph, now on the desk where I sit writing. Two serious young men in uniform with gloves and sabers. In 2006, while in Germany visiting Walter kin, I learned from my cousin, Fritz Meier, that they were my grandfather's brother's sons, Fritz and

Wilhelm Walter, who died on the Russian Front. Pop would always point in an embarrassed excuse to the striped epaulets on their shoulders to say, "That means they're in the band." I keep the photo on my desk for the same reason that I occasionally wear a Confederate Army belt buckle. Who am I to think it couldn't have been me?

My last day on Mon Louis Island, I was left with Pop to spend the night. Mommee and Daddy were in Spring Hill setting up the house. Next day they would pick the two of us up. My grandfather was a withdrawn and forbidding man, or so it seemed at the time. Later, I could see that having lost his own home and business, he had resolved to respect the young couple with whom he had to live by adopting a life in the background. There was at least one crack in this unemotional posture which, if I'd been older, I might have responded to. It was earlier, weeks before we moved. My parents were gone. My baby sister Patsy and I were with Pop in his bedroom. Patsy had pulled herself up by means of the spread on his bed. Pop knelt on the floor, calling her. He and I saw her take her very first steps toward him. He cried as he held her.

But that was forgotten as I settled in for the evening and next day with this silent grandfather. The house was strange, stripped, empty. A quirky reality set in. I asked if I could let a chicken in the house, a chicken whose habit it was to stand on the kitchen steps.

"Let her in," Pop said—not a moment's hesitation. Wow, the rules are gone!

Next morning I was handed a bowl of cornflakes and the tin of canned milk. After the chicken, in for a dime, in for a dollar: "Can I put chocolate syrup on my cereal?" He handed me a small tin of Hershey's chocolate syrup. We became close, with our chicken and chocolate syrup secret.

Fourth Grade was a pivotal year, which I survived under the corrupting but charming Miss Murty, also known off-campus as "Mrs. Murdoch." Charming as in the way of snakes with birds. Each class passed to the next class that Miss Murty was the widow of a Confederate soldier. How could that be? She was old but not cadaverous. The answer was that a young Miss Murty had married an old veteran to get his state Confederate pension. She was Catholic. We began class with a "Hail Mary" or "Our Father." We learned to sing "The Bonnie Blue Flag":

Hurrah, hurrah;
For Southern Rights, hurrah.
Hurrah for the Bonnie Blue Flag
That bears the single star.

I assume the purpose of this was to fulfill a unit on music and commit to memory the order in which the Southern states seceded and also to praise the president and vice president of the Confederacy, all of which followed the opening stanza.

We would also recite "The Conquered Banner," the poem by Father Ryan, S.J.: *Furl that banner, / Furl it sadly. . . .*

This was important because Father Ryan was not only "the poet laureate of the Confederacy" but he became a Mobilian, and his statue could be visited in Ryan Park. When I was grown up, out from under Miss Murty and involved in the civil rights movement, I visited the unlocked and empty Episcopal Church of the Holy Cross (founded 1847) in the Black Belt village of Uniontown, Alabama. In it a stained-glass window depicts the Confederate Battle Flag, not sadly furled but sadly ascending into Heaven.

The layout of the fourth-grade classroom was a schematic of Miss Murty's domination. A big bank of windows on the north wall poured natural light into the room. Along that wall was the first row. Immediately in front of first row was the seat of power, her desk. That row she called the A row. Supposedly for "A" students but also for kids from established Spring Hill families and other of her pets. Some A-row kids were honored by having her squeeze into their desk to "help" her grade papers. A and a few B kids got to sit in her lap at her desk and eat candy treats from the desk drawer. I was in B row. In increasing shadow were the C, D, and F rows (we didn't have an E). To these rows were relegated kids from lesser families, the dumb, and those unfortunates whose parents had come to Mobile for "the war effort."

In the last seat on the last row sat one of the newcomers, not only last of the last but the most in shadow, far from the northern light. This kid and I have a friendship that has endured to this day. But not then. I was a B-row kid and looked only to A-row kids. My friend-to-be was Henry Greene Cole IV, from Georgia. From her desk Miss Murty would entertain the class by rebuking Henry's failures. Diagonally, Henry was the farthest from her desk, but not from her invective. I recall one taunt: "There you sit, I see you, your eyes the size of blueberry pies!" Then this (she always referred to herself in the third person): "Miss Murty met a mother at the bus stop." She made it clear Henry was the subject. "This mother told Miss Murty how worried she was about her child. You know what Miss Murty said? 'Just let me keep him for a while, and I'll straighten him out.'"

I no longer attribute paranormal powers to my elementary-school teachers, so I wonder how Miss Murty knew that Henry was a member of that Cole family who had been supporters of the Union through the War and were rewarded with political favors in Georgia during Reconstruction? I only learned this from Henry five years later. Indeed, Henry was the namesake of the first Henry Greene Cole, who moved to Marietta, Georgia, in 1837. This Henry was an outspoken Unionist. He risked his life over and over as a notorious Federal spy during the war. After the war, he became a prosperous businessman in Marietta. It is easy to see how the Coles were proud of him and why. My friend Henry, a newcomer to Mobile, kept this from his new friends. The rest of us expressed our teenage rebellion as lovers of the Confederate past. Louis Tonsmeire and I bought Confederate flags from the Annin Flag Company in New York. The legend was that years after the war, Jefferson Davis's widow appeared in the company's offices. Withdrawing a hat pin from her hair, she plunged it into her finger. Handing a bloody handkerchief to the clerk, she asked that any Confederate flags produced duplicate that hue of red.

A few years ago, I developed a one-off monologue about Miss Murty. In researching it, I asked Henry and other survivors to give me their memories. Henry's was not like the rest of us, who cloaked our recall in humor. He told me fourth grade was the worst time of his life.

Miss Murty's effect on my B-row existence was to make me long for the grossly unfair attentions she lavished on the As, one of whom is my closest lifetime friend, Louis Tonsmeire. Mobile County had no kindergarten; the county ran an eleven-year system: seven in grammar school, four in high school. We didn't miss a thing from that lost year. What is middle school for anyway?

Louis and I met the first day of first grade. The Walters were still unpacking from our move. On that stressful first day, many mothers came with their kids to first grade, which let out early to ease the shock. (I hear that today's parents come with their kids to the first day of college.) Mrs. Tonsmeire asked my mother if I could come home with Louis to play. We've marched through life pretty much together and are now retired Episcopal priests with aching or artificial joints.

Back then it was troubling to see my buddy Louis bathed in the stronger light one row over. His sister had been queen of the school's May Festival some years earlier. This social plus helped guarantee his placement. I became so upset by being on B row and by a fear of stumbling while reciting the multiplication tables that I developed stomachaches and was allowed to stay home a few times.

My mother soon figured things out. She was not angry with me. Having lost her father while a baby, she'd turned to her grandfather, Dr. Jacob G. Michael, for a father. She was smart, and he was born to spoil her. She'd run the thermometer up by means of the radiator to skip school, and he would go along with it; or worse, he'd let her stay home to teach her to make elaborate, artful nineteenth-century bandages, even let her go to class the next day with her arm in a sling they'd been practicing on. She told me she was going to meet with Miss Murty. I must have been gripping the iron brackets of my desk when I later heard Miss Murty maliciously repeat to the class exactly what my mother told me of the meeting. I was waiting for my name to be dropped. But I was saved. Miss Murty made clear that a sweet boy had not felt Miss Murty cared enough for him, but Miss Murty would make it up. Later I was promoted to A row, and Miss Murty even wedged her behind in beside me a time or two to let me "help" her grade papers, a bonus only a few A-row kids received.

She was loyal to her favorites. Our school had no cafeteria; we brought bag lunches. We could, however, order half-pints of milk. Seventh-grade "milk boys" delivered trays of little bottles to each classroom just before Big Recess. When a true uber pet—the son of Mobile's weatherman—was the milk boy, Miss Murty, to our nervous laughter, would drag him into the cloakroom for what we believed was a private hug.

Each fourth grade would beg Miss Murty to scare the first graders the way she had scared them when they were first graders. She would oblige. When first grade was in the hall after their dismissal, she would invite them into her room while her students waited, holding their breaths. She would seat the victims in front of her desk and sing very softly: "The Worms Crawl in, the Worms Crawl out." The last line, when she had the little kids hypnotized:

> *The worms crawl in,*
> *The worms crawl out,*
> *The worms play pinochle*
> *On your snout.*
> *Did you ever think*
> *When the hearse goes by*
> *That you might be the next to . . .*

Then she shouted,

> *DIE!*

On a good year, this would cause tears, toppling over, running from the room.

She was, you should have gathered, a good performer, moving dramatically and imitating different voices. Miss Murty had a unique way of explaining why the Yankees attacked us. It went this way.

She would preface this unit by explaining the bond between Southerners and New Englanders. Of all Americans, we two groups spoke English close to how the British spoke it. That is, we spoke English correctly. However, she gave the edge to New Englanders. After establishing this bond, she would explain that New England ship captains were the ones who brought "the slaves" to America and became rich selling them to us. She explained an architectural feature: the widows' walk. From that cupola, the wives of the captains would look to the sea, awaiting their menfolk who would return with rum but no "slaves." She was right here. See the documentary film *Traces of the Trade*. Then see *OOM*, a documentary that explores recent racial angst in Mobile and complements *Traces of the Trade*.

Miss Murty threw herself into it: "Well, those wives began to say to their husbands. . ." Here she would cock her head and sweep a hand over it to imitate a woman combing out her hair, "'Bring us some of those slaves to cooooomb our long locks and do for us. Why should those Southern ladies have all that and not us?'"

We would be told that the husbands resisted, but the New England ladies would not let up. They pestered their husbands until they couldn't stand it anymore. "All right," they said, "we'll bring you some!"

"And you know what, children?" Her voice was almost a whisper as she reached the climax. "It's hot in Africa; colored people can't live up North; it's too cold up there." Then came the screech that electrified all first-time hearers:

"They all *DIED!*"

Her coda was an analysis of the cause of the War Between the States (the term we were taught for the Civil War). "Those women said to their husbands, 'If we can't have 'em, they can't either.' They went on that way, children, until their husbands couldn't take it anymore either and started the WAW!" Until I wrote this, I hadn't seen that Miss Murty's two dramatic masterpieces both ended with death: "Die!" and "Died!"

We stumbled out of this Gothic Confederacy into the world of a redheaded, young, beautiful New England schoolmarm.

I was eleven on entering fifth grade at Spring Hill Elementary School. It was 1943. To the shock of our class, the fifth-grade teacher was a beautiful, young, redheaded war bride from New England—Miss Anderson had followed her husband to Brookley Air Force Base in Mobile; now he was assigned elsewhere. My new but inseparable friend Max Rogers and I were in love with Miss Anderson. A new regime was beginning.

In only one way that year did our Miss Anderson fail to delight us. She gained a reputation for this slip-up. One winter day it began to snow wet, floppy flakes. My grandmother, who was born in 1876, told us the last time it snowed in Mobile was in her high school days at Barton Academy.

Children from all the rooms poured out onto the playground. All but us. Miss Anderson calmly taught on. "Miss Anderson, Miss Anderson," we screeched, "let us out!" Miss Anderson explained that the first snow took the impurities out of the atmosphere. We should wait awhile; maybe the snow would be clean by Big Recess. One of us did the unheard of—broke from his seat and pounded down the hall to Miss Lining, the principal. Miss Lining came to the fifth grade to tell Miss Anderson that we had never seen snow, so she should let us out. Which she did with sweet apologies. We fifth-graders only got slush, a scum of which was only available along the tops of the pine benches. It dribbled through our hands, never to be thrown. But who would not forgive her?

Our school was too underfunded to have an adequate library. We were encouraged to bring "pleasure books" from home. These the teachers would read to us at a designated time. In an act of perverse affection, we brought her *Eneas Africanus* from Max's daddy's library, putting it into her hands. I'm sure Big Max had something to do with the selection. He came from the Rogers family plantation in Gainesville, Alabama, where the book was, I'd imagine, a family favorite.

Max and I had only flipped through the book, but we realized, in the murky way of eleven-year-olds, that Miss Anderson was not of Miss Murty's world. So bringing that book to the young, beautiful New Englander was a test. Sit back, see what happens. Next day Miss Anderson handed the book back with a bland look. Why, she would not say. But we knew. An early bit of chinking fell from our polite wall of racist culture. I will come back to *Eneas Africanus* shortly.

After her test, Miss Anderson asked Max and me to her apartment for milk and cookies. The world turned upside down! Even to see a teacher out of class, dangerously loose in the grocery store, was scary. But in her little apartment, up the outside back staircase of our neighbors the Greys' house . . . it was blissful. We grasped that she cared enough for us to trespass the bar that kept student and teacher apart out of class. It was only when I was an adult that I realized her needs—lonely, away from home, separated from her new husband. Where would she look for companionship? Hardly in the teachers' lounge with Miss Murty. Not that our school had a teachers' lounge.

When I was discussing all this with Louis Tonsmeire these many decades later, he said, "Do you remember the trouble I got into with Miss Lining?"

Besides being principal, Miss Lining taught seventh grade. Louis recalled that Miss Lining had introduced us to the old chestnut that America was a melting pot where all us descendants of immigrants were pureed into Americans. Louis asked Miss Lining how that could be, everyone all boiled up? What about colored people who seemed very separate? Miss Lining shushed him. Louis told me he really wanted to know, so he kept asking. At home his mother told him Miss Lining had called to say Louis was causing a disturbance in class. I asked Louis if he knew one of Miss Lining's presumed forebears was G. D. Lining, recorded in Scharf's *History of the Confederate States Navy* as having been first assistant engineer aboard the rebel gunboat *Morgan* during the Battle of Mobile Bay. He hadn't heard that. We agreed that if so, it made sense.

---

7. My Father's Love

As I write, a sadness comes that my brother, David, missed out on a cascade of toys and the love they carried because Daddy was caught up in our mother's dying when David came along in 1946. Doubly sad because it was David who inherited our father's skill. Grown up, as founding owner of his company, Reefmaker ecosystems, David patented bulwarks and reefs that protect and augment the shoreline and provide habitat for the fish—snappers and other marine life—that Daddy loved. David maintained the equipment and made and put down the large concrete structures himself. When I visited him down at the Gulf, I visited my father. I also enjoyed visiting my father through this chapter. I see now that in my formation, while in awe of my mother's gutsy articulation of her moral and spiritual being, I was also molded by my father's loving me with his hands, "skilled at the plane and the lathe." He made toys for my sister, my friends, and me. These cunning things he created bore his love and made me a useful man.

One was a 1938 "Phantom Flash" rise-off-the-ground rubber-band-powered model airplane made of balsa wood and rice paper. (Old guys have recreated the "Phantom Flash." See Google. I've bought a kit, and the plane awaits its resurrection after seventy-three years sleep.)

Until he held it in his hands, I'd not seen it. It's 1938, I'm six, and we are on Mon Louis Island. Joe Summerlin has harvested his corn. We are walking to the field on a hot fall day. Daddy winds it up and shows me how to launch it into a barely moving headwind. Had he tested it before? The balance is perfect. It slowly gains altitude. And gains and gains and gains. Today I know that the rubber bands had long run out. The prop is freewheeling. The Phantom Flash is a hundred feet over us. Daddy watches without a word or gesture. Then it is gone, too high to see.

"Will it go across the Bay?" I ask.

"It might."

Then Daddy tells me what a thermal is. Joe's cornfield was just hot enough, the breeze just faint enough. An invisible elevator of hot air, just at the right place, bloomed up into the sky, and the Phantom Flash was lifted, not to be seen again. I wasn't disappointed. What did I know? It seemed that's what such fragile creations were meant to do: fly once, fly away. If Daddy had cursed and waved his arms, I would have known better, but that he never did.

Another toy was a little wooden tugboat driven by a reconfigured eight-day clock movement.

With a few cog wheels removed and a hay-wire shaft coming out to a propeller, you had propulsion. Daddy used eight-day clockworks for toys because of the powerful springs. I will now lose intuitive readers, as defined by Carl Jung, by describing this propulsion system in detail. The clockwork sat in the hollowed-out hull. If the shaft had just gone on down through a hole in the stern, the boat would leak. So a copper tube was run up into the hull, ending well above the waterline. It would ask too much of toy engineering for a single shaft to run freely from the clockworks down the tube to the propeller. Daddy made an elegant universal joint that freely coupled the drive shaft to the propeller shaft. (Daddy was of the late nineteenth-, early twentieth-century tribe of toy makers for whom the power for toys came from wind, rubber bands, steam, or springs.) The shaft from the clockworks ended in a dog leg. It touched the prop shaft, which ended in a right angle.

Easy running.

Our Mon Louis property was low, and a drainage ditch ran along one side. I remember a Creole friend playing in the ditch with me and the tugboat.

I've searched for the name of this next gadget. It draws the arabesques that you see on the background of our paper money. His was composed of three, maybe four, wheels attached to one flat board. A sewing machine belt ran around all of them. One wheel held a piece of paper. Another wheel held a flat rod with holes to insert a pencil at different positions on the rod. The pencil rested on the paper. When the wheels were turned by a knob, the pencil moved and the wheel with paper moved, creating a design on the paper. Moving the pencil to different holes would produce different designs.

My sister's dollhouse Christmas present was fully electric, powered by an Eveready dry cell. My mother was the interior decorator. The stove, refrigerator, and much of the furniture looked like our own. She was good for fine stuff with Daddy's jigsaw.

A sailboat about eighteen inches long. Sails by Martha Walter.

Boat hulls were made of stacked ¾-inch planks. Each cut so that when stacked and glued the shape roughly conformed to the hull. Thus:

With a rasp and sandpaper a finished exterior was produced. A deck glued on top, and there was a sailboat with even a lead keel.

A steam turbine. Start with a World War II green, stainless-steel oxygen flask the size of a cantaloupe. This has got to be a real memory. A movie: Van Johnson at the controls of a stricken B-17, or a Liberator, or maybe a B-25. It's in flames. Van has a mask over his face. A hose is connected to a twin of our surplus oxygen flask. Van slips the mask off, risking death by smoke inhalation so as to tell the crew how to save themselves—but probably not himself. Here was that flask. We could hold it in our hands. We had no oxygen with which to fill it. We had oxygen later in 1954, while my mother lay at home dying.

Daddy attached a copper tube to the flask and rigged a kerosene flame under it. He had saved a little brass turbine that had been part of an elaborate 1920s car-washing tool. The copper tube now directed a jet of steam onto the spinning turbine, making a satisfying whine. *NTAA—Never throw anything away.*

A two-foot World War II submarine powered by a lengthy string of rubber bands encased in a castor oil-filled brass tube running the length of the hull. (Rubber encased in castor oil will not oxidize.) Daddy had saved some aluminum sheets from a scrapped airplane. (NTAA!) The metal was finely corrugated and made decking on the sub that looked real, surmounted by a deck gun. It was a devilish powerful toy. The slack rubber bands when unwound extended from the tube about ten feet. We used a hand-cranked drill hooked to the propeller to wind it. It was immensely satisfying to wind away at the slack strands to make a row of twists along their length, then a row of twists on top of the first twists, then twists onto the second set, and so on until the twisted rubber shrank itself into the brass tube. You had to hang onto the four-blade brass prop with skill and strength not to lose all that time spent winding and to keep from getting gashed.

One of its trial runs was at the Spring Hill swimming pool. My grammar school classmate, Jo Anne English, was also enjoying the pool. Jo Anne had much-admired, butt-length hair. Jo Anne was underwater going one way, and the sub transected her passage. She erupted from the pool screaming, the heavy sub hanging down her back, a ball of that glorious hair wrapped around the propeller. Our pool was no marvel of filtration. It was lined with cypress boards, had a sand bottom, and was replenished with tannic-acid-stained water from the Spring Hill Pumping Station Lake. There was no way in that water that Jo Anne could have seen what was bearing down on her. Jo Anne was helped out. Daddy laid the child down, the sub alongside her. He untangled a bunch of hair, but the kernel of the tangle resisted. He was getting out his pocketknife when Mrs. English arrived, yelling, "Don't cut my child's hair!" After a bit, Mrs. English conceded that some would have to go. Daddy promised the minimum, and the poor child was free. The sub was later lost, not at sea, but in Fowl River. Diving planes set too steeply, it nosed into the bottom and snagged onto something.

A failed masterpiece, a three-foot model of the battleship USS *Missouri.* It was made in honor of the Japanese surrender, which was signed on the *Missouri's* deck.

When Daddy needed real power, he turned to wind-up motors scavenged from Victrola record players. One such powered the model's two propellers.

You stuck the crank through a hole in the bow. It had three turrets with three cannons, each machined on a metal lathe. Each cannon could receive a fire-cracker, the fuse of which stuck through a hole in a threaded nut on the base. Almost touching the nut was a brass pin wired to a Ford Model T spark coil, powered by a dry cell. The spark coil was to have had a clockwork- or rubber band-powered timer. (Some of Daddy's model airplane buddies were said to have rubber band-powered timers in their planes set to release parachutes. One legend said a guy could parachute a mouse that way.)

In theory the ship, under power from the Victrola motor, could at some point fire a broadside ignited by the spark coil. The technical problems of propulsion and firepower were myriad. Daddy lacked the patience to overcome them. Sometimes I would set the battleship out in the backyard and touch matches to fuses hanging out the back of the cannons.

My father aimed too high, bless him. He built me a Sherman tank. Big toy, about two feet long. The shape came from boards glued together, then shaped by rasp and sandpaper. The concept was to use metal timing chains from car engines, turning on their sprockets, for tank treads. Today automotive timing "chains" are plastic belts. That's the part that, if it breaks, your engine fries. These metal ones did look just like tank treads. Daddy took the body of the Sherman to his shop, the Mobile Cylinder Grinding Company, to fit the treads. This was around 1944. I was twelve. I didn't hear anything about the tank for a while. Then, down at the shop, Daddy showed me the sad truth. When the tank was pulled with a string, the wooden body was not heavy enough to give the treads traction. It just slid. It slid across the shop floor, which was encrusted with a bumpy concretion of grease and metal filings. If that surface, which was never removed, couldn't provide traction, nothing could. I never saw the Sherman again.

Totally successful was the army of toys made for me and the boys I played with. The jeeps were made from wooden apple boxes scavenged from Greer's Wholesale Produce. The wheels were turned on the Craftsman wood lathe (rubber wheels were unavailable during the war). He even turned some big wooden wheels for a Radio Flyer-type wagon he built for us.

Some of the boys had utility trailers for their jeeps. I did find a pair of rubber treads off those little Japanese wind-up tanks that disappeared from the counters of Kress department stores on December 7, 1941. Out of that set came a half-track truck. For amphibious landings, he built barges and a "Sea Mule," which was a military tug with a clockwork motor. This allowed us to practice landings across the discharge creek from that same swimming pool where the *Jo Anne English* was disabled by an American submarine.

An easy toy. Twist two stout wires into a helix. Drop a spool (kind that holds thread) onto the twisted wires. Make a propeller out of aluminum sheet metal. Cut a slot in the center of the prop. Drop prop down the wire onto spool. Push up spool quickly. Propeller spirals up the wires. Off it flies.

The Diver. Some ideas came from *Popular Mechanics* magazine. I suspect the Diver plans did. To make the Diver, you needed an evaporated milk can for his body, a smaller can for his head. Dowels for arms and legs, a cork, wood screw, some lead for weight. That's about it.

You soldered the little can onto the big can for the Diver's head. Before that, you put a cork with a wood screw inside the head. The head of the screw hung down in the big can through a small hole. This produced a valve—Cork up, valve closed. Cork down, valve open. Put lead on the Diver's feet to just allow him to float with his head and shoulders out of the water. Turn him over, and in a hole in his bottom put in dry ice. Dry ice was available to us, as were tubs of ice cream, because Daddy had a deal with the Sealtest Ice Cream wholesaler.

Throw the Diver off the wharf at the Alba Club. The cork resting in his head allows air and CO_2 to escape. He descends, water enters his head through mouth and eyes. Therefore, the cork valve closes. His body fills with CO_2. He rises. Water spews out his mouth and eyes. What a relief for him! He sinks back to his unseen work on the bottom. And so on.

The fun was to have no safety line on the Diver and become antsy, not grabbing him until just before the dry ice ran out. We never lost him to the deep.

Not that we could have afforded a tankful, but no helium was available during the Second World War and after until Congress repealed the law that put helium under government control. Roosevelt would not allow Hitler to have helium for the *Hindenburg* or its airship successor, which was under construction at the outbreak of war but never completed. People remembered the dirigible bombings of England during the First World War. Hydrogen is flammable; helium is inert. One incendiary bullet could bring down a hydrogen-filled dirigible.

Daddy knew how to make our own hydrogen-filled balloons in spite of the government hoarding the helium. Take a whiskey bottle, drop slivers of aluminum in it, add water, then lye. Pop a balloon over the top. The lye and aluminum produce hydrogen and heat. Too much lye causes the brew to boil up into the balloon, ruining everything. Barring that, in an hour the balloon is ready to tie off with a string and float. Daddy showed us how to balance the lift with bits of paper tied to the string so that the little aerostat would ease around the house with equipoise.

When the war ended, the Marine Junk Company and Zieman's were glutted with surplus. Daddy was at the two places at least once a week. He tipped off Boy Scout Troop 17 that "Bags, Sleeping, Arctic, Army" were available, ripproof and stuffed with chicken feathers. They could even be zipped together to make a double. For scouts with a yen for the southern hemisphere, there were "Hammocks, Sleeping, Tropical, Army." These slung you protectively under mosquito netting and provided a little roof to protect from jungle rain. I didn't buy one; hammocks mess up my back. C-Rations and tins of hardtack were all over the place.

One afternoon in our backyard, three-quarters of a barrage balloon appeared all spread out. Daddy couldn't say right off what we would do with it, nor could he say what we'd do with a bulletproof wing tank from a mighty big bomber—probably a B-29. It was the size of a couple of septic tanks. My buddy Henry Cole and I were deposited inside the wing tank to harvest hundreds of self-locking nuts and bolts, holding together a maze of struts designed to keep the tank rigid. It was hot, confined, and dark in there. We never did find a use for the tank. But my mother sewed ponchos for us from the barrage balloon fabric. These worked pretty well in squalls while fishing out in the Bay.

The surplus prize was yards and yards of rubber rope which barrage balloons used as lacing, like corsets, to keep them rigid as the gas expanded and contracted. The descendant of that rubber rope today is called bungee cord. I was fourteen. Daddy didn't want the rope. Inspired by him, my friends and I wanted it, but we didn't know what for.

That didn't last long. Thanks to Daddy, I was starting on my own toys. The first use for the rope was an uber slingshot. To make it, we tied two multi-strands of rubber rope, about twenty feet in length, way up two adjoining trees. The pouch for the projectile was a croker sack big enough to hold a brick. The triggerman would back up, holding the pouch until he couldn't resist the pull. Another would hold him around the waist and continue; then another behind him and so on, until the triggerman's feet were off the ground. A brick would go a hundred yards or so, making a thrumming sound like incoming artillery. It was fortunate that Spring Hill College had an abandoned clay pit for target practice.

Then there was simple 1940s bungee jumping from the water oak in our front yard. This was so gentle a use as even to attract my sister and her girlfriends.

My friend Pat Campbell and I, inspired by illustrations in our Latin books, built a full-scale "onager" catapult from some heavy timbers we found. The energy came from rubber ropes, not the twisted horse hair of the Roman originals. The trajectory of our onager was high and erratic. It was so heavy that we had no way to get it further than Austill Lane, where I lived. It threw brickbats. Given the proximity of our neighbors' houses, even our undeveloped teenage brains said, better not do this anymore. The catapult itself became surplus military equipment.

The best of the rubber rope uses was as a splice into water-ski towline. I do believe Daddy was the first on our side of the Bay to buy skis after the war. Our fourteen-foot runabout and its twenty-two-horse Evinrude provided a fast tow. Boys and girls from St. Paul's Church came down to the Alba Club to learn to ski. One of the St. Paul's girls had skin for which the word "creamy" was invented. She arrived in a black wool one-piece swimsuit, strapless. Beginners, including me, will often hold on to a tow rope after falling off the skis. Daddy was taking a turn towing this girl who fell off and hung on, peeling her suit near about to her ankles. I was marooned on shore, too far away to see anything.

With rubber rope added to the towline, you could dig the skis down in the water, stretching the rope as the boat flew on. Coming up on the skis rocketed you even past the boat. Care needed to be taken not to ram the towboat. Then you paused at the end of the tether, sank down, and did it over again.

Daddy's ingenuity—and his teaching by doing—went beyond toys. There was the dimmer for Jesus, Mary, and Joseph.

St. Paul's young people produced a Christmas Pageant in '48 or '49. It was staged in the chancel behind the three graceful arches that divided chancel from nave. With the church in expectant darkness, how fine it would have been for a rheostat to bring up the chancel lights after the Holy Family had taken its place. Daddy said store-bought rheostats would cost too much, besides the difficulty of installation. But, he said he thought he could rig something up. My sister, Patsy, was to be Mary.

He and I showed up at the church with an obsolete glass battery jar (of the sort that powered radios before homes were electrified), a box of salt, a rubber tube, a stout copper wire, sharpened at the end, a dowel, wire, and tools. We spliced into the circuit that supplied the chancel lights. The ground wire, attached to a lead weight, went into the battery jar filled with saltwater. The hot wire was attached to the rigid, sharpened copper wire. That wire could be guided into the saltwater through the rubber tube. Daddy made me the stage electrician. My job was to insert the copper wire slowly down the tube by means of a dowel taped to the wire. We gave it a test. The tip of the wire touched the water with a fizz, and slowly descending, brought up the lights from off position to glowing filaments, to dim orange and full light. My safety training was minimal but adequate. "Brother, don't touch the hot wire, don't touch the saltwater. You could get killed." It went well. Crouched behind the choir stalls, I watched my sweet sister appear out of the darkness.

This is how fathers raise sons in the best of worlds: show, explain, then hand the thing off—now you do it. With obvious risks and implicit trust. Stepping back, I trust you. Now grow up.

8. *Books to Edify the White Southern Child*

The book, *Eneas Africanus,* that Max and I used to discomfit Miss Anderson was part of a body of Southern literature that tempted us to forget a gruesome war. I was raised on some of these books. I believe this literature has value for young people if read at the right time, the right way, for the right reason. We shy away from these books because they are a body of literature that wavers from one side or the other of a red line, which itself wavers. A line that tries to divide the racially correct from the incorrect. We try to corral them once and for all, segregating what children should read or not read about race in the United States of America.

The following will be, as one of my biblical commentaries puts it, "an excursus," which translates to "getting off the track," doesn't it?

Take an easy one, *Huckleberry Finn.* The war is won. It's acceptable, a classic. There is not even a quibble about at what age a child should read it. If a kid is old enough to fall into its power, the kid is old enough to understand Twain's hatred of racial injustice. That war is over; but, yeah, I know, the terrorist skirmishes go on.

Eneas Africanus is poorly written, racist, and pathetically sentimental. I had fun googling and reading it just now. But it can be read against the grain for edification. Perhaps a bright high school student or a college student interested in nineteenth- and twentieth-century white racist ideation might benefit. Of the books in this class, *Huck Finn* is at the ultraviolet, acceptable top, *Eneas* at the infrared bottom.

The forgotten and forgettable *Eneas Africanus* was printed in 1920 by the author, Harry Stillwell Edwards, in Macon, Georgia, where, like Joel Chandler Harris of the *Atlanta Constitution,* he was in the newspaper business. The story goes like this:

Yankee forces are threatening Major George Toomey's plantation. The Major entrusts his faithful slave, Eneas, with a great chest of silver, the most precious item of which is a silver cup that has been in the family since the seventeenth century. All Toomey brides must drink a draft of pure spring water from it on their wedding day. Eneas is given two horses and a wagon full of hay in which to hide the chest. He's told to ride off and return to the Toomey place when the shooting is over.

This work of fiction is written as if it were fact. Eneas performs fantastic feats of sly courage, folksy wit, and dogged loyalty as he travels for eight years and 3,350 miles through seven states. The running gag is Eneas's total illiteracy and zilch-to-negative sense of direction. One soon suspends belief that this formerly enslaved man continues to be "loyal" after passing from chattel to free person just to return some white folks' silver. Edwards is incapable of presenting his character as brave and intelligent. The only virtue he's interested in is Eneas's loyalty to a once and future master. Even worse, the author finds as laughable the virtue he celebrates. Eneas is a wily fool, a minstrel figure. His inability to pronounce "Toomey's place" and his hopeless sense of direction allow the author to have helpful strangers direct him to every Thomasville in Dixie—and there are plenty of them. Finally this African Aeneas ends the epic by rolling into the old Toomey place at the very moment the Major's daughter, freshly married, is longing to drink from the missing cup.

During his eight years of wandering, Eneas has acquired a "yellowhammer" wife, a bunch of kids, and become a preacher. From this narrative I learned that yellowhammer (the common flicker, *Colaptes auratus*) is not only the name of the Alabama state bird and the battle cry of Alabama's rebel troops (who were clad in butternut brown, thus "Alabama Yellowhammer!") but also a term for the light-skinned black women of Alabama.

I grew to hate Harry Stillwell Edwards while doing research about his book. He puts into Eneas's mouth, as he greets his former owner, that he has brought a healthy yellow woman back to work on the old place. The reunion of Toomey and Eneas is depicted as farce, and Eneas gets little thanks from the Toomeys as he hands the chalice to the Major so the Major's daughter can quaff pure spring water from it. The verse engraved on the cup is too sappy to repeat.

Then there is the romantic *Diddie, Dumps and Tot.* We didn't have it in our home library. But it was beloved of many Southern white children from its inception in 1882 up until, let's say, the early 1950s, by when their parents were too ashamed to read it to them.

Diddie, Dumps, and Tot are little girls who grew up on their daddy's plantation, a thriving business enterprise based on slavery. The author, writing under the name Louise Clarke Pyrnelle (1850–1907), was born and raised on the Ittabena plantation in Perry County, Alabama, just out of Uniontown. She was an Episcopalian. If she worshiped at Holy Cross Church after the War, she would have gazed at that Confederate Battle Flag winging it sadly up to Heaven. She *is* the three little girls, Diddie, Dumps, and Tot. She has the voices down pat—unsurprising since she spent time on the stage as a "dialect speaker," not to mischaracterize black dialect but to faithfully reproduce it, a strange business to our present sensibilities—and is an accurate chronicler of what she saw, if not of what she would not see or could not. I've never been able to definitively apply "would not" to anybody. To me, "could not" is always possible.

This reminds me of a striving black family, my parishioners in Jersey City. The father had a good job. How they protected their kids! Hoped for them. One beautiful daughter was pegged to go to New York as a model, maybe an actress. At home in her bed, she gave birth to a full-term boy. She lay silent in the blood, the cord uncut. I was told this allowed the blood to drain away from the baby, and he died. Thing was, and I believed them, no one in that family saw she was pregnant. They could not.

Pyrnelle and her husband were lay Episcopal missionaries traveling in Georgia, Alabama, and Florida. When I was rector of St. Andrew's Church in Birmingham (1985–1999), I learned Mrs. Pyrnelle had been a member toward the close of her life. Her grave is in Selma, Alabama, far from bustling Birmingham. So I feel she lies quiet, ignorant of the mentally handicapped, the SSI recipients, artists, gays, lesbians, alcoholics, blacks, straights, and even Republicans who belong to St. Andrew's. We whites' personal brands of racism are as countless as the stars in heaven. She might have been happy in my 1990s parish, a quick learner. Unlike other Southern white race books for kids, Pyrnelle's has an apologia in her Preface.

> Nor does my book pretend to be any defence of slavery. I know not whether it was right or wrong (there are many pros and cons on that subject); but it was the law of the land ... and born under that law a slave-holder ... surrounded by

negroes from my earliest infancy, "I KNOW whereof I do speak;" and it is to tell of the pleasant and happy relations that existed between master and slave that I write this story of "Diddie, Dumps, and Tot."

When the story begins, everybody is happy; the human chattel are happy, the enslaved African preachers and the old storytellers are happy, the house servants are very happy, the slave-owning father, Major Waldron, is noble and happy. The little girls are in a blissful heaven—until the War sweeps over them and they grow up into a peck of trouble. After that calamity, Major Waldron sleeps on Malvern Hill, where he "Nobly died for Dixie." Mrs. Waldron is in the "State Lunatic Asylum." The big house and the gin are burned; only four chimneys stand. Diddie married at eighteen on the eve of the Rebellion. But word came from Forrest's Cavalry:

> *And ere long a messenger came,*
> *Bringing the sad, sad story—*
> *A riderless horse: a funeral march:*
> *Dead on the field of glory!*

Then Diddie is widowed and poor; the land can be neither sold nor worked. Tot, the baby, died young. Dumps remains a spinster to devote her life to her mother. Their misery reflects the course of the author's family, who lost their plantation and wealth in 1865.

Of the freed blacks, Pyrnelle allows that some are pretty well-off, but many are dissolute. One, once a favorite, is now in the state legislature telling lies about Major Waldron's prewar management style.

Setting aside Pyrnelle's blinkered sensibility, the book is a mine of thought-starters. While not fit for infant ears, it would be good for junior or senior high schoolers, perfect to teach reading against the text and explicating what can be wrong with ideas one reads about, as well as what an apologia is.

It is a detailed snapshot of the era. She accurately records spirituals, games, sermons, songs, and even a version of "Br'er Rabbit and the Tar Baby." It would be easy for young people to discover and discuss the person standing behind that camera.

When Pyrnelle wrote in 1882, there was oppression, lynching, and torture of blacks in the former Confederacy. A vigilante white culture was searching for a more efficient replacement for slavery than night-riding. A system of dominance was found and legalized, but not until the former Confederate states were given the right to absolute white rule, beginning around 1900. Until then, there was no uniform legally established segregation, no omnipresent Jim Crow.

In Pyrnelle's idyllic, pre-War world, the races are jammed up-close and personal. In *Diddie, Dumps and Tot*'s Chapter VII, "Poor Ann," we read about the queasiness felt by both enslaved and free when a slave trader camps outside the Waldron plantation to display his goods. Major Waldron allows the girls to go shopping with him, queasy or not. At the camp, they see a small tent. The trader apologizes, "There is a sick yellow woman in there that I bought in Maryland. . . . I doubt if anyone will buy her, though she has a very likely little boy about two years old." The Major looks in. Pyrnelle writes, "Lying on a very comfortable bed was a woman nearly white. . . ." Poor Ann tells the Major and the girls, who have crowded in with their father, that she wishes to be sold to a decent home so people there will be kind to her little boy after her death. The girls begin to cry. Diddie strokes the woman's "long black hair" and impulsively assures her they will give her "a home."

Major Waldron leaves to talk this over with his wife. He returns to buy Ann and her son. Soon after, Ann dies and the boy grows up on the plantation enslaved. To be sure that the very small or the very clueless will get it, the author makes clear that the little boy has been given a decent name, "Henry," and Pyrnelle adds, "a very pretty child he was. He was almost as white as Tot." No horror of miscegenation here; Pyrnelle is no foe of race mixing. She's a cheek-by-jowl mixer-upper. With her truthful ear, she records Diddie's, Dumps's, and Tot's dialect as that of the enslaved house servants who mothered them and with whose children they played. But not exactly like. Pyrnelle's written dialect shows that the girls also picked up touches from the Major and Mrs. Waldron. Pyrnelle performed on stage in New York City and elsewhere as a dialectician, happily a forgotten art, but she was a gifted and appreciative student of black dialect.

I do believe that years ago when I served as rector of St. James Church in Eufaula, Alabama (1959–1961), I could hear the ghostly echoes of house-servant Africans in the accents of the privileged granddaughters of Diddie, Dumps, and Tot.

To say Mrs. Pyrnelle was not a segregationist is not to say she wasn't several kinds of racist. She would have just made it to the fainting couch had she spied a row of whites chopping cotton under the lash of a black overseer.

My other grandfather, Frederick Cade Marsh, of Franklin, Louisiana, died when his only child, my mother, was nine months old. He was the son of John Bronson Marsh, whose bitter humor let him jot the following on the back of a Confederate bill:

> April 9, 1865. This bill was paid to John B. Marsh for services rendered in the Confederate States Army as Ordinance Sergeant and this was given to my son Frederick Cade Marsh.

By April 9, 1865, John Marsh knew that the $100 bill was only a souvenir, just as it is today. It hangs framed in my office.

I have a book that belonged to my grandfather Marsh, published in 1905, two years before Pyrnelle died. *The Color Line: A Brief in Behalf of the Unborn,* by William Benjamin Smith. Mr. Smith believed that Ann and Henry's polluted blood, if unchecked, would cause the extinction of civilization. A different cut of racism than Pyrnelle's.

The Waldrons accept the likeness of Ann and Henry to themselves and their chattel. I don't believe it was entirely a patronizing acceptance. It reflected, for them, the way things are. Smith, however, sees a biological horror. In a third-person pep talk to himself, he said he must

> guard himself especially against the emotion of sympathy, pity for the unfortunate race, "the man of yesterday," which the unfeeling process of Nature demands in sacrifice on the altar of the evolution of humanity.

Smith was a statistician teaching at Tulane. Starting with the premise that one drop of black blood could eradicate millennia of white morality and intelligence, he called us white folk to the barricades:

> . . . nay! It is a tremendous and instant peril, against which eternal vigilance

is the only safeguard, in whose presence it is vain and fatuous to cry "peace, peace" when there is no peace, a peril whose menace is sharpened by well meant efforts at humanity and generosity by seemingly just demands for social equality masquerading as "equal opportunity."

Flipping through *The Color Line,* I could find no suggestion about what that "sacrifice on the altar of evolution" might entail. But we know today, don't we? Who should study *The Color Line,* which is a book for grown-ups, is not my main interest. *Diddie, Dumps and Tot,* if read against the text by older teens and college students, could shed some light on white racial views and the human ability to deceive ourselves or, better to say, be deceived by the demons inside and outside us that distort the moral world. "The man of yesterday," wow!

Little Black Sambo was a story for small white children and was still being read innocently to me and my sister by my mother and grandmother. *Eneas Africanus* is not worth redemption, but *Little Black Sambo* cries out for rescue. The hero is an appealing, courageous little boy who in a world of fantasy tames savage beasts into something really tasty, a simpler version of *Where the Wild Things Are.* He and his mother and father need different names; that's no fault of their own, and the older illustrations are ugly stereotypes (except for the tigers). The text is not patronizing. The prose is so perfect to the ear, especially the characters' lilting names, that it would take a gifted writer and illustrator to redeem it, charm intact. May such a one arise.

A book I enjoyed when old enough to read for myself was *Ol' Man Adam an' His Chillun.* The author, Roark Bradford (1896–1948), was born white on a Lauderdale County, Tennessee, plantation. He grew up alongside black sharecroppers, played, sang, and worshipped with them. He carried all his life, one critic wrote, an inner conflict. He had a deep respect for black culture but doubts about its value. If true, a sad ambivalence. Was his literary success about a folk he thought might not matter? The stories in the book are retold Bible stories, mostly from the Old Testament. They are derived, distantly, from black preachers he heard.

Bradford's ambivalence, like a curse that cannot be shaken, entered Harper and Brothers offices with a vengeance, and then into a Broadway musical based on the book, and then a movie based on the musical.

Each chapter of the book is provided with a line drawing by A. B. Walker. In Chapter One we see a sexy white girl, Eve, naked as a blue jay, with long *straight, blond* hair flowing behind her to her ankles. Chapter Two shows a hayseed white country boy, Cain, flirting with a "gorilla gal" seated in a tree because as he says, "Yar is me waiting for a woman to git married wid and it ain't no woman to git married wid. . . ."

What's going on? Lord have mercy, all the illustrated characters are 1920s-style white folks, including "de Lawd," who is the spittin' image of Colonel Sanders! Not one black person is illustrated, yet all the verbal characters are black. On the flyleaf, the publishers touted the book's retelling of Bible stories as "racy." Perhaps the blacks are drawn white to protect white males from thoughts about some Halle Berry Eve. Realistically, Harper Brothers probably didn't think it would sell without this crazy disconnect between the all-black characters and the illustrated "racy" white ones.

Many who don't know the book know the 1930 musical version, *Green Pastures*. It gave an unprecedented breakthrough to the members of its all-black cast. It ran seventy-three weeks on Broadway and then toured the country. This gave black artists their first national recognition. Then, lo and behold! In 1936, Hollywood released the movie *The Green Pastures*. An all-white cast bopped around acting like simple black folk.

The editor of the 2002 *Time Out Film Guide*, John Pym, is as ambivalent as Bradford or Harper Brothers. "There is nothing intrinsically offensive about this all-white cast's use of all-black stereotypes to illustrate the artless simplicities of gospel religion of Deep South slavery," says Pym. At the end of the review, Pym kind of gets aholt of himself to write something negative: "What is offensive is the way in which the depths of plangent suffering that inspired the spirituals is totally ignored." Poor black folk, plangently suffering but artlessly simple and being portrayed by white actors. This book is best left to historians of race in America or very sharp teenagers. Got to say, its stories are really funny.

Uncle Remus, however, deserves a full-throttle campaign to be read to black and white children and enjoyed by their grown-ups. Doubt such will be launched. That is sad. Here is the title page and printing history of the copy I was given when a kid.

> *Uncle Remus, His Songs and Sayings,* by Joel Chandler Harris, New and Revised Edition. With over One Hundred Illustrations by A. B. Frost. Grosset and Dunlap Publishers, New York. By arrangement with D. Appleton-Century Co. Inc. Copyright 1880, 1895, by D. Appleton and Company. Copyright 1908, 1921 by Esther LaRose Harris.

My copy also bears the once-familiar bracketed announcement that begins, "[This book while produced under wartime conditions . . .]"—World War II, that is—and so on. It shows its provenance by being small, oxidized, and shedding pages.

"The Preface and Dedication to the New Edition" is by Joel Chandler Harris and is directed to the incomparable illustrator, Arthur Burdett Frost. No one ever, not ever, will put clothes on animals of the South so well. His animals are as far from Disney cute as the earth is from the sun. In praise of Frost, Harris writes:

> But it would be no mystery at all if this new edition were to be more popular than the old one. Do you know why? Because you have taken it under your hand and made it yours. Because you have breathed the breath of life into these amiable brethren of wood and field. Because by a stroke here and a touch there, you have conveyed into their quaint antics the illumination of your own inimitable humor, which is as true to our sun and soil as it is to the spirit and essence of the matter set forth.

Today the charge of "dialect" is fired at the book. Dialect is equated with racism. As if Uncle Remus is a simpleton not to have picked up the white Southern tongue. As if Mr. Harris maliciously depicts him as limited. Like Pyrnelle, who studied performance and dialect recitation in New York, Joel Chandler Harris saved for us all a sophisticated wit that cannot be expressed in Standard English. Unlike Harry Stillwell Edwards, who is blinded by his belief in racial inferiority and doesn't trouble to record dialect accurately, Harris's use of dialect is studied and deeply respectful. It ain't easy to set on paper or read out loud. I recall my mother reading to us from her 1906 edition of selected stories, a book from which her mother read to her. She struggled each time she opened the book. It's like learning to ride a bicycle. Halting, wobbly, tentative, but then click! Off you go and Remus is there: real, intelligent, and compassionate.

Harris said this about concern for dialect:

> The dialect, it will be observed, is wholly different from that of the Hon. Pompey Smash [a stock pre-Civil War minstrel figure] and his literary descendants and also from the intolerable misrepresentations of the minstrel stage, but it is at least phonetically genuine. Nevertheless, if the language of Uncle Remus fails to give vivid hints of the really poetic imagination of the negro; if it fails to embody the quaint and homely humor which was his most prominent characteristic, if it does not suggest a certain picturesque sensitiveness—a curious exaltation of mind and temperament not to be defined by words—then I have reproduced the form of the dialect merely, and not the essence, and my attempt may be counted a failure.

Harris was familiar with the work of ethnographers who pointed out to him the universal reach of the stories—variants from Native Americans from Canada to Brazil, from the peoples of India, Southeast Asia, and Upper Egypt.

Uncle Remus is noble. Uncle Walt didn't get that. Disney cute doesn't work with Remus. So *Song of the South* is confined, thank God, to the Disney vaults. I recall an attempt to rehabilitate Uncle Remus by making him sound like Andrew Young, our former ambassador to the United Nations. I'm at a loss myself. I don't know how to bring Uncle Remus back on the stage as long as our tetchiness, black and white, prevails. Maybe someday—for other children, of all colors. What a loss. In chapter thirty-eight, "Why the Negro Is Black," Remus gigs us white folks so subtly we don't know we've been skewered. The "little boy" notices one night that "the palms of the old man's hands were as white as his own." He asks why, to which the old gentleman replies, "Toby

sho de pa'm err my han's w'ite, honey . . . en, w'en it come ter dat, dey wuz a
time w'en all de white folks 'uz black—blacker dan me, kase I done bin yer so
long dat I bin sorta bleach out." After a quiet time spent waxing some shoe
thread, he goes on, "Niggers is niggers now, but de time wuz w'en we 'uz all
niggers tergedder."

Remus goes on with the tale of the discovery of a pond ". . . some'rs in
de naberhood" in which if people washed, "dey'd be wash off nice 'en w'ite."
Everyone heads to the pond, the more "soople . . . make a break fer de pon,'
and dem w'at wuz de soopless, dey got in fus. . . ." Soon the water is used up.
". . . w'en dem yuthers come 'long, de mostest dey could do wuz ter paddle
about wid der foots en dabble in it wid der han's. Dem was the niggers. . . ."

Today, academic mortars lob shells into opposing trenches over which of these
older children's books are bad guys or good guys. In Huntsville, Alabama, an
admirable local bookstore carried these books and more old-timers like them.
I felt like looking over my shoulder for the correctness police when I stopped
by. I heard of a collector of Jim Crow signs and racist artifacts who wished
to open a museum to display his collection. This caught him between the
trenches of that battle, a place many smart alecks deny exists. He hated these
artifacts' original message but hated worse those who wanted his collection
suppressed. He believed people black and white would get it if they could
see these things. He must be white because I know there is a devoted trade in
this tasteless memorabilia among black folk. For me, it's time to read it, look
at it, and talk about it—not sell folks short on understanding context. Let's
celebrate the liminal.

Puts me in mind of the "Pornography Room" of the Naples Museum, where
once only incorruptible upper class, white European gentlemen were allowed
to gaze on the erotic materials saved just for them by Vesuvius. Not long ago
it was believed by science and religion that women and young people were
too underdeveloped morally, too soft in the head, to view such stuff, stuff that
could lead them to hysteria, self-abuse, and ultimately to slipping the leash of
those gentlemen who alone were strong enough to take it.

There is no Pornography Room in the Naples Museum today. We should
let Uncle Remus out of the Race Room. Sambo, too, after a name change and a

makeover. Maybe even *Diddie, Dumps and Tot*, discreetly garbed in footnotes. *Huckleberry Finn* has been out for years. Yes, a few crazies try to put him away every so often. The price of rational discourse is eternal vigilance.

9. Max and Me

The 1946 *Revised Handbook for Boys*, known as the *Boy Scouts' Handbook*, lists on page 488 the fifth of ten requirements for the Civics Merit Badge. It reads, "Attend a political meeting or town council, a session of court or other public civic meeting and make a full report of his observations." I joined Spring Hill's Troop 17 at the required age of twelve. Starter rank was Tenderfoot. Some merit badges, such as Civics, were reserved for the more seasoned ranks. So I was thirteen, as was my buddy Max Rogers, when we decided to get the Civics Merit Badge. My certificates, still around, show I was awarded Civics, Cycling, Forestry, and Cooking on August 12, 1946, at a Court of Honor. Max's father, Big Max, was a lawyer, which may have explained our choice of "court session."

I asked my grandmother if she knew any judges. Widowed early, she depended on professional males in Mobile and had quite a stable. Her blue eyes brightened: "There's no finer man in Mobile than Judge Edington." Max and I put ourselves in the last pew of Judge Edington's court, the lone spectator citizens. We hadn't asked if we might come because we'd learned the courts were open to the public. For a while we were alone on the last bench in the courtroom; this was a bit intimidating. Setting the mood for serious business. Judge Edington appeared and seated himself. Then a rumpled lawyer walked through a door on one side of the court. Later, from the other side, a second lawyer appeared, more blowzy than rumpled. In tow were two wretched black men whose condition made the lawyers look elegant. Their clothes were soiled and raggedy. They were hunched and hangdog.

Seven of us in the court. Two of them—to Max and me, to most white people—completely unlike us other five. As Max and I watched, from what seemed an increasing distance, Judge Edington and the two lawyers had themselves a fine time joshing and jibing the men, reducing them, if possible, to creatures of even less worth. We were too far away to make out the words, just the chuckles, the shucking and jiving.

He's the judge—my grandmother's "no finer man." Why doesn't he stop those lawyers?

I don't want to over-remember my revulsion. I was only going on fourteen; my range was limited. I recall thinking while leaving the courthouse that if the judge was one of Mobile's finest, I wanted nothing to do with these men. With that came the inevitable belief that no other white people in Mobile felt as I did. I was not then focused on the two black men, but on what I had just learned about my family and my world.

That is a true recall because I know I said nothing about my feelings to Max, to my family, or anyone. When I went before the Board of Review of dads and scoutmasters to prove I'd met the requirements for the Civics badge, I trashed Requirement Five, which ends, ". . . make a final report on his observation." I made no final report. I also trashed Scout Law Number One: "A Scout is Trustworthy." Law One gets doggedly specific, "If he were to violate his honor by . . . not doing exactly a given task when trusted on his honor, he may be directed to hand over his Scout Badge." Of course I wasn't going to "make a full report of his (my) observation." I took that to be the "given task" I was going to violate. I knew good and well the Scout edifice did not want to hear my observation.

Max's family had come to Spring Hill during World War II, bringing pizzazz, smarts, and excitement. They bought a large tract across from St. Paul's Episcopal Church: "The old ____ place." Standing went up when it was said, "So-and-so bought the old ____ place," rather than "a lot" or "a house."

The Rogerses built what we called "a modern house," irregular in floor plan, curvy, with walls of glass bricks and an enclosed "patio" with a polished brick floor and bamboo furniture. The halls and living room were papered with the metallic paper that once sheathed the interiors of mahogany tea crates from

China. There was a doorless, drive-through garage, not yet called "a carport." On the other side of the garage was a small apartment for George. Like Big Max, George came from the Rogers plantation in Sumter County. George was young, handsome, good-natured, and black—probably Spring Hill's only live-in cook and butler. George let Max and me visit in his rooms until he got married. A couple of times when we came home from school, George let us fill up on doughnuts lifted directly from a kettle of bubbling oil. Correction: they made a detour for powdered sugar.

The Rogerses further supplied Spring Hill with talk and awe by their annual St. Paul's carol parties. Big Max always led in song, and my mother often played the piano. They kept pea fowl loose on their property to wander, to nest, to multiply, and to scream. Our rector, the Reverend Robb White, once threatened to shoot them if they continued to gather, as he believed, across from the church on Sundays to scream along with the sermon. The Rogerses brought extravagant Southern-style names to Spring Hill. My friend Max was Charles McPherson Adustan Rogers, the IV. His father's law firm, McCorvey, Turner, Rogers, Johnston and Allen, was perched almost at the top of our then tallest building, the Merchants' National Bank. From there, Max and I would fly paper airplanes and, not often, drop water balloons out of fully operable sashes.

Big Max had been raised on the Rogers plantation just outside Gainesville, Alabama. In town one found Rogers General Store and St. Alban's Episcopal Church (established in 1879 and once full of the Rogers family, by 2010 it had four active members). The Rogerses' soil was in the heart of the Black Belt, a geological feature that runs across central Alabama from Mississippi to Georgia. Its black soil once grew abundant cotton until it was exhausted by the planters who had previously exhausted the soils of Virginia and would move on to exhaust the cotton-bearing soils of Texas.

The area's chalky hummocks are felicitous to red cedars, which crave lime. I was told so many cedars grew on the bare land of southwest Alabama that a pencil factory once operated on the plantation. It was not there when Max and I would visit during summer vacation. Off we went on the train from Mobile. We got off in Livingston, alerted to check out the eternal domino game played by chicken-necked old white men in the town square gazebo. The players shared space with a cool artesian fountain. They didn't have to leave for water.

We would be met in Livingston by Aunt Suddie in her pickup. I only remember Aunt Suddie and Uncle Barnes Rogers living in the big, one-story plantation house. I assumed they were Big Max's brother and sister; I never asked. We had fun! We could ride docile horses, cool our feet in the Victorian spring house, carefully downstream from butter, milk, and eggs. We peed in the big chamber pot that nested under the four-poster we shared. We'd visit Rogers General Store and walk to the bridge over the Tombigbee to drop firecrackers off the bridge.

I didn't want to write this: One type of firecracker we bought would shoot a projectile up, which would then explode. Somebody in the store said we should not miss the black men's Saturday craps game, held in a hollow behind the store. Behind a screen of bushes, we set up one of our fireworks like a mortar, so as to angle its little bomb up and over the craps game. We heard it go off and caught a glimpse of men looking confused, and then we ran away. Would we have done that to craps-playing white farmers? No.

Back then on Saturdays, as all old-timers know, these Black Belt towns were always thick with cars, wagons, and people, black and white. That was then. I heard a few years ago that food stamps were all that was propping up Gainesville, its majority-black population having gone North.

Max and I had an adventure with black kids our age who lived on the plantation. It was more strange than fun. The boys asked if we'd like to go out with them after dark; did we have a flashlight? There was a glimmer of dominance in the invitation—they asked us, it was at night, we didn't know what they were about, or where we were going. Matters were turned around.

We followed the bobbing flashlight beam down chalky washes and up hummocks. Nothing but dark cedars reaching up. The game was simple—find roosting songbirds and swat them with a stick. When our leaders had two or three, they built a fire to roast them. I tasted one: smoky raw meat. I believe what was then a game had probably come down from past generations as a necessity.

Aunt Suddie organized more carefree events for herself and us white kids at her own special place, a grassy slope shelving into a gravel beach on the Tombigbee River. A trip in the back of the pickup truck took us there to gather fool's gold and clams that might have pearls, and to swim to the sandbar with one tree.

One day at the plantation, I found Uncle Barnes sitting in the breezeway between the house and the kitchen. Max and I had just finished lunch, but Barnes was eating alone. I asked what he was eating. "Chicken Foot Perloo," Barnes said. He loved it but had to eat it in the breezeway because no one could stand to see the yellow chicken feet stuck every which way in the gummy rice. Barnes explained you couldn't eat a chicken foot with the scales on it. After a plunge in boiling water, the scales would fall from the feet, which could then be added for a slow cook in some rice and butter. That was your perloo.

I have always been fond of gummy food, so I must have shown enough interest for Barnes to warm to the subject. The feet of most creatures have a lot of cartilage, so chicken feet leach into the rice their tasty goo to flavor and bind the grains, he explained, and then offered me some. Unlike my reaction to the songbird roast, I took a generous taste of this dish and have wanted a mess ever since. Once I got close. In a San Francisco Chinese restaurant, I saw Duck Feet and Rice on the menu. Close, close enough. I ordered it only to be told they were out of duck feet.

This moment with Barnes and the perloo deeply affected me. Barnes was gentle and shy. He would come in from the fields, bathe, eat, and say little. Aside from the perloo talk, I don't recall him ever speaking to me. On the breezeway we clicked. I was interested in him. He cared enough to explain to a kid from Mobile why he ate chicken feet and was pleased I liked them too. I appreciated how gently he accepted being banished and that he seemed pleased I didn't think him odd.

During the civil rights movement, twenty years later, I had reason to doubt Suddie and Barnes would have much use for me. Then in 1986, forty years after those enchanted swims, I received a letter from Mrs. John A. Rogers, asking if I recalled her Aunt Suddie taking us to her spot and telling me she still went there. She wanted me to know she appreciated the work I had done with the black women's cooperative, the Freedom Quilting Bee. Her appreciation brought tears. I remembered my high school Virgil: *sunt lacrima rerum*—"these are the things of tears." A sentence so compressed it can be translated many ways. One way: "To think on these things of the past and all the meaning they now bear brings one to tears."

In 1999, a young historian named Susan Youngblood Ashmore began taping me as I talked about civil rights days. I figured she would use my tales and those of a couple of others to write a little something. Years went by, and now we are close friends. In 2009, when she gave me a copy of her book, *Carry It On: The War on Poverty and the Civil Rights Movement in Alabama, 1964–1972*, I was rocked back at the book's scope, attention to detail, and high level of scholarship. She had scoured hundreds of sources: from Lyndon Baines Johnson to Sargent Shriver to Ma Willie Abrams of Wilcox County. I consumed it all: text, sources, bibliography, index—visiting old friends and opponents. Naturally, I focused on opponents, finding unrevealed reasons to bolster my anger at their duplicitous and self-serving ways. Then I read the first two words on page 202: "Barnes Rogers"—not Barnes Rogers in 1946 but Barnes Rogers in 1966:

> Barnes Rogers, his son, John, and Barnes's two sisters owned twenty-four hundred acres in northern Sumter County and had rented parts of their property to tenants for thirty years. In January 1966, they decided to shift to timber production when the Hammermill Paper Company offered as much as three times the amount their renters had been paying. The new arrangement did not allow the tenants to work the land, although they could continue to pay rent for their housing. Left without any cotton acreage, several farmers had no way to support themselves. R. W. Williams had lived on his place for fifty-one years under a handshake agreement that rolled over year after year until January 1966. He rented six acres from the paper company, paying $105 a month for land and a sharecropper house, so he could at least grow his own food.
>
> Not all of the Rogerses' renters fell under this new arrangement. Some worked on property not reserved for the paper company. Robert Thomas lost the ability to farm his usual thirteen acres when he inquired about his cotton allotment check. When Barnes Rogers tried to get Thomas to sign over his ASCS [Agricultural and Soil Conservation Service] check, Thomas refused

Ma Willie Abrams in the doorway of her house in Wilcox County; its walls and ceilings were insulated with glued-on sheets of newspaper, magazines, and pages from calendars.

because his landlord would not give him enough time to read the document. According to Thomas, Rogers "Just wanted us to go on and sign it. He just have a mark there for you to sign." Thomas did not budge. "Yeah, I wanted to know how much it was and he didn't want to tell me," Thomas later testified to the Alabama State Advisory Committee to the U.S. Commission on Civil Rights, "and I told him I was going to see about the check. Well, it wasn't too long before I got a letter that he wasn't going to rent me any more land. . . . [A]ll I could see was he got mad about that." The cotton farmer had also participated in mass meetings conducted by the Sumter County Movement for Human Rights, and he believed that Rogers had canceled their agreement in part because of those civil rights activities.

Mr. McCorvey: One day in the law offices of McCorvey, Turner, Rogers, Johnston & Allen, Mr. Gessner McCorvey called Max and me into his office. We were around twelve or thirteen. That had never happened before. His office was gloomy, its walls looming with leather-bound books. It was a little scary; he was big and old. Important, too, because his name was the first in the string we loved to rattle off as fast as possible. He attempted joviality, but it rang hollow. I was never approached by a pederast, but that is what it must feel like. He handed us a picture. He was laughing and wanted us to laugh. It was a photograph of a black man doctored up to make him appear to be an ape.

I left his office feeling dirty. I didn't mention to Max how I felt. We said nothing about it. I was revulsed, but that didn't come from identifying the photograph with the warning word "racist." It was Mr. McCorvey himself who repelled me, not the concept of bigotry. That sensibility was not then available to me.

In 1948, the politics swirling around in Mr. McCorvey's law firm also appeared on the playground of Spring Hill Elementary School. The "Dixiecrats" had walked out of the Democratic National Convention, and the boys' side of the playground was tense with challenges about whom our parents were going to vote for. No one was very clear what the fuss was about, but some parents were hot about something, and it spilled over onto the boys' side of the playground. We never knew nor cared what the girls' side was talking about. My folks, though New Deal Democrats, didn't vote at that time; they explained later that they'd been too poor to pay the poll tax during the Depression ($1.50 a year), tax and interest cumulative. They did tell me they supported the national party. I asked them what Max had meant when he was challenged about how his daddy would vote. Max had said, "He's going fishing." My mother explained that he wasn't actually going fishing. The Walters fished a lot, especially for speckled trout in November. It meant that Big Max was caught between some powerful people—some for Truman, some for Strom Thurmond. So, no vote at all.

Prior to 1966, the ballot symbol of the Alabama Democratic Party.

As an adult, I learned that Gessner T. McCorvey, at the time he tried to corrupt me, was chair of the Alabama Democratic Party Executive Committee. In 1948, he co-opted the state party for the Dixiecrats, who hated Truman for his pro-labor leanings and the civil rights plank he helped insert in the party platform. McCorvey threatened political annihilation to any Trumanites in Alabama. On July 29, 1948, all of Alabama's electors pledged to Strom Thurmond. Big Max, off fishing, would not have voted that year under the Democratic Rooster, as I later did several times. That was the longtime ballot logo of the Alabama Democratic Party. You pulled the lever under a crowing rooster, over whose head and beneath whose claws were banners proclaiming "White Supremacy for the Right." The state party committee removed the banner in January 1966.

But the white supremacy logo was still in place in 1965 when Stokely Carmichael, then the SNCC chairman, explained to newly registered black voters of Lowndes County the virtues of the black panther logo over the rooster. A separate Lowndes County political party could give the 80 percent black population control. SNCC, always strapped for cash, had lifted that logo from a local black, segregated high school's football team. Stokely explained that panthers were quiet, went about their own business, but if attacked would defend themselves. The birth of the Black Panther Party in Lowndes County is captured in the documentary film *Lay My Burden Down*. I did not until now put the rooster and crow together as further white blindness to injustice. What I do recall is the rage and fear of many Alabama white folks that SNCC would threaten them with a panther attack. The same folks who went to the polls to vote under the rooster crowing "White Supremacy."

How pleasant it would be to end this chapter celebrating the farewell flight of the Rooster and Jim Crow. They are still around, tricked out in disguises. The feathers barely show. They can still fly, sometimes here, sometimes there. As late as 2010, the two had perched on the roost of a candidate for governor of New York named Paladino, who entertained millions by his racist emails. Unlike Edington and McCorvey, he denied his race hatred with a laugh. I'd rather deal with the two who were out in the open.

10. *High School*

The Mobile Optimists sponsored an oratorical contest on April 27, 1949. I represented Murphy High School, chosen from among the students taking Speech. Speech was composed of Mobile's talkative upper-middle-class kids, among whom I believed myself to be the only one with stage fright, which I fought with humor. Example, my speech: "Why I Will Never Be an Episcopal Minister." The Optimists required the speech to be written by the contestant and be delivered from memory, no notes allowed. The subject was "Youth Look Forward to Their Civic Responsibility." It took days to do the memorizing.

After the Admiral Semmes Hotel fed us, the contest began. As I spoke, the text was spooling through my brain, an interior teleprompter. As my mouth was finishing a sentence, my brain would scroll down the next one or two. Then the screen went blank; the next sentence balked. My mouth was going to run out of information. I had a second or two lag time to decide what to do. I'd not been told to leave the typescript at home; it was secure in the breast pocket of my new Robert Hall suit. I pulled it out, confessed I'd lost my place, found the missing sentence, and folded the speech back into its pocket. My brain reeled off the rest of the sentences flawlessly.

I sat. That's it, I thought, that redheaded guy from McGill is going to win. Roman Catholic McGill High was Murphy's rival.

I won. As the black waiters cleared the tables, the businessmen told me my cool recovery had cinched it, even though I had broken the memorization rule. It was on to the regionals in Jackson, Mississippi. If I won there, on to the nationals. That part was news to me and a little scary. I'd only been out of Mobile County once when I was about five. My parents took me, along with their best friends, George and Corinne Gaillard, to visit Corinne's folks' Mississippi Delta plantation. I only recall a "Gone with the Wind" house and that I picked a few bolls of cotton. Where did the money come from in 1937 for this trip? Yet we could afford a side trip to the Memphis Zoo. I recall a clear picture of Monkey Island but not what became a family story: "When Little Francis Wet His Pants Laughing at the Monkeys." No need to say more.

Somewhere around Memphis one night, we saw lights twinkling on the far shore of the Mississippi, just as we'd seen our house lights at night when in a skiff off the shoreline of Mon Louis. So I was reported to have said, "Is that Pop over at our house?" I was ready to come home.

Now I was to leave home a second time with an unknown Optimist. In my own room at Jackson's Heidelberg Hotel, I spent a night of panic. All the ways I could mess up, pass out, blank out, throw up, or walk off. Late that night, I knelt at the bed in an act that spoke of my lack of orthodox piety. I prayed to the man in my family I took to be the bravest, my great-grandfather, Dr. Jacob G. Michael. He was mediated to me primarily by his daughters: my grandmother and two great-aunts.

Michael genes had defied the odds. Those three Michael girls and their four brothers (long dead) produced seven girls and no boys. No replacement male came along for fifty-three years—then me. Perhaps this predisposed his daughters to hold their father up to me, the Successor. Why I thought him the bravest I don't know, except I did know he was in the War. The Michael girls told of no war exploits or acts of bravery. Truth be told, many stories were genteel put-downs of his male foibles, feminine critiques even as they adored him.

In an eccentric memoir, *Clerical Errors* by Louis Tucker, the author, a querulous Episcopal priest who visited the Michaels' Hygeia Hotel for services and knew Dr. Michael well, said of him: "... an old Confederate surgeon, with mustache, goatee, but yet not quite the Type; he was responsible for so many lives that he had almost lost the reckless twinkle, although he had the eyes." By "Type" and "reckless twinkle," Louis Tucker was referring to his admired father and similar Confederate veterans who still had killing in their hearts, ready if messed with. But Papoo was all I had that night before the contest.

Next day at the Heidelberg, a flubless speech. I didn't win. My handler said I deserved to win, but most likely, small-minded judges from Mississippi were put off by my emphasis on Mobile's Mardi Gras as a source of civic pride.

My Mother and Father John Cole: While I was in high school my mother suffered a radical mastectomy. Breast, muscles, ribs, lymphatic system scooped out, then blistering x-rays. With her medical knowledge she knew the prognosis. I still see her swollen arm strapped up as she lay in bed in an attempt to drain the lymphatic fluid. She and her doctor, Norberne Clark, were friends as well as patient/physician. They agreed he could thread tubing through the sunken chest area, around her side, to drain the fluid into her back. This done with a long needle and no anesthetic. Later the cancer metastasized to the bone. This is not said to curry sympathy but to lay a baseline for what she did with the rest of her life.

She came to a deeper abandonment to God. A "conversion" as the term is used in classic mystical theology. It irritates me to have to fritz around, putting quotes to "conversion," to claw the term back from evangelicals, who use it to mean a non-repeatable event. No, hers was that good old-time, sixth-century conversion that is an ever-new, repeatable process of opening to the infinite of God. At first she prayed for healing with her friend, Gladys Fields. They lovingly fought the rector of St. Paul's to provide Unction for the Sick, a practice for which his Low Church upbringing had not prepared him. Which he did.

When we moved to Spring Hill the church had a pedal-powered reed organ. My mother became the organist, and to rest her feet from pumping my father crawled under the church and hooked a vacuum cleaner motor and fan to the organ. When she was in too much pain to play the organ, she took voice lessons from her friend, Clarendon McClure, a venerable Mobile musician who came to my help years later. She joined the choir, and when that was too difficult she took to composition.

I have a 1951 setting of hers to the hymn "Prayer is the Soul's Sincere Desire." Tucked into the sheet music are two newspaper clippings showing the active life she was leaving. One picture shows her racing an outboard in the "Mobile Outboard Regatta." The caption reads, "The picture at the bottom is a feminine entry in the races, Miss Martha Marsh, who was the only woman pilot." The other clipping shows her in her boat, *Golliwogg*, a name she chose from Debussey's "Golliwogg's Cake Walk." Given the last act of her life I wonder if she knew the dictionary definition of golliwogg: "a grotesque black doll used by Florence K. Upton (died 1922) in a series of children's books." Daddy told me she used a ten-horsepower Caille, the lower unit of which held a murderous forward-facing propeller. All other outboards I ever heard of put the prop on the rear of the lower housing. So if you fell out and the motor turned the boat onto you, as they were wont to do, you might at least be hit by the gear box of the prop first. The Caille, however, was a submerged meat grinder. Nowadays all such boats, like jet skis, have

My mother, Martha Marsh (Walter), in an innocent time when she was about ten years old, wearing a costume for some occasion.

kill switches tethered to the operator. (I can hear my father saying, "Buncha sissies.") The second clipping shows a winner with the caption: "Miss Martha Marsh of Mobile in the Polliwogg [sic] winner of the women's outboard motor race at Bay St. Louis, Miss., Sunday. The event was run in a blinding rainstorm, with the course defined only during lightning flashes." I'm glad she raced outboards. I owe my life to it—one day a good-looking guy named Francis Walter Jr. helped her out of the *Golliwog*.

After the Second World War, Spring Hill had gotten a doctor, a Tennessee veteran. He arrived in a Model A Ford. Martha went to work for him as a lab and X-ray assistant—the kind of work she had once given up to marry. Can you believe lab techs once sat right in one's doctor's office peering at a microscope slide scored into tiny squares counting how many eosinophils and leukocytes were in each square? Today who gives a thought to the tireless robot off Lord knows where that does that? Even after the brutal surgery she had lost none of her brand of childrearing. For some reason she was doing urinalysis on me. I asked how I was. "All normal," she said looking at me. "There were a number of sperm cells but it could have been a wet dream." To that there can be no reply from a teenaged boy. My brother, David, was still needing a little help on the toilet while she was spending a lot of time in bed. She would get up and tend to him. Then she stopped. Then there was the cry that still hurts me, David calling, "Somebody," instead of "Mommee." Martha told her mother that it was hard to not go to him but she was preparing David for her death. David says that far from being an emotional help it made him feel she no longer loved him.

She kept up fishing trips as long as she could. There is a snapshot of her standing on the wharf outside our boathouse at the Alba Club. She's in a wet nor'easter smiling like the devil, a little hunched to favor the left side of her chest.

Lent 1951 I was in my freshman year at Spring Hill College, living at home, a ten-minute walk to the campus. One Wednesday Mommee was attending a Christ Church Lenten Preaching Service. Mobile's Episcopal churches would sponsor these and the area clergy would sit in the chancel. She could see men up there she had known for years, vested in cassock, surplice, and stole. As she was leaving the service she saw a black man wearing a clerical collar. He was in the last row of pews. One assumes everyone else saw him but she was the one who walked over. And said, "How do you do, I'm Martha Walter."

"I'm Father John Cole," he said.

"What church are you from?"

"The Church of the Good Shepherd."

"And where is your church?"

"It's downtown on State Street."

Let's say that's when the axis of her world jumped its bearings.

"I've lived in Mobile," she said, "since I was a baby and I never even knew there was a colored church in Mobile."

Father Cole said, "It was established in 1854."

That night my father, grandmother, my sister Patricia, and David sat immobile at the supper table as she poured this out with fire in her eyes: "Then I said to him, 'Why aren't you up there?'"

"Up there" was the chancel, with its now-departing clergy. Father Cole's answer was profound. I believe it came because the two of them had been lifted out of chronological time into *kairos* time. In everyday speech it would be called "a defining moment." *Kairos* is Greek for qualitative, not quantitative time: a period in which something special happens. In this case the *kairos* shaped future time for Martha, me, my family, who knows who else?

"You'll have to ask them that," he said.

That could have been the end. But no.

"I turned around," she said, "went down the aisle to the door into the parish hall and headed to the rector's office."

The rector, the Reverend J. Sullivan Bond, said, "Come in, Martha." She did, to ask the question Father Cole would not answer. She found the embarrassed answer she received not an answer to her newly honed grasp of the Church as the Body of Christ where all can be incorporated.

We sat stunned at the supper table. Martha was as alive as ever she would be. I hope I remember correctly: that I was transported, proud of her, and ready to explore the truth she had realized.

Table talk wasn't over. "I've been thinking about what I should do. They must have a Women's Auxiliary. I've decided to find out who is president of the Women's Auxiliary of the Church of the Good Shepherd and I'm going to pay a call on her. I don't know what I'll say. This is all I know to do, right now." Those words meant a social call. A white woman calling on a colored woman in her home. Not standing out in the yard. Not a note with no courtesy titles.

Martha learned the president was Mrs. Effie Goode. I came to know her after my mother's death. She was the wife of Dr. Escus Goode, a dentist. She and her husband were part of Mobile's black elite. Mrs. Goode had dark red hair, a creamy complexion, elegant bearing, and a living room full of stuffed chairs and couches.

Came the second supper table talk. The first thing she said was, "As I came in, Mrs. Goode used an expression I haven't heard since I was a girl, 'Let me rest your coat in the bedroom.'"

What was coming next? This is the gist of it, and sure, it's honed by the many times I've told it to myself and others.

"Mrs. Goode, I'm here because I don't know what else to do. I'm just one

My grandmother, Marie Catherine Michael "Bobbin" Marsh, and Volena Gardner.

woman. I have picked you, to say to you, that I've lived here all my life and never questioned how colored people are treated by us. But now I know. I want you to know I will no longer be part of it. I don't know what I will do, but I will never again be part of it."

Shortly before she died she asked Father Cole to bring her Holy Communion. I was home for Thanksgiving from first year in seminary. I had leave from the dean to come early and stay as long as necessary because she was close to death and did die the Sunday before Thanksgiving Day, 1954. After she died our maid, Mrs. Volena Gardner, told me that Martha had asked her to keep her friend, Gladys Fields, from visiting because in her narcotic haze she felt that Mrs. Fields's prayers were keeping her alive and in pain. Volena said she and my mother then prayed.

Father Cole administered the sacrament to my mother, me, my sister, my grandmother, and Volena. My sister made it clear to the rector of St. Paul's that Volena would sit with the family during the burial liturgy instead of in the back pew where she was supposed to sit. For a few God-drunk people, there is an unbreakable weld between justice and that which St. Paul meant when he wrote "No longer live I, Christ lives within me." Others may call that Christ something else.

Ushers and Junior Advisers: High school kids at our church belonged to "The Young People's Service League" which my constant friend, Louis, and I joined with enthusiasm. This was a couple of years before my mother's death.

Our lives have run parallel through grammar school, high school, college, the same canonical process to begin the road to ordination, riding in the same car to Sewanee to seminary (though not roommates—enough is enough). We were ordained together at St. Paul's, Spring Hill. Finally we disengaged. He to marriage and parish work in the diocese of Alabama; me to New York City. Now we are retired priests, still close, with similar achy bones or replaced joints.

No such aches in high school. Then we enjoyed Boy Scouts, exploring Mobile's Civil War fortifications, serving at the altar, and especially the fellowship and girls of St. Paul's YPSL. Our becoming day students at Spring Hill College avoided the disjunct felt by freshmen away from home, and we contrived to continue our earlier way of life even though now college students. For instance, we were quite the favorites of the pretty young faculty advisor of the Murphy High School Ushers Club. Ushering opened the world of drama and music to members of the club because the school's large stage was a favorite venue for tours. We asked the advisor if we could stay on as ushers even though we'd graduated. She capitulated for a couple of years until she said we'd gotten too tall to be mistaken for high school kids and she could get in trouble.

This allowed us to see Tallulah Bankhead in *Private Lives*. We ushers had been promised an audience with Miss Bankhead in her dressing room after the show. We did see her during curtain calls, waving a Confederate Battle Flag, but not backstage. Pressed hard, our faculty advisor finally admitted that Miss Bankhead was too drunk to receive us. I then realized I had noticed her weaving as well as waving a flag. It was my first time to see a sure-enough intoxicated person. And it was Tallulah!

We decided to pull the Usher's Club deal on the YPSL. We asked to become a new thing, "Junior YPSL Advisors." This was after my mother's epiphany. Louis had heard about it from me. We were both ashamed and intrigued about this hidden Episcopal Church in Mobile. We asked the adult advisors if we could create a program to introduce the existence of black Episcopalians. We would never have gotten so far with it had not the adult advisors been Mr. and Mrs. Yandell. They were what we called Yankees, though I don't believe that they were Yankee-born. That tag meant they were part of the population explosion that transformed Mobile during the Second World War. Though it was true that most of the wave of newcomers were not technically Yankees, certainly not the Mississippi poor whites working in the shipyards. The Yandells thought the idea was nice. Not radical—nice. This was the program: The first Sunday evening the kids would be given a multiple-choice quiz and time to discuss it. The second Sunday Father Cole would talk about Good Shepherd and black Episcopalians. How I wish I had a copy of our quiz. It started slow: "Are there any Negro Episcopalians? Yes or No." The only hot question was one that got the jump on the "What Would Jesus Do" bromide. "If you were on the bus and a Negro sat beside you would you get up? Yes or No." This was something that could possibly happen to them because Mobile's version of Jim Crow on buses was (in theory) that whites began seating behind the driver and moved back. Blacks were to begin at the very back and work forward. This would, pardon me, create a gray area when they met. (When the Montgomery Bus Boycott was being planned an early proposal was only to request the adoption of the "Mobile Plan.") The next question was, "If a colored person sat next to Jesus would he get up? Yes or No."

The Yandells approved it all. I asked if I could be the one to invite Father Cole. I wanted to meet him. I was entering my mother's *kairos* time; easing into it.

I didn't have a driver's license. I didn't get one the moment it was possible. Postponement dealt with the challenges and uncertainties of vehicular dating and male socializing. The latter consisted of driving around looking for beer. Thanks to my German forebears we had beer and wine on the table. Children got watered wine in jelly glasses. It was said my first beer was sucked from my mother's thumb. As for dating, that had to do with anxiety.

Mommee waited in the car as I walked up to the shabby rectory next door to the church. Father Cole accepted the invitation simply and graciously. Louis and I gave the quiz to our kids, discussion followed. Father Cole was up for the next Sunday. During the week the Yandells called the two of us over. At this time the parish was without a rector. The all-male vestry had some of the canonical authority normally vested in the rector. The Yandells told us the vestry would not allow Father Cole to come.

"Why?" we asked.

"They said young girls would be present."

The Yandells were more surprised than we and much embarrassed to become enforcers for the vestry. To take me off the hook, they offered to hand Father Cole the insult rather than ask me to do it.

"I invited him. I'll uninvite him."

I could have had any number of emotions. I felt two: guilt, with a big helping of anger on top. Who were these men to contradict my mother's moral vision? As I see it now, it was also my remembered encounters with Judge Edington and Gessner McCorvey. There was a dawning that in our world this was an overarching issue.

Father Cole was as gracious as before. Said he wasn't surprised; he'd figured that would happen. I hadn't, not at all. I began to look around the room as if I had days to do so. I saw the bare pine floorboards, the lumpy chairs. I saw his library, floor to ceiling, covering half the walls. I thought of my father building the bookshelves along one living room wall up to my bedroom door. As I lingered in kairos time I thought idly of our library. *Funk & Wagnall's* outdated encyclopedias, Wheatley's three-volume *Diary of Samuel Pepys* (expurgated), *Tristram Shandy*, the strange, racy *The Merry Nights of Straparola*, privately printed. Mom had acquired that in 1931, "No. 310 of only 1000 copies." That contentious pair, sitting together, *Mother India* and *Father India*. The book, hidden but not really, on the shelf up at the ceiling delicately introducing sex to young married couples, which Max and I sneaked out of the house for information.

There was also a line of unusual books, each exactly 3 x 4 inches, bound in thin, green, leather covers. The publisher was "Little Leather Library Corporation, Copyright 1921." Even new they were the victims of cheap leather and oxidizing paper. Each book was a gem of a reprint. I've only saved five. One is *Lays of Ancient Rome* by Thomas Babington Macaulay, another a Hans Christian Andersen fairy tale. When my grandmother and mother left Mobile for Brookside, Massachusetts, so that the smarty-pants sixteen-year-old could begin pre-med studies, Martha bought the series in Boston so she would have these little pearls designed to be read on public conveyances. I don't think I could have stood her then.

Lord have mercy! Here comes my first computer metaphor. Might I say that during that fugue state in Father Cole's study, I was downloading my social justice program for later use?

I snapped out of it, apologized to him for my being white. Later, at home, I flipped. I rejected the white culture into which I had been born and nourished. A little later, I was ashamed again, identifying myself as inescapably part of Mobile's white culture and therefore guilty. I am thankful to have stayed in this back and forth identity dance for much of my life. Toward the close of Act One in one's life the unformed gets rigid sometimes to bad effect. I'm thankful not to have wasted my soul's energy rejecting my past, hating my peers and my family. Just as glad, too, I didn't allow the fire to flicker out and—making a few quiet apologies—sink back to being a mostly satisfied white guy.

Leaving Father Cole, I found myself on the rectory walk to the street. I see that walk as well as I see the pen in my hand. Beautiful tan and brown Old

Mobile bricks, herringbone-laid, no mortar. While standing on the bricks I drew a life-altering conclusion: He has more books than we do, and he can't come to our church.

A definition of crisis in the *Oxford Universal Dictionary*, 1933, reads: ". . . a state of affairs in which a decisive change for better or worse is imminent." Under "pathology" it reads: "The point in the progress of a disease when a change takes place which is decisive of recovery or death." Another take on *kairos*.

White Southerners don't have these race conversions so much now. Too much cleansing water has swept under the bridge.

I looked at the bricks again. I heard in myself: *I will never be part of this system again. Never. Ever.* I will fight. I will never give up. Ever. My mother sat waiting in the car as I came down the walk.

11. *The Michael Sisters*

From my infancy I was treated as exceptional, an elitism infused in me by the Three Sisters: my grandmother and two great-aunts, the three daughters of my Michael great-grandparents. They called each other Minnie, Ida B., and Marie, and they were the ground of my childhood. I was the Three Sisters' favored one. I know they wanted me to be a doctor like their father, but none ever mentioned it. They believed whatever I chose to do with my life would be perfect. They could not help but spoil me—after the birth of their brother, Ruffin, in 1879, no males had been born to the Michael line until I arrived in 1932.

The oldest, Minnie Josephine Michael, was the calm, slow-moving sister. A spinster, she referred to herself as "an unappropriated blessing." We children called her "Arminnie," a corruption of Aunt Minnie. She was born April 24, 1866. Her father, Dr. Jacob G. Michael, thought it safer for the birth to occur at his mother's home in Demopolis, Alabama, but the baby was then whisked across the Tombigbee River to the little settlement of Belmont, where Dr. and Mrs. Michael had relocated in the last weeks of the Civil War. Then came Ida Bolivia Michael Hempstead, who bore three daughters; her husband made money, and long after his death, some of it helped me through college and seminary. The youngest sister was my grandmother, Marie Catherine Michael Marsh, whom I called "Bobbin."

Great-aunt Ida Bolivia hated to be photographed and pretty much avoided her likeness being taken throughout her life. She also hated her Christian name, would not allow it to be used. Her two sisters called her "Ida B."; I called her "Mamie." Her granddaughters, Ann, Betsy, and Peggy, called her "Mamaw" (and called my grandmother "T" or "T-widey," an obvious corruption of "Auntie"). Every Christmas I got a new five-dollar bill from Mamie—if not new from the Merchants' National Bank, at least washed and ironed.

I once asked why somebody would be named "Bolivia" and was told in a voice that said, "Don't ask that again," that she was named after a relative—which could have been said of everyone in our family, save my sister, whom my mother boldly decided to name "Patricia Mary."

Years later, I learned from a distant cousin that the father of these three old ladies had a brother, John Edward Michael. John married Bolivia McQuire. Bolivia's father, Wesley McQuire, was born in Tennessee in 1803, died in Mobile 1877. Wesley was a passionate libertarian (or just hated the Spanish). He named his daughters Uruguay, Paraguay, and Bolivia because these nations had thrown off the Spanish yoke. Yet my great-aunt Ida Bolivia was the least political of all animals. Out of affection, or maybe respect, Great-grandfather Michael named a daughter after his sister-in-law's child.

The Three Sisters admitted they were captured by two vignettes—of pickles and pine trees—told by Marie and Minnie (Ida B. was no storyteller). Their father would give the three little girls each the price of a dill pickle. They would walk up the railroad tracks leading to the little town of Citronelle about a mile away.

At the grocers they would each buy a dill pickle, dipped up from the great pickle barrel in the middle of the store. When they set off for home each held a pickle wrapped in newspaper. Marie would have finished her pickle way before they got home. The story never said she begged licks from her sisters' pickles. I doubt she did. Minnie would pace her pickle to the walk. Arriving home at "The White House" on the hotel grounds she would have just finished it off. Ida B. would save her pickle, maybe taking a lick or two, or a nibble on the way so she could enjoy it at home. It was never told if she lorded the pickle over her sisters. I doubt she did.

Marie married Frederick Cade Marsh of Franklin, Louisiana. Their daughter, Martha, my mother, was nine months old when he died. An officer in the New York Life Insurance Company, he left my grandmother financially secure. But knowing little about money, depending on the advice of others, she made unwise investments. Who today remembers the Handy Dandy Grocery Store concept? A thing before its time. A shopper could walk down the aisles and take her own selections off convenient shelves, rather than depending on the grocer to get them for her. An investment winner!? It folded. Or the stock in Black Giant Mines Company in Salome, Arizona? Marie also spent money on my mother, Martha, who was not a greedy child, just very smart and possibly spoiled. She was given a Mason and Hamlin parlor grand, a harp, a ten-horse outboard motor, and a racing boat. At sixteen she skipped a grade in high school and enrolled in a pre-med program at Brookside Hospital, Brookside, Massachusetts. She wanted to be a doctor like her Michael grandfather. She and Marie, Southern-born and -bred, set off for New England. Two years later Martha dropped out. They said they were homesick for Mobile. Marie said all the food in Massachusetts was white and boiled. They brought home antiques. Back in Mobile, Martha, who had learned enough to be a lab tech and operate the primitive X-ray machines of the day, found work with old Dr. Sledge who, I think, delivered me.

Minnie worked as a typist for the L&N Railroad for thirty years. At her hundredth birthday party an L&N official gave her one hundred roses and told the guests, "Miss Minnie has lived more years in retirement than she ever did working. We're losing money on her." At her death, she had just enough left.

I know Ida B. was helping both Minnie and Marie at the last. Ida B. married a successful businessman who owned a slice of the Waterman Steamship

Company and brought lots of bananas into Mobile from our banana republics. Her sisters told me that Ida B. would say she earned every penny of her wealth being married to Walter Hempstead.

That was about the pickles.

The pine trees had to do with a frequent guest of the Hygeia Hotel, who may have wanted to become a gentleman caller, who often came up from Mobile by sternwheeler on the Mobile River. He told the Michael girls that around half way between Citronelle and Mobile, on a bare marshy point, were three pine trees standing together. They made him think of them. Next time one of the sisters had reason to go to Mobile by boat, she kept an eye out for the pine trees. On returning she told her sisters that the three trees huddled together on a muddy point were the scrawniest, ugliest, sickliest trees she had ever seen. That would have been either Marie or Ida B. While all three were not overawed by the male sex and would say so, Minnie was too gentle, too genteel, to speak so harshly.

The hapless flatterer never gained gentlemen-caller status.

When I was a child, being sick and at home was heaven. Bobbin cooked whatever I asked for. My trays had hand-cut paper doilies cushioning hot, toasted milk-bread or soft-boiled eggs. (I can still cut a mean doily if my dear wife, Faye, is abed.) From the house on Dauphin Street, Mamie sent up to my sickbed port wine gelatin and homemade custard with whipped egg whites and cinnamon on top.

Was I ever read to! Mamie was too far downtown to read to me, but the other two did. My mother also read to me, including some of her childhood books, which that old Civil War vet who had laid "Bolivia" on a daughter read to her.

Snapshot of Bobbin, 1940s: As has been said, my grandmother was the nervous sister. We needed to make a little noise coming up behind her, or she might yelp and jump. "My Land, you scared the living daylights out of me!"

When their parents died in the 1920s, Bobbin sold the house on Dauphin Street and moved into a stucco house further downtown. There Bobbin, Arminnie, and Arminnie's spitz dog, Teddy, lived together with Ruffin, their brother, now a widower, and of course my mother. Teddy gave Bobbin and Ruffin something to fuss about, but when Teddy died, Ruffin sniffled, "I loved that damned dog."

Then Bobbin moved out to Halls Mill Road on the then-outskirts of Mobile. Great-uncle Ruffin moved with Bobbin—the Michaels stuck together. At an earlier time, Great-uncle Boyd, his wife, and their two spinster girls, my grandmother with her parents and my mother, and Mamie with her husband and three girls lived on Dauphin Street within a few blocks of each other. Their progeny, six girls, did not lack for playmates. Once while at Bobbin's, I asked Uncle Ruffin who he was going to vote for in the 1940 presidential campaign. He said, "Willkie." A shock. I had never met anyone not for Roosevelt, though I was only eight years old.

In Bobbin's backyard on Halls Mill Road was a tall pecan tree that provided a large crop of paper-shells each fall. Her tree was subject to an annual invasion of eastern tent caterpillars. These smart little buggers construct silken tents, some as large as a half-bushel basket. The caterpillars laze around inside the webs, safe from birds and other predators. Foragers go out seeking fresh, tasty leaves. If they find something nice, they leave a chemical trail back to the tent, which the stay-at-homes sense and follow. They feed and quickly return to the tent for safety's sake.

Bobbin kept bamboo fishing poles in the garage. Having avoided the job as long as possible, she'd get a pole out of the garage and tie a length of baling wire to the tip. At the loose end of the wire, she'd tie a fuzz ball of rags.

My sister and I once watched her at the task, while griping that "Ruffin should do this." She poured kerosene on the ball of rags and lit it. To destroy the caterpillars, you had to stand directly under a web and thrust the ball of fire up through the branches to the web.

Bobbin would hop, twist, and shriek, a bouncing ball of fire high above her head. Many a "Lord, have mercy" as the flame above destroyed a tent, raining tent caterpillars down upon her: fuzzy live ones, toasted ones, oozing ones, blackened ones, dead still-prickly ones. They'd be in her hair, on her shoulders, stuck on the bottoms of her shoes. She was brave, never running out from below a nest or dropping the pole.

Snapshot of Arminnie: In 1957, I had the St. Paul's tape recorder again. The seven-inch reels turned slowly, forgotten, while my sister Patsy, her little boy, Michael, Arminnie, my father, and I visited at Patsy's home. I asked Arminnie to tell a familiar tale. Always ready for that, she transported us to Belmont, Alabama, sometime during the 1870s. Here is a transcript:

> You see, I was born the year after the War was over and a lot of men came down from the North and they tried to excite the Negroes—they hadn't been rightly treated and all that.
>
> And so the men, my father was among them, he was a ringleader; in fact, they formed a Ku Klux Klan because something had to be done—you know, to keep down the rioting.
>
> One day everybody in Belmont where we lived were very excited because it was rumored that the Negroes were gonna—there was going to be an uprising of the Negroes.
>
> So my father had to go out with the Ku Klux Klan, and that would leave my mother at home with the children. I think there were some smaller than my oldest brother and I. [Boyd Denny Michael was the firstborn in 1865.]
>
> So she conceived the idea of hiding us out in the apple orchard in the high grass and weeds. And my father and his other Klansmen got on their horses and they started up the road; they were armed, of course, and they—somebody— spied an old log, and these Negroes were lying down. Behind it with their guns, you know, they were armed.
>
> And my father stopped his horse—I think he was riding a white horse— and they all stopped and my father called out, "What are you all doing there?"
>
> And they told him they were gonna have their rights.
>
> "Now if you'll wait a minute and just calm yourselves and come forward like brave men, we'll talk this over."
>
> So the Negroes did. They all had great respect for my father. In fact, if he told one of 'em a sick person wasn't going to live an hour, they knew he wasn't going to live but an hour.
>
> So that rioting was quieted.
>
> I'll tell you where [the Klan] used to meet. In the cemetery—by a large headstone. Kind of behind that. And my father was never one of the first ones

to get there because he was scared. [Laughs] In Belmont, if he was coming home late [from seeing a patient] and passed that place, he would put spurs to that horse and fly.

Well, he was a Ku Klux, and I'm proud to this day that he was because there was no way in those days to enforce law and order in those troublesome days.

No "nigger," always "Negroes" with a long "ē" on the first syllable, which stuck out in those days. I am proud that the little girl hidden in the weed patch grew up nice to say "... the Negroes hadn't been rightly treated." You will also note the legendary accretions to the story. Dr. Jacob G. Michael rides a white horse. He is the head of the local Klan. He settles the hash all by himself, no violence. This Dr. Michael is given away in an earlier stratum of the tale when Jake Michael appears, a young man scared of graveyards, who puts spurs to his horse even in passing one and won't be the first to arrive at a Klan meeting among the tombstones.

In 1968, I visited Belmont and had that rare experience of a childhood tale becoming real before my eyes. We made a turn; there on a rise was an 1840s Methodist church, beside it a graveyard with one monument in the center higher than all the rest. I sat myself down at its base and conjured.

At age one hundred, Arminnie read the newspaper and watched television news. Not the least political, she supported Mobile's integration. "What," Arminnie once said to me, "has gotten into the Klan? They didn't used to be this way." The three Michael sisters spoke on the telephone every day. I'm sure Ida B. gave Arminnie her favorable opinion of Mr. John LeFlore, her postman, the black, masterful leader of Mobile's effective and peaceful integration. When I learned of her connection with this legendary figure, I asked Ida B. what she and Mr. Le Flore talked about, how they got on in those tense days.

"He was very nice. I liked him."

See, all in the family.

Back in Mobile again the summer of 1958, I visited Arminnie at Whaley's Convalescent Home in Spring Hill. She rarely complained of anything at Whaley's, certainly not her aches and pains, if she had any. Except margarine. Very occasionally she would mention to me her aversion to margarine but always in a whisper because she didn't want to hurt the feelings of the staff.

One visit I asked her what of all things to eat she missed the most. "I would give anything for a plate of raw oysters," she whispered.

I told myself that come hell or high water, I'd get her some oysters before I left for New York. This would not be easy. Our family admired Mrs. Whaley, the founder and owner. The Whaleys began the convalescent business in their own home, where Arminnie, one of her first customers, lived for many years. Later, as the Whaleys prospered, a facility was built in the backyard. Arminnie lived there now. Mrs. Whaley was a kind but controlling person. Arminnie—articulate, ancient, friendly, and cultured—was her star boarder. Mrs. Whaley always introduced Miss Michael to families considering the placement of a relative.

A plate of raw oysters would threaten Mrs. Whaley's total control, simply because she'd never thought of serving them, and they were not part of her routine.

It had to be done in secret. Such places all have long hallways. At the end of Arminnie's hall was an exterior door leading to a small area for deliveries. At ninety-two, Arminnie was still allowed to go for a push in a wheelchair around the shady lanes past the old houses of that part of Spring Hill. I asked Mrs. Whaley if I could take Arminnie out one day; the staff rarely had the time to do it. Yes, I could.

One sunny day, I parked by the service entrance. Left in the car's trunk were paper bowls, napkins, silverware, paper cups, McIlhenny's tabasco sauce, oyster crackers, and, in a little cooler, the oysters and a split of champagne. We got to the car unnoticed, hung the loot on the back of the wheelchair, and off we went. As usual, she was able to tell me who had built or who had lived in many of the houses: "My boy, you know your third-grade teacher, Miss Gaillard, lived there with her father, that old Mr. Gaillard, the lawyer. I never liked him. He practiced law until he was a hundred years old." (As to Mr. Gaillard, Bobbin came home from town on the bus one day and told us how irritated she was that Mr. Gaillard had not gotten up to give her his seat. However, he was one hundred years old.)

We went as far as Mary B. Austin School, where I had survived Miss Murty. We stopped under some young live oaks to have our picnic. The oysters and champagne tasted all the better for being illicit. We ate up everything but some oyster crackers and hot sauce.

As we headed back, it began to sprinkle. I pushed harder. The little mercy of our thick-leaved trees postponing the raindrops soon gave way, and by the time we were through the back entrance, we were damp, not wet, damp.

The next time I visited Arminnie, Mrs. Whaley stepped in and asked if she could see me in the hallway. She lit into me. "I know you took her out in the rain. Miss Minnie was up all that night with a stomachache. What did you give her?!"

I confessed to oysters. I think I left out the hot sauce and champagne. "You should never have done that! She could have died!" I was thinking, "And you'd lose your best advertisement for Whaley's, wouldn't you?" How unfair of me to draw such a conclusion.

The oysters didn't kill Arminnie; she lived comfortably at Whaley's for another twelve years.

The best snapshot I have of Great-aunt Mamie, or Ida B., the middle sister, is of her sitting in an upholstered chair in her parlor. Of course, I do not forget the five-dollar bills I got for Christmas or the checks to Sewanee for my seminary education. I have no snapshot of her like the other two because she lived downtown, we lived in Spring Hill, and she was sedentary—not lazy, but comfortable in her favorite chair in her sunny parlor.

Her husband, Walter Hempstead, was said to have a violent temper. On a quiet Sunday afternoon, he'd invite Mamie and the girls "out for a drive," as we used to say. Sometimes because of his inability to master the car or because of a mechanical problem, they'd be stuck somewhere, the females all dressed for Sunday motoring and cowering in the Hudson Super Six, while Uncle Walter raged around the car, throwing tools.

Someone mused to her once how blessed she was to be married to wealth. She said, "I earned every penny of it."

When I went there for a visit, things were always the same. I know she liked it that way.

12. Nice Parents—The Michaels and Simisons

While I was at Spring Hill College, the City of Mobile put benches at the bus stops. With eyes opened on Father Cole's front walk, I could see a racial dance at the bus stop across from Greer's Store in Spring Hill. There was rarely a black person on the bench, and only if no white people were at the stop or anywhere near. If a white person approached, the black sitter registered it from afar and got up. Not up the way we whites would. A slow slide, a look to the side away from the white person's approach, then an oblique drift to a certain spot where both races understood no whites ever stood to wait on the bus. The white person then would approach in a certain privileged but not haughty way. This projected that he had not noticed that a person of color had been sitting where he now seated himself. Ignore and be ignored, without rudeness or exaggerated servility.

My great-aunt Minnie was a bus rider. "Arminnie," I said, "if you were on the bus bench and a colored person sat on it, would you get up?"

"No."

"Why not?"

"It wouldn't be nice."

"Who taught you to be nice?"

"My mother and father."

How were Arminnie's parents nice? Her mother, Margaret Ann Simison, was born November 26, 1841, in Mount Vernon, a river village thirty miles north of Mobile. The Mount Vernon Arsenal was a Federal outpost until the Mobile Rifles came up from Mobile on January 4, 1861, to seize it for Alabama—or some constituency, because Alabama did not secede until one week later. No shots, the Federal troops marched quietly away, leaving a trove of munitions.

Jacob G. Michael, a newly graduated physician working at the Marine Hospital in Mobile, was in that militia. He stayed on at the Arsenal as a deputy acting assistant surgeon in the Confederate Army, a lowly rank that he spent the rest of the war trying to elevate. He married Miss Simison on April 29,

1862. She was twenty; he was twenty-two. She moved from her father's house to join her husband in the Arsenal; family lore reports they lived in its most striking part, the tower. It was all still there in 2000.

Memoria reminds me how young they were. That is not easy for me to grasp because I know them from photographs, Jacob (Jake) as a goateed old gentleman and Margaret (Maggie) as recalled by her granddaughter, Margaret Wells:

> I can see Memo now sitting in her little wicker rocker by the west window of the front room—her hands never still—making buttonholes or whipping lace for our underclothes, or during World War I teaching me to knit washcloths for the soldiers. Always dressed in a shirtwaist and skirt, a tucked black silk waist, with high collar in the summer.

Their children called them Poppa and Momma. Grandchildren: Papoo and Memo. Endearing names used by children freeze upon the deaths of their recipients. So Papoo and Memo are what we greats, great-greats, and more to come will call them. Is it just us Southerners, black and white, who call each other by the baby-talk names of their kids?

I shall call this young couple Maggie and Jake as they stand together at the edge of our homegrown and deadliest war. After their children came, they called each other Mrs. Michael and Doctor, a custom of honorifics lingering on until our day among old, rural black couples.

Maggie's father, Boyd Denny Simison, was born in 1805 in Carlisle, Pennsylvania. This description of him comes from the *Denny Genealogy*, a fat blue book that even includes my sister and me.

> He first came south at the time of the Mexican War, when as a Major, he brought a company of volunteers from Carlisle to New Orleans.... Major Simison was told to go to the Arsenal at Mount Vernon for further orders. Here he was told that the war was over and to muster out his men.

Like many men in the North, Major Simison saw a future in the Deep South. The Creek War was over. The Creeks and Cherokees were marched to their deaths or corralled in semi-captivity in Arkansas. Alabama was now a state. Steam was on the rivers. The *Genealogy* goes on:

> Later he went back to the Arsenal since his cousin Nancy Denny had married the Commandant, Edward Harding, and he decided to settle there permanently.

The Major prospered. In 1841 he married Martha Taylor Barnett of "an old Georgia family." Wasn't long before she gave the Major his firstborn, Maggie.

Major Simison is the first "aha" to my curiosity about enslavement among my people. You bet he did! He used enslaved Africans to work his land grant, his sawmill, and the fiery kilns of his brickyard. His woodcutters pulled virgin cypresses from the swamp with oxen and split pine and swamp poplar for his woodyard, fueling the steamboats. Family lore reports he got the government contract to build a brick replacement for the old earthen "Indian Arsenal." The *Genealogy* says he built with his bricks "the high wall around the Arsenal." The Major provided his family with an eight-room log house. Maybe Maggie had her own bedroom!

The *Genealogy* continues with more details about Major Simison.

> Various stories have come down about his political interests. One says he was an abolitionist, but was forced to become a slaveholder because part of his wife's dower was in slaves.... Another story relates how he and a relative, with $37,000 in cash carried in a money belt around his waist, made the long journey to Lynchburg, Virginia, to buy slaves for himself and others.

If Boyd Denny Simison had a conflicted conscience about slaveholding, it exactly aped that of George Washington: money and position trumped abolition.

In crinkled old tissue paper, I keep two locks of hair, one from the Major and one from his wife, Martha, cut from their heads after death. These, carefully labeled, were sent to Maggie probably by her sister, Lizzie. Martha's is blond and silky. I used to believe that the Major's lock could not be his. Not that of an old man. When the *Denny Genealogy* arrived, it reported "he had reddish sandy hair and blue eyes." Like many Scotch-Irish, he died with reddish sandy hair.

Did Jake and Maggie own slaves? Ida B., their daughter, says emphatically, No: "Mother used to tell us that Grandma Michael (Jake's mother) would say everything she put in the bunghole her sons let out by the spigot." I treasure the spigot remark; it is the oldest voice of a forebear. This woman came from the Alsace-Lorraine in the 1830s, was widowed in Demopolis, and is said to have operated a grocery store or perhaps a cotton warehouse. Ida B. denied she had anything like a plantation. And it is true these Alsace-Lorraine settlers were not quick to acquire enslaved people.

So did Maggie have a slave dower? We know the couple had no money at the close of the war. Jake's letters prove that. But one Civil War letter to her contains two hints:

Camp Watts
Sunday February 12, 1865
My Darling Wife,
. . . Night before last I was attacked with severe itching all over me; in the morning I discovered large raised patches particularly over my arms and legs, it afterwards spread all over me and I assure you it was almost intolerable. I got some simple cerate from the surgeon and made Wilson apply it all over the eruptions which seemed to relieve the itching. . . . I think it was nettle rash.

Jake had left Maggie and their son Boyd at the Mount Vernon Arsenal while he attempted to join the Army of Northern Virginia. Not to fight but to secure the rank of acting assistant surgeon instead of deputy acting assistant surgeon. This would have included a pay raise (in worthless Confederate scrip). Blocked by destroyed rail lines, he ended up in Camp Watts, near Notasulga in east central Alabama. I suspect the rash was from anxiety. Then this:

Wilson seems to get along very well; he does nothing but gets our wood and water and makes the fires. I think he is rather tired of the place.

Nowhere else in his letters does Jake use a single name to indicate someone. He either uses courtesy titles or, with acquaintances, the whole name, such as "Frank Hardie." On such grounds as the singular "Wilson" and his menial tasks, I do believe he was Jake's enslaved body servant, perhaps from Maggie's dower. Wilson disappears after this. Where did he go after the Surrender? Where are *his* great-grandchildren?

On my way to college classes, I would stop by Arminnie's, who then lived in a cottage across Austill Lane from us. It was our habit to read "Family Morning Prayer" from the *Book of Common Prayer*. After that, I would tell her how things were going across the lane; she offered a broader palette: how things were going on Rickarby Street, which meant the duplex that Ida B. shared with her daughter, Elizabeth, and her girls, Ann and Betsy. Arminnie would update me on "the Michael girls," spinsters Josephine and Elizabeth, on in years now, who still lived alone in the home of their father, my great-uncle Boyd. The Michael girls were severe and withdrawn. My enforced visits as a child were never easy. My mother would warn me to sit up straight before we got out of the car. Didn't matter; Josephine would be on me not to ruin my posture by slouching on their hard parlor chairs. But I was once privileged by them to see Uncle Boyd's kidney stone, which they reverently kept in a little jewelry box. Later, they stunned me by the gift of his elegant mechanical drawing set. They had to show regard for me because I was then the only living male descendant from Jake and Maggie, their grandparents.

Time permitting, Arminnie would range on to distant relatives in Demopolis and over to the Mount Vernon Simisons, with whom she kept up. Arminnie cared about keeping up with extended family, serving them and us as a catalyst to reaffirm who we were. Christine Jacobson Carter in *Southern Single Blessedness* explains that Southern spinsters often were "the glue" that held family and social networks together, the "communicators, caretakers, surrogate mothers, family servants, and benevolent women extending feminine virtues to individuals and organizations."

No Simison keeping-up-with for Ida B., who dismissed her mother's kin as "the bootlegging Simisons" and would not speak of them. This relieved her of having to keep up. Nor did my grandmother, Bobbin, keep up. Her indifference grew from an aversion to "going places." Showing interest would require an occasional trip up to see them. As reported, Bobbin was the stick-in-the-mud Michael girl.

Occasionally, when I visited her Arminnie would get out the Hammel's Department Store box—Maggie's Box. In 1921, when Maggie died, it became her daughter's. Now it is mine. Rather, its contents are; the box is long gone.

Maggie was a Class A saver. On February 19, 1882, as recorded by her hand, she began to paste onto thin cardboard sheets her newspaper clippings from before and after the War, placing them into the box with other treasures. Some clippings are frivolous: Advice on etiquette, jokes, serialized fiction like "Cured of Coquetting" and "A Rival's Revenge." Just the ticket for a teenage girl. Others are dark: Long lists of troop deployments, including Louisiana Guards, Mobile Cadets, Gulf City Guards Company, Major J. B. Walton's Battalion, the Washington Artillery, and the Crescent Rifles.

At sixteen, Maggie had left Mount Vernon, making the long trip down the Tombigbee to its confluence with the Mobile. Then on to the port of Mobile, where she boarded a packet taking her down the Bay into the Gulf, coasting along the Mississippi Sound, then up the Mississippi River to New Orleans to board with her aunt Eliza (Simison) Roper and attend M'me Loquet's Female Collegiate Institute. Most of the militias she recorded were from around New Orleans. Miss Simison must have been one popular girl. She penciled marks by many of the men's names and "Killed" or "Wounded" by some. Fifty names in all.

In its own cardboard box is a little charm, a tarnished silver star the size of a fifty-cent piece. On the front are engraved the words:

Recepn Come
J. Rowan
June 1st / 57.

And on the reverse side:

Miss M. A. Simison

I believe the star is an invitation to a ball. Gregory Waselkov, in his book, *A Conquering Spirit*, about the Creek Indian War, records how four barely civilized young adventurers in the frontier Mississippi Territory planned such a ball in 1810. Serious business—so serious that an argument developed among these tetchy men about who was to hand out the invitations. The argument resulted in a duel and a death. No evidence Maggie's ball went badly. She returned to Mount Vernon in 1859, after her graduation.

Among a packet of letters are two to Maggie from an obvious if undeclared admirer, Frank C. Smith. His second letter is dated January 13, 1862, and indicates that Frank is now soldiering in the Gulf City Guards attached to the 3rd Alabama Regiment. He reminds her a little peevishly that he is the one who has been mailing those war-related clippings to her from New Orleans. Too bad for Frank—in two more months Jake will have won her.

Another clipping covers her graduation, undated, but in a metal tube originally intended to hold maps are family diplomas from 1859–1960. Hers is dated May 27, 1859. Jake studied briefly in New Orleans in the medical department of the University of New Orleans that same year. Did they meet? No evidence. The acid—Memoria's enemy—in the clipping has eroded a few words:

> _____ would have given a Muhammedan a lively idea Of his houri paradise _____ Exercises in music afforded Excellent entertainment _____ to be most creditable to the abilities _____ pupils and teacher _____ M'me Loquet. Diplomas awarded to Miss Emma J. Kendij of New _____, Miss Simison of Alabama, Miss Orine Wilson and Miss Mandell of New Orleans.

Another clipping from the war years tells us that M'me Loquet, at a later graduation of the

> . . . admirable Collegiate Institute for Young Ladies [exhibited] a little bag made of a Confederate flag, containing $200, the amount which it Had been contemplated to Expend in prizes and which Her noble-souled girls had accepted only to hand over to the soldiers.

It was to be in another world as my great-aunt untied strings and unwrapped tissues, telling stories, each entitled mentally by me "Who We Were." Such stories stew a bit and are reissued as "Who We Are."

Jake's wartime surgical kit would be unwrapped: lances, a bullet extractor, and, so beautiful, a set of shining surgical needles fixed in red felt, gold-plated, curved like eyebrows. Silk thread, as strong and white as it was in 1861, waits in a packet alongside the needles, never again to be guided between the eyes. Then, always a surprise to me, a pair of creamy kid gloves worn by Jake on their wedding day in 1862. They appear to be too small for a grown man. Do kid gloves shrink after a hundred and fifty years? I will google that someday.

Across our lane, in Bobbin's cedar chest, under her father's lap robe, rested his .32 rimfire target rifle and the wartime .44 Remington cavalry pistol. I suspect Minnie was afraid of them. I can hear her sister, my grandmother, say, "For Heaven's sake, Minnie, give them to me!" Bobbin was often impatient with her placid yet cautious elder sister.

Memoria snuggles in an apartment in my brain. The nameplate on the door reads, "THE PAST, PLEASE RING." She should snuggle. It is the best-appointed place in my skull, unlike the low-voltage recesses that cope with the present and, may I be forgiven, the cranny that plans for the future. My brain: a trial to my wife, Faye, and nothing to joke about.

On occasion Daddy would drive Arminnie, Patsy, and me to Mount Vernon. No bootleg or stills or socially unacceptable Simisons did I ever see—only friendly cousins who flocked around Arminnie because she cared. We always had to catch up on Natalie Simison because, as a school teacher in Mobile, she was never there. Born in 1876, the same year as Bobbin, Natalie was the maiden daughter of Uncle Sam, who was Maggie's younger brother, my great-great-uncle. Uncle Sam also fought in the war, said to have been a scout with the rank of private. It was let out on one of those Mount Vernon trips that Natalie had Uncle Sam's Confederate uniform. I wanted it. My mother said, "Let's try to get it!" Arminnie may have misunderstood my interest, remarking that were I to get it, it wouldn't fit. Uncle Sam was too small. But the uniform evaporated in a mist of "We-can't-find-it" and "But-we'll-look-again." I recall Natalie had reddish-blond hair.

It was not easy for Arminnie to broach subjects she considered indelicate, but how could she not, with delight, tell us Simisons and Walterses that Uncle Sam eschewed outhouses as newfangled and until his death repaired to his own log out in the woods.

On one trip, we were led to the swamp to pick mayhaws, which Bobbin cooked into pale red jelly. Mayhaws are the small, round, reddish fruit of the thorny hawthorne tree. It resembles a crabapple and ripens from mid-April to early May, hence the name mayhaw. Our leader said there were plenty enough on the ground for us, but the preferred method was from a skiff poled up a narrow slough. Gatherers would beat the overhanging branches with a pole and then skim up the floating haws.

I was offered camping privileges on an old barge tied up at Simison's Landing on the Mobile River. It was enclosed, had a woodstove and bunks. My buddies and I had fun camping on it and tromping in the swamp, thinking we were deer hunting.

Many years later I was leaving Mobile after a visit and decided to detour to Mount Vernon to see the Arsenal where Jake and Maggie first lived together. It had reverted to the State of Alabama and once served as the "Negro Insane Asylum." Though "served" is too generous a word either for that ancient facility or the state's financial support of black folk. Major Simison's brick wall now kept clients in, not attackers out. I drove to a visitors' parking lot and took out a camera. My heart was full of young Maggie, her new-wife feelings, her fears; her abandonment in 1864, left there with her infant son and her husband gone to seek money and preferment in the Army of Virginia, two months before that Army ceased to be. As I focused on the old stockade, a female security guard walked out of a little house and told me I couldn't take pictures because it was a mental hospital and the patients couldn't be photographed.

"I just want to take a picture of that building, the one with the tower—not people." I paused. "You see, er—my great-grandparents lived there during the war. She was a Simison."

The strictures of security fell away, replaced by a big smile. "I was a Simison before I married. Who was your great-grandmother?"

So we jawed a while, agreeing we were cousins. "Look," she said, "take a few pictures; I'll watch if anyone comes."

It was a family tale that the couple "lived in the tower." There it was, looked a little cramped for newlyweds. Memory had gravitated toward the romantic here. I took pictures. I have her name and address still: Mrs. Gayle (Simison) Long—Cousin Gayle.

13. Seminary and Racism

In the fall of 1954 when Louis and I drove up to Sewanee in my 1948 Chrysler, we had the dim knowledge that the faculty of the seminary had been "replaced." In Mobile, our rector, Milton Wood, had little, if anything, to say about this. As we unpacked our suitcases, we were ignorant, for sure, that an ecclesiastical and academic war had just played out. We learned that when talks had ceased and compromise was impossible, the Seminary faculty—save one—had informed the trustees that if a black student who had applied to the seminary was not admitted, they would resign. He was not admitted. They resigned along with the university's chaplain. At our arrival that September, we found a new faculty being cobbled together from older and retired men and a couple of new guys.

Episcopal seminaries hope to produce priests and deacons in three years—first-year students are called juniors; second-year, middlers; and third-year, seniors. We found the rising middlers and seniors to be riven and in shock. Some of their fellows had followed the departing faculty; some had stayed. What an earthquake! I recall none of the upperclassmen talking to us about it. I am shamed and surprised that Louis and I and our incoming class were so oblivious. Why was I? I was cocked and primed by my Mobile race baptism to become engaged and partisan. Perhaps it was that my Mobile transformation was interior, personal, and related to my mother. But the Sewanee affair involved the Episcopal Church and scores of people, many of whom were powerful and, no doubt, more intelligent than I. Even so, I knew the defenders of this white privilege were dead wrong.

How could we have been so asleep when there in our class of '57 was Merrick Collier of St. Matthew's Parish, Savannah, the first full-time black student at the University of the South? The shock of the resignations had so rattled the regents and trustees that they recanted, admitting Merrick. He was not the applicant who had triggered the ugly reaction, but he was black. This eruption and Merrick's short stay at Sewanee has been covered by Will Campbell in *And Also with You: Duncan Gray and the American Dilemma* and by Donald Armentrout in the *Sewanee Theological Review,* and by me in the *Keystone Newsletter of the Sewanee Trust.*

Oh shoot, just two Merrick stories. He was handsome, funny and irrepressible. It was then a custom at Sewanee to show *Gone With the Wind* annually at the little campus theater. Louis and I, my roommate Walter Peterson, and our two Arkansan theologs, Joel Pugh and Scott May, decided to go. Merrick joined us. I know we were aware, but barely, that we were "integrating" the theater. It then had what was called "the slave gallery," where the university's black employees and their families sat (the gallery itself is long gone, marked now only by a handrail oddly embedded against a wall). Merrick was not one to say, "See you later," and slink up to the gallery. As the credits rolled, Joel informed us that it was the custom to stand and cheer when Scarlett shot the Yankee deserter on Tara's staircase. The film opens with a little black boy riding the wheel of a bell to call the hands in. I can't see that without a pang of love. My mother drove us once from Mon Louis up to Mobile, where the Roxy Theatre was showing the movie. When that bell rang, she gave my shoulder a fierce clutch, smiling like the dickens at my seven-year-old self. It startled me—why was she reacting that way? Because to her, that was us Southerners and her grandfathers, her people, who she was, and she wanted me to know who I was. The fact that the little boy was enslaved didn't register.

Back to Sewanee. We came to the Tara staircase. Bang! We all stood to cheer, except Merrick who sat with composure. I decided, surrounded by so many upright bodies, that maybe none but us seminarians had seen his non-action. Came the Atlanta staircase, a domestic scene, Rhett and Scarlett are having a fight. Does he push? Does she lose her footing or fall intentionally? Anyway, at this point Merrick stood and cheered—alone. Then sat, composed. I was proud of him but more engaged in wondering if we were going to be set upon by undergraduates. Nothing happened in the theater. It was dark when we emerged for the longish walk to St. Luke's Hall.

Beyond that lay the KA house. Kappa Alpha was/is an extension of the Confederacy. We were not bushwhacked. Just before Homecoming weekend, which the seminary also observed, Merrick informed us he had a confederate (with a little "c") in the KAs who had given him two tickets to their Old South Ball. He planned, he told us, to come as Robert E. Lee and his Savannah girlfriend as Scarlett O'Hara. With Merrick, one never knew what was real or joshing. Rumor brought back to St. Luke's Hall that the KAs had heard about the insult and vowed at some drunken soiree to kill Merrick if he and Scarlett set foot on the dance floor. It was a fact that our interim dean, the Right Reverend Edmund Pendleton Dandridge, did tell Merrick to go home for Homecoming. This became prudent in retrospect. We juniors had prepared a skit for the alums, the middlers, and the seniors.

We heard later that just before our show, two local guys with paper bags over their heads pushed two alums into a restroom. The priests, unused to danger, assumed the men were juniors dressed for the skit and started joking with them. When pushed to the wall and asked, "Where's that nigger?" they quickly recalibrated, telling the guys they were visitors and knew nothing. The masked men fled. As we ran through the building looking for other trouble, some of us found on the basement landing of the Fourth Entry, an inadequate, partially burned pile of small branches and twigs. We attributed to alcohol the inadequacy of this pitiful arson attempt because another rumor alleged that the intruders had been drunk.

My buddies and I, including Merrick, lived in the Fourth Entry. Each floor had two apartments, each holding two students. Merrick had an apartment to himself.

I keep saying rumor. It was not, and still is not, the policy of Sewanee to report embarrassing events or encourage dialogue about such events. The final rumor, weeks later, was that the guys were caught; one was kin to the sheriff of an adjoining county. The vice chancellor, Dr. Edward McCrady, so went the tale, offered the sheriff two rail tickets to Chicago, suggesting the two guys might like to live up there awhile.

When the second semester began, Merrick was gone. Nothing official was said. We asked why. Bishop Dandridge, not a cleric given to follow-up questions, said he had left. What pains me is that, to my knowledge, no students or faculty reached out to Merrick after he left. I did not.

Academic Fireworks: During my middler year, I attended a book sale at the home of Dr. Eugene Kayden, a Russian-born Sewanee scholar who was the first to translate the poems of Boris Pasternak. Dr. Kayden turned these sales into thoughtful social events by quizzing buyers about their choices. I'd heard of the massive study of race in America by Gunnar Myrdal and saw a used copy suited to my budget. Dr. Kayden wanted to know why I was buying *An American Dilemma*. I told Kayden my heart told me segregation was evil; the book would supply the head knowledge. What diocese, he wanted to know. When told Alabama, he predicted a rough ride and wished me well. Five years later, June 1961, Dr. Kayden suffered his fifteen minutes of celebrity. He was notified he would be awarded an honorary doctorate by his university. The occasions on which Sewanee had shown its backside on Jim Crow had diminished after I was a student. This one was a national mooning. Kayden refused the honor. *Time* magazine was titillated; other media sources picked it up. Kayden refused to receive the degree alongside Thomas R. Waring, the fire-eating racist editor of the Charleston *News and Courier*. We thought at the time the paper was and most likely ever would be an antediluvian rag. We were wrong, and in later years the paper gained a good reputation as one willing to address racial issues, perhaps even liberal by South Carolina standards.

In any case, Thomas Waring was the kinsman of another educated segregationist, Dr. Edward McCrady, our vice chancellor (read "president") of Sewanee. Dr. McCrady had resisted the integration of the university to its bitter, divisive end. Even after Merrick left, he continued his struggle.

A couple of Thomas Waring's quotes will suffice: of other nations, ". . . the whiter they are the better the country"; and when Tom Mboya, a Kenyan activist and Oxford graduate, visited the United States, Waring described him as: ". . . a man only lately come down out of a tree." The faculty had twice managed to kill the idea of awarding Waring an honorary doctorate of civil law. But in 1961, the regents overrode the faculty. Dr. Kayden was to be pulled on stage with the wacky notion that all would be peace and harmony if he, a supporter of racial justice, and Waring received hoods together. The vice chancellor was quoted in *Time* as saying the double bill would be "a true ministry of reconciliation." "Reconciliation" was a race term used back then by white folks who could manage six-syllable words. One of our bishops even wrote a book about it. It meant back then, "Let's you all calm down."

Dr. Kayden refused the honor, ". . . until a happier time when there is no ideological conflict in the South." Waring took his degree without the reconciling symmetry. Later, Kayden accepted a degree from Sewanee.

I treasure my copy of *An American Dilemma*. I referenced it in a sermon at St. Andrew's Church in Birmingham in 1968. A young woman with reddish-blond hair was so taken with the book and/or me she bought herself the paperback version. Nine years later we were married. Thank you, Dr. Kayden, for melding the two copies into our one library.

The only seminary discussion of the looming struggle to free black America that I recall came during an evening wine and cheese reception for us seniors at the home of the new dean. The subjects for discussion were things we might deal with as new pastors. One question came up that evening as it was gearing up to surface, not only in the dean's living room, but in the great, wide world: What would we do in our first parish if on a Saturday evening a black man came to the rectory to ask if he could worship at our church the next day? It appeared we had no pure segregationists that evening, at least none willing to fess up. It was a question most of us had not, would not, or could not consider. Most did not respond. One response was the old saw: "Not now, but one day." Another was stretched beyond the grave: "We'll all be one in Heaven." Maybe a couple of us said, "Welcome him." The careful added, "Let key vestry members know ahead of time. If you're canned, so be it, pick up and move on." One said that since he would be a freshly ordained deacon and canonically under the rule of his bishop, he would ask the bishop what to do and then do that. He may well have become a bishop himself.

That was the question of the evening. The dean asked it. So many better questions could have enlivened the evening: What do you plan to do to reach out to the black community? What will you teach young people in your parish about the church's complicity in the slave trade?

The word for such questions these days is "proactive." Neither the word nor its spirit were in evidence that evening. Who could blame the dean? "Proactive" wasn't even in my 1973 *American Heritage Dictionary of the English Language*.

Opportunity in New York: In the latter part of my senior year, March 1957, Bishop Dandridge informed me that the General Theological Seminary in New York City had selected me for a two-year fellowship with an $1,800 annual stipend. With food and lodging supplied, my needs would be more than met. I would tutor freshmen and middlers and work toward a master's of divinity degree. A letter soon came from Carpenter House, the Birmingham headquarters of the diocese of Alabama. The Right Reverend Charles C. J. Carpenter, DD, LLD, said how proud of me he was and that "while we need men very badly in the work in the diocese, we also want our men to be as well prepared as possible, and I feel that this offers you a splendid opportunity for preparation which will enable you to be more effective when your active ministry begins."

Even with support from Bishop Carpenter, I was apprehensive. I went to FitzSimmons Allison, our youngest faculty member, for advice. He pointed out that I'd lived at home during college and was just finishing three years in a mountain wilderness: "Go! New York's full of things to stretch your mind and spirit."

In Birmingham, I met with Bishop Carpenter, who was generous, saying that I should definitely accept and return to Alabama in two years to begin a parish ministry, something I wanted to do. "The more education you fellows get, the better." He never dallied over decisions affecting the seminarians and young clergy who sat nervously before his desk. Bishop Carpenter finished our meeting with a favorite, wise saw: "Consistency is the hobgoblin of little minds." He took this line from Ralph Waldo Emerson's 1841 essay, "Self-Reliance." Bishop Carpenter was very tall and very sturdy. I think he associated his size and strength with the breadth of his mind. Commenting on a prominent Episcopal "divine," who had attacked one of his segregationist statements, he told someone, "He's just a little fellow."

Ordination Conflict: After graduating from Sewanee and before I left for New York, Louis Tonsmeire and I returned to Mobile and were ordained to the diaconate at St. Paul's on July 17, 1957, on the feast of the obscure St. Osmund (d. 1099). I was well into Myrdal's *An American Dilemma*. The book intensified a dawning worry: Where could I be posted in two years and not get railroaded out of the diocese of Alabama? Then before the ordination, a real-life dilemma reared its horns. It had to do with the promise I made on Father Cole's brick walk: Never, ever, be part of "this" again. "This" being the injustices of white racism.

Shortly before the ordination, the ladies of St. Paul's told Louis and me that they were preparing a luncheon after the service. It was to be for us, our families, and the Mobile clergy and spouses. We were to invite the clergy. It was to be held at the Alba Hunting and Fishing Club on Dog River. My grandfather, Franz Walter, had been a member; my father was a member. We kept our fourteen-foot runabout in a stall out on the boathouse wharf. I'd grown up there—Spanish moss, the boat ways, the swimming dock, the skiffs for use of members, the big boat wharf, the clubhouse with its ancient tarpon leaping over the fireplace. The Alba Club was old Mobile, a bit out of fashion, getting on in years, perfect for our luncheon. It was not the Spring Hill Country Club.

As I warmed to this kindness, Father Cole disturbed it like the single toll of a bell. A sound I knew. The first peal had struck when he and my mother met, again when I met him carrying the refusal of my church to allow him into its fellowship, and third when he brought the Sacrament to my mother the last time. Now a fourth stroke, not that Father Cole was aware of these effects. A fifth toll would come two years later.

It was a simple syllogism. We were to invite the Mobile clergy, Father Cole was a member of the Mobile clergy, ergo, Father Cole would be invited. Except that in the calculus of Jim Crow in the 1950s, such a syllogism was null. The likelihood of the Alba Club allowing him past the gate—also null. It occurs to me that the Latin *alba* comes from an adjective meaning "white" or "dead white." It is referenced in Roy Osborne's *Telesio and Morato on the Meaning of Colours,* from the Roman satirist Juvenal, who used it in this phrase from "Satires" (1.111): *Nuper in hanc urbem pedibus qui venerat albis,* referring to a slave who came to Rome with chalked feet to show he was for sale.

Forgive me, Father Cole; after reading the above, I dwelt on an image of you standing at the gate of the Alba Club, dusty, disheveled, bare feet splashed with whitewash.

Should I invite a man to a meal where I knew him to be unwelcome, because of a system designed to benefit me and beggar him? My front-walk conversion said, No. What to do? Answering that took so much energy that I had little left to imagine that my opposition would release a cascade of misery and misunderstanding onto my family and fellow parishioners, all of them dear to me. The St. Paul's ladies had likely never given a thought to the possibility of a Father Cole in their circle, just as my mother had not. Had they given a thought, had it appeared as a little blip on the screen of their luncheon, wasn't it true that it would be immediately covered over by the proprietary wings of Jim Crow? My mother had come out from that dark shadow. Could they?

I went to Louis. Laying out my position and feelings was hard on us both. He said Father Cole wouldn't come, invited or not. It would be his decision, not mine. Writing him an invitation was only a formality. I think he also counseled that this was no way for me to begin ordained ministry. I should wait to gain experience and find other like-minded people. Besides, he said, "You aren't paying for the meal and serving it. The Women's Auxiliary is doing that for us."

I said, "What about me now?" I'd chosen not to float along in a lie any longer. I put my friend in a spot. It hurts me after all these years. (After writing this, so indelibly recalled, I telephoned Louis to ask what he remembered of it. He said he remembered nothing of it! Didn't happen! Well! I stick with Memoria's version.)

I told him I was going to see Mrs. _____, who was in charge of the luncheon. She had been a friend of Mother's, and I had gone from first grade through high school with her daughter. I sat in dread in her living room. I was to attack something for which she could feel no guilt. After beating around the bush, I said I could not invite Father Cole because the Alba Club was barred to him. I couldn't not invite him either because he was a member of the Mobile clergy. Mrs. _____ became angry. Who could blame her?

I suggested that the meal could be moved to the church's parish hall, where one could hope he would be seated. Mrs. _____ pointed out that the man would not come no matter. There was no problem. I soldiered on about the parish hall, wishing I could evaporate and reappear in a world without race. That not occurring, I said, "If it's at the Alba Club, I won't attend."

Mrs. _____ was still more furious. I'd never experienced one of my mother's friends being angry with me. I became a ten-year-old who had violated the Sweet Child Code—not only that, but in the home of one of my mother's friends.

It is our opponents who sometimes clear a cloudy vision from which we have been seeking direction. They contradict it, point out its weaknesses, and appeal to what everyone else does. Perversely, this can help us. Yeah, that's why I am doing this. Mrs. _____ let me have it. Her parting words still guide me: "Francis, you're going to have Communion with him; do you need to eat with him too?"

I'd grasped it before—of course I had—but not fully until the gift she gave with those words. We Episcopalians say over and over in worship the Nicene Creed. It includes, "We believe in One . . . Church." Therefore, only one meal for one people.

I left her with nothing agreed. But on the day, there was no Alba Club; the parish hall was used. Father Cole was invited. He did not come. I had wounded men and women who helped raise me. I imagine the meal at the club would have been catered. Now, I suppose the ladies had the extra work of preparing and serving the one in the parish hall. I was treated with love and respect. No one said a word about it, not to me or my family, ever. They did a good job, leaving aside Jim Crow.

Ordination to the diaconate was a day of promise and sorrow. I don't regret throwing an apple of discord. Yet, I wonder how many of those hardworking women regretted my earlier going-to-seminary gift from them of heavy leather suitcases—top of the line.

Built by Slaves: St. Paul's is proud of its founding date, 1858. Father Cole's parish, Good Shepherd, had its start in 1854. I like that—beat us by four years. At times we used to add to the 1858 boast: "built by slaves." What did we mean by that? Constructed by the forced labor of human chattel? Heavens no. It meant, "We're Old Mobile; we have standing." It took the second liberation one hundred years later to allow, as a side effect, the meaning of "slavery" to batter its way into the white brain. In 2008, St. Paul's celebrated its 150th anniversary. The parish archivist reprinted, among other documents, that Mr. _____ and Mr. _____ gave the labor of X number of slaves for so many days for building the church. Contribution gratefully accepted. In that year, 2008, there was no boast "built by slaves." No comment at all. Progress. Perhaps a smidgen of apology, a word of repentance, will be offered for the labor of enslaved persons when St. Paul's celebrates its 175th anniversary.

When I was confirmed at age twelve, I received a gift from two old stalwarts at St. Paul's, Gladys and Warren Fields. I carried it in my pocket for years. It was usual for confirmands to receive pious presents, a Prayer Book, a Bible, and especially three-ribbon bookmarks with silver tokens dangling from their ends: a cross for hope, a heart for charity, and an anchor for faith. The Fields gave me a pocketknife. It told me I did not have to leave being a real boy to become a real Christian.

14. New York City, General Seminary

As I came off the plane to set foot in New York, which Cousin Eugene called "Pavement Land," I flinched at what I took to be the beginning of a murder. Not so. Only the raillery of two baggage handlers. After moving to my quarters I dashed to a window overlooking Twenty-first Street. Something terrible happening. I froze going over the usual riffs: should I call the police, but what if? What if this isn't life-threatening? It was the driver of a small van expressing his feelings to a man blocking the street to make a fuel oil delivery. Mr. Fuel Oil was also expressing his feelings. Things got better. I was soon charmed and calmed by the kindness of the inhabitants of our Chelsea neighborhood, people not unlike Mobilians: the owner of the corner grocery, Twenty-first and Ninth Avenue, endlessly patient with new seminarians from all over the earth puzzling over new labels and strange fruit. Such a small grocery, but I knew from my grandfather's produce days that I was offered "select" and "extra select" fruits and vegetables not often on the rail cars serving Walter Produce.

There was the old "Jelly Lady" across Ninth from the seminary entrance. She bought fresh fruit from local markets, brewing up glowing jellies. Her tiny shop was also home where she slept in a chair. A block down the avenue was the Italian barber who told me he had lost his faith years ago from all he heard from seminarians. No barber in Mobile or Sewanee ended a shearing as he did: I was startled after my first cut to feel a neck massage from a little electric motor he'd strapped to his hand. If that was not enough, a dose of Lilac Vegetal and a finish of talcum powder.

There's more. My students liked me. I hadn't known what to expect about that. I was the outside tutor. The rest had been selected from General grads. I was invited by one of my tutees from Lancaster, Pennsylvania, to a crucial hockey match. Never saw so much ice. And a weekend in Paterson, New Jersey, at the home of another tutee where I was astounded by small porchless houses packed row by row. Greg walked me to a favorite childhood spot of his, a boggy, underdeveloped piece of land. It was freezing out, everything bare and barren except one skunk cabbage in full leaf. I had never seen one before. Looking up from the skunk cabbage I could see the Empire State Building to the east. I choked up. I was homesick for Gulf Coast vegetation: always green, never bare. The skunk cabbage helped.

News filtered slowly at General Seminary. No cyberspace then, no Twitter or blogs, only an anemic bulletin board with a few posts about the interesting people from all over who came and went. As an unmarried tutor, I took my meals at the faculty high table. One evening I took my seat beside a large-bearded, large Russian Orthodox cleric.

We introduced ourselves. He was the Bishop of Odessa and the Exarch of the Patriarch of Moscow. As an exarch he had the prickly task of mediating the separation of the Russian Orthodox exiles in America from the Patriarchate of Moscow, then under the thumb of the Soviet state. But dinner was not the time for diplomacy. He wanted to know of my plans for marriage. I was still in deacon's orders, not yet a priest. He may have thought the Episcopal Church was like the Russian Church, which allowed priests to be married only if they married before admission to the priesthood. This allowed for a pool of celibate priests from which bishops could be drawn. Bishops had to be celibate. So the consolation prize for a celibate priest was the chance to become a bishop. This explained, I believe, his inordinate interest in my ordination/marriage plans. The Exarch was jovial, a take-charge guy. Explaining that Russian was the greatest of languages for lovemaking he invited me to Odessa where there were plenty of handsome young Russian women eager to marry.

The refectory often served ice cream. The rumor was that the family who endowed the seminary included in the endowment perpetual ice cream. The Exarch liked ice cream and I learned a use for the beards of the Orthodox clergy. There once appeared a decent-sized dribble of ice cream on his beard, but with swift downward strokes of both hands it disappeared.

"Have you met Father Scott?"

"Who's he?"

Michael Scott was no bearded exuberant guest. One hardly noticed him. Unassuming, shy, Franciscan in spirit, and a fearless follower of Ghandi's nonviolence, he was easy to miss. We began to hear that he had something to do with securing the rights of African natives through the United Nations.

He lived a slot-car existence in Manhattan. Upon his arrival from London or Africa, our government restricted him to those streets taking him from his point of entry either to the United Nations or the seminary where the dean had offered him hospitality. Nowhere else. This restriction emanated from my almost namesake, Francis Eugene Walter, the Red-baiting chair of the House Un-American Activities Committee (HUAC). Father Scott was a third-generation Anglican priest. He and his father had served among poor and working-class people, which led them to support the labor movement in Great Britain. Of course, in those days, so did the Communist Party. Scott considered but eventually turned from the Party as incompatible with the Gospel. HUAC considered consideration equal to membership, hence the visa restrictions. The tutors invited Father Scott to a sherry before evensong. We heard what he was up to at the United Nations. It came out that he had no typewriter. When my former temporary quarters at Sewanee burned, we theological students living there lost everything. My most poignant loss was my great-grandfather Jacob Michael's gold pocket watch which had been on my desk to alert me to head to dinner at Gailor, the dining hall. Good it performed this last service because all of us theologs were at dinner when the building caught fire. My parakeet, Tweety Bird, perished—onlookers told me she was chirping "Nearer My God to Thee" as the upstairs gallery gave way beneath her.

An insurance agent sat us down to list losses.

"Typewriters?"

All hands but mine.

"What about you?"

"I don't type; never had one."

"You're gonna get one anyway."

So it was little loss to offer the Smith Corona portable to him.

As a priest serving in the Union of South Africa, Father Scott ended up posted, as he phrased it, to South West Africa, a territory under the control of the Union of South Africa, which was part of the British Empire. Today, thanks to Michael Scott and many thousands of others, South West Africa is Namibia, a free, independent nation.

Even Germany snagged colonies in Africa. How many of us Americans even wondered why in the 1951 movie, *The African Queen*, Humphrey Bogart and Katharine Hepburn tangled with a German gunboat on Lake Victoria during World War I? South West Africa became a German colony. It was a large hunk of Africa sitting on the northeast corner of the Union of South Africa, with a long Atlantic shoreline. Among the original inhabitants attacked, impounded, starved, and exterminated by the Germans were Herero tribespeople. In turn, hoping for independence, the Herero and other tribes still functioning after the "Herero Genecide" of 1904 attacked the Germans during the First World War. After the Armistice the European powers flocked like buzzards to pick over the German and Turkish colonies. The League of Nations awarded South West Africa to Great Britain under a "Mandate" to develop the population and resources to prepare for self-rule. So much for native independence. Worse still, the Crown ceded execution of the Mandate to the Union of South Africa, a member of the British Commonwealth. Independence? Development? Go figure. This betrayal was made even more unassailable by the demise of the League of Nations. The native people of South West Africa turned to the United Nations after the Second World War. By then, Father Scott was serving in a Herero mission. As soon as the Herero attempted to petition the United Nations for independence, the apartheid government of South Africa forbade them visas to leave the country. Father Scott, as a subject of Britain, could not be restricted and was able to represent South West Africa in person at the United Nations.

This struggle is complex and difficult to condense. I recall one effort by

Scott and his base of support in London, the Africa Bureau. Have the UN recognize young Queen Elizabeth as the true holder of the Mandate. She in turn would fulfill its purpose by giving operational control to England with guarantees of its eventual independence. Fairy dust.

Scott was sickened by what the native population continued to suffer, now under the British Crown. In 1947, he began his long quest to secure independence with human rights for the territory. After the 1952 Mau Mau Revolt in Kenya, four people in England had organized the Africa Bureau. In his book, *A Time to Speak*, Scott wrote that the Africa Bureau came about because of "their common interest and sense of urgency about Africa in the context of the post-war world." The Africa Bureau became a leader in addressing colonialism in Africa. It also gave Scott the closest thing he ever had to a home/home base in London.

As soon as the South African government realized that officials of the Herero tribe were at the UN petitioning for removal of the Mandate from South Africa, it restricted their travel visas. Since Scott's visa could not be restricted by South Africa, he began a lone ministry of representing South West Africa at the UN. Not satisfied with keeping people of color from petitioning for their independence, the government of South Africa in 1950 declared Father Scott a "prohibited inhabitant or visitor to the Union of South Africa," which to the government included South West Africa. So again Scott could neither return for consultation to the native people of South West Africa, which he alone was representing at the United Nations, nor, thanks to HUAC, travel in the U.S. to raise money and plead their case for independence.

Michael Scott became my spiritual advisor to fit me to return to Alabama. At one of our times in his rooms, he told of visiting an old Boer farmer whose views on race were hardly his own. The story was intended to equip me to accept with love and patience people whose views I could not accept. I failed that a few times. When *A Time to Speak* was published in 1958 he gave me a copy inscribed:

> With gratitude and all good wishes for your work in Alabama. "For us there is
> only trying, the rest is not our business." —"East Coker" [T. S. Eliot]
>   Michael Scott

In the book I found a longer version of the evening spent with the old white farmer. It is so revelatory of Michael Scott that I reprint the passage here:

In one district of the Transvaal I was asked to interview an old Afrikaans-speaking farmer. He received me very courteously in the old-fashioned tradition of his people. He had a large farm which had been afflicted by drought, though there was a promise of rain in a changing wind. He sat at the head of a long table. His sons were seated on one side of the room, the eldest nearest him, and the womenfolk, his wife, sisters, and daughters, on the other side. He was tall and well-built, with blue eyes, light hair, and beard, and he motioned me to a seat beside him at the head of the table. By his left side was an enormous family Bible, on which he rested his arm.

He began by saying that he had heard I would like to speak with him and had set apart this time. It was right that white people should discuss their differences, especially when these concerned the native people who were placed under us. He believed that I had taken part in, or attended, some conference abroad about the natives and he would like of course to hear what the representatives of other nations had had to say about our problems. But first he would like to say what he thought about them himself. These were people and problems which had to be lived with, not merely discussed. He and his forefathers had been living with them side by side for many generations now. Therefore it was right that I should also be given an opportunity of listening to him.

The old man thereupon expounded his views at great length and expressed the fears that he and many of his people felt. The natives were getting altogether out of hand. They expected too much. The towns were ruining them. They paid them higher wages than the farmers could afford and taught them a lot of wrong things. The able-bodied native men went away to the towns and left their children and women as squatters on the farmers' land.

Of course some farmers were bad employers. They did flog the natives, especially now that some of them were getting cheeky. He did not flog his natives. Occasionally he had to give one a beating, but it was very rare, and at this his sons nodded in confirmation. I think he was telling the truth. Some of the farmers did not feed their natives properly, he said. They were unhealthy and had not enough energy to work. The Native Farm Labour Commission had found that. Then they flogged the natives to try and get more work out of them. He was all against that and was always saying so in public. They were spoiling the labour market in the Western Transvaal though he had kept many of his "boys" for a long time.

The "coolies" were out of places in the country. They were always making trouble for the government, and it wasn't right that they should have all the trade with the white people in the district. The Farmers Cooperative was the proper trading organization for the farmers to patronize. He would like to see all the coolies sent back to India. The natives and the whites would get on better. The Indians were doing a lot of propaganda in the country about breaking down the colour bar for non-Europeans. That of course was impossible. The Lord in His wisdom had made people of different races and nations. The different peoples He had distinguished by different colours. It was therefore not right to want to mix them all up. And for a people like his own, living in a continent like Africa, it was right that they should cherish what had come down to them and had been preserved by their forebears. He then asked me to tell him what the matters were that had been discussed at the United Nations.

I outlined the course of the United Nations debate on racial discrimination and the treatment of Indians in South Africa. I said this question of race was one which now affected every nation in the world. It was not merely our South African problem. Other peoples were beginning to take a pride in their race and were beginning to ask for freedom as his own forbears, the Voortrekkers, had sought freedom. The United Nations had come into existence because that freedom, like peace, was indivisible. It would grow or die. We could not have it for ourselves and deny it to others indefinitely. We must begin to move forward with the rest of the world. I quoted from a speech by Mrs. Vijylaksmi Pandit, ambassador of India, at the United Nations:

"We write a Charter to promote human rights, and then proceed to ask for a committee to define them, for a Court of Justice to interpret them. That way lies disaster.... Let me therefore state the real issue involved in this resolution, which affects not only the Indians in the Union of South Africa but all the people of Asia and Africa. For us, it is not the mere assertion of certain rights and privileges. We look upon it primarily as a challenge to our dignity and self respect...."

The old man listened in a rather puzzled way, his lips pursed dubiously. He had opened the Bible and was turning the pages slowly. It had become very dark as huge billowing clouds rolled in front of the sun, casting their shadows over his lands.

He said, "Yes, I have read in the papers some of the things that were said about my country. Mrs. Pandit said, for instance, that Jesus Christ could not come to South Africa. That was a very wrong thing to have said. Of course Jesus Christ is here in our country. Every morning we have our prayers. All the family is here. I call in the servants and I read a chapter to them. And we say our prayers here in my house. 'Wherever two or three or are gathered together, there am I,' He said. Of course He is here in my home. I cannot understand how any white man could sit and listen to a 'coolie' woman saying such things about his country."

Gently I tried to bring home to the old man a truth which he had never really faced, and which would be quite abhorrent to him. I explained that what Mrs. Pandit had meant was that under the immigration laws of the country and the Asiatic Land Tenure and Indian Representation Act all Asiatics were prohibited from entry, and those that were here were discriminated against on the grounds of race, not on the grounds that they were as God had made them to be.

For the purpose of that particular Act, Asiatics were defined as peoples whose national home was in Asia. (Jews had been exempted under the Act.) But Jesus Christ was born and lived in Asia and was regarded as an Asiatic by every other nation. That is what Mrs. Pandit had meant by her remark.

The poor old man seemed utterly taken aback. "Jesus Christ . . . an Asiatic." His eldest son, who had been sitting forward on his chair with his hands on his knees and his elbows out, stood up and walked up and down with his fists clenched. How could any man sit still and listen to another white man saying Jesus Christ was an Asiatic? Clearly to him I was a renegade to my race and my religion. By now it had become quite dark and had actually begun to rain. On the wall was a picture of Jesus Christ with blue eyes and a straw-coloured beard, holding a lamb. It could almost have been the old man himself when he was younger. He followed my eyes to this picture and rain drops came quicker on the roof. There was suddenly a splitting clap of thunder and the rain descended in full fury on the corrugated iron roof. Speech was impossible because of the noise. And we sat, each preoccupied with his thoughts. The old man was obviously pleased about the rain, but was too preoccupied and too polite to change the subject of conversation to the weather. His eldest son had gone out to see what the prospects were, whether this was a passing thunder shower or whether it might be a long rain.

After we had sat for a while longer the old man rose and went to the window. There were huge puddles forming all over his lands. The hills were obscured by a gray curtain of rain. He raised his arms as I went over and stood beside him. "You see," he said, "the Lord is blessing us today." I had not the heart to make an obvious quotation from scripture which came to mind. Since further conversation was not easy, and his farm track was likely to be impassable if the rain continued, I said good-bye, wished him and his family well, thanked him for his courtesy and restraint, considering how much he differed from my point of view and how strongly he felt on these matters, and took my departure. He promised he would think over what I had said. And I had a feeling that he would when he was alone, and not under any necessity to put up an argument to defend his religion or his race.

Back in Alabama and the struggles of the civil rights movement, I never sought or welcomed such conversations. I lacked the humility, the power to accept possessed by my mentor. This is almost always true when the wrong-headed opponent is in authority over me.

In 1958 Father Scott was called to London, and he asked me to represent him at the United Nations. Overwhelmed as I was, it meant only the modest office of observing, recording, and passing on committee deliberations germane to South West Africa. This involved registration at the UN as a nongovernmental agency observer or some such title and being issued a card that would get me into buildings and hearing rooms to make notes. The freedoms of 1958 are impossible to imagine. No background check, no questioning, no fingerprints or eye scans for me. After flashing my card at an entrance, I was free to roam to locate some panel or hearing the Africa Bureau wished me to cover. Then I was free to wander. Magical moments were a descent into the basements of the UN where recordings of meetings were stored. I'd be directed to a neat little room with a platter, stylus, speaker, and buttons to stop and start the equipment, then order the material I had been asked to copy. The information was stored on wafer-thin floppy vinyl records big as family-size pizzas. The records turned at a stately 16½, not 33 rpm.

Today struggles, warfare, the extermination of thousands are over. South West Africa only lingers on old maps. On March 21, 1990, the Republic of Namibia took its place.

During the two years at General, I did a decent job as tutor and failed as fellow. My master's of sacred theology topic, "The Logos Christology of William Porcher DuBose," never saw ink and paper. Grace Church in Jersey City, courting Elizabeth Mitchell of Florence, Alabama, who was working in New York City for Putnam/Coward McCann Publishers, and my work at the UN ate up the time for academics. Or so I told myself. No one, not the dean or my faculty advisor, chided me or even mentioned my neglect of work on the master's. This was the first time I was only responsible to myself. No report cards, no one to report to except my conscience. My conscience gave me a "B." I still wish letters from General would have "Graduate" on them instead of "Fellow."

Because of my relationship to the Africa Bureau I received two invitations in 1958 to events that shaped the future. The first was to a New York screening of "a dramatic documentary," *Come Back, Africa*, written and directed by Lionel Rogosin. It was scripted and filmed, often on the fly, undercover, using South African amateurs playing parts in real places. Its purpose was to reveal the injustice and cruelty of apartheid. When Lionel arrived in South Africa, he had cans of unexposed film, little money, and a pack of lies. *Come Back, Africa* told the story of people living out the psychic, social, and physical violence of apartheid. Lionel found opponents of this system—white and black—willing to help him at the risk of their lives. The lies were for the authorities. For urban exterior shots, Lionel got permission to do a supposed documentary on street musicians while using his amateur actors to carry the story line in front of the performers. For one native character who, with his wife, leaves his homeland to work in the mines, Lionel told mine owners that he was doing a documentary for a mining juggernaut in the United States which was very impressed with

South African mining techniques. Ah, flattery! To do this film, Lionel told the officials he had developed a story demanding that his character, Zacharia, had to portray a miner. Lionel, "Zacharia," the camera, and camera operator went deep into the mines. "Zacharia" was filmed alongside real miners showing the conditions under which they worked. Lionel also filmed in native unlicensed shebeens. We'd call them honky-tonks. There he discovered the nineteen-year-old singer and soon to be activist, Miriam Makeba; later he bribed and lied her passage to the U.S., where we all got to meet her at the screening. Following the story line, Zacharia's wife took work as a domestic in a white area, effectively making it impossible for the couple even to visit. Her scenes and those of her "employers" were played in the homes of white actor/volunteers.

I heard most were from an Anglican group opposed to apartheid. Sheets covered the windows to hide interior shots. Lionel told us that as each film was exposed it went raw into a can to be rushed to the airport, getting it safely out of Africa. The film (restored and as of 2019 available on DVD and streaming) played its part in alerting the world to the reality behind the word "apartheid."

In late 1971 during Selma Inter-Religious Project days in Alabama, I called Lionel, with whom I'd had no contact for fifteen years, to ask if he would film a strike of the Gulf Coast Pulpwood Cutters Association. (More about that later.) Of course he'd come, get right on it. Didn't hear from him for a while. We learned he was sidetracked in Atlanta staying longer in that big hotel that is hollow in the center. It seems a man had killed himself leaping into the hollow. Lionel had become fascinated with the event and tarried in Atlanta. I recall him telling me, when we located him, that the poor man had fallen right onto the lobby bar. Lionel was exploring if a story was there. He did get to us and began filming. What was filmed is awaiting editing and restoration by his sons to approximate the movie he intended.

I'm a slow-moving introvert. Not Lionel. He was all forward propulsion to justice, rolling out his own future and ours.

The second invitation was to hear a talk by the Reverend Fred Shuttlesworth of Birmingham. Shuttlesworth was fresh from one of the Klan bombings of his home and family. The host for Shuttlesworth's talk was the Southern Conference Educational Fund (SCEF), a new organization to me. SCEF was a mostly white, left-leaning group which had been righteously working in the South for many years. In those blessed years their work meant to HUAC and the Senate Internal Security Committee (SISC) the same as working for the violent overthrow of the government of the United States of America.

The work of American Communist Party members in the civil rights movement is downplayed. The nation has simplified and burnished the myth of its embrace of freedom for people of color. Things have to be simple so small children and adults with withered attention spans need only learn of Martin Luther King Jr. and his "Letter from Birmingham Jail," Rosa Parks and the bus seat, and maybe a tip of the hat to Harriet Tubman.

Communists? Whoever heard of the Southern Tenant Farmers Union, with black and white members, around Reeltown, Alabama, 1932, near Notasulga? A few people with socialist and communist high ideals helped it form. Black union members Cliff James, John McMullen, Milo Bentley, Ned Cobb, and forty other armed men in Cliff James's cabin. They would not surrender to the High Sheriff every speck of their dignity; they would question and call to account that the Law belonged to the banks, the furnish merchants, and the landowners. The Law surrounded Cliff James's cabin. When the Law, unused to resistance, ran off, wounded Cliff James then made it to Tuskegee and a black hospital. The Law returned, reinforced. Others died. No gains, no rights. At the end of a poem about this event, "In Egypt Land," the poet John Beecher attached this:

The sheriff removed Cliff James from the hospital to the county jail in December 22. A mob gathered to lynch the prisoner on Christmas day. For protection he was taken to jail in Montgomery. Here Cliff James died on the stone floor of his cell, December 7, 1932.

There has to be a corner in Heaven where all the failed attempts to bring mercy and truth, justice and peace are gathered together in one hall, and are visited often with angelic song and dance. The first book I read to report matter-of-factly the role of the left in the movement was *Carry Me Home,* the Pulitzer-winning history/memoir by Diane McWhorter.

That 1959 morning as I walked into the hotel conference room to hear

Shuttlesworth, my goodness, there was Eleanor Roosevelt! Shuttlesworth gave a rousing, unscripted account of the strategies developing in Birmingham and of his beatings and the latest bombing of home and family. He bounced around the podium filled with joy. King may have been the brave, inspired voice of the movement, but at that time in the struggle Shuttlesworth was the revved-up engine of forward propulsion.

We hearers sat at round tables, holding about six. After Shuttlesworth we were given time to meet our seatmates and tell something about ourselves. Mrs. Roosevelt began moving from table to table to chat not about civil rights or Birmingham, but about us, who we were, where we were born or lived, what we were doing. It was not possible to be awestruck. I thought, "She looks like my grandmother and great-aunts, Bobbin, Arminnie, and Mamie. Dresses like 'em too." Her visit to our table was not a performance, not a ploy to get anything, but Mrs. Roosevelt herself, a woman totally aware of her position, but guileless.

On the way out I spoke with Carl Braden who with his wife Anne were Southern Conference Educational Fund field workers. SCEF sponsored the event. Anne's book, *The Wall Between,* recounted the couple's earlier efforts to sell a house in a white section of Louisville to a black family. Anne relates the sale, the burning of the house, their arrest, trial, and convictions, Anne's stay in jail and Carl's fifteen-year prison sentence in 1954 for sedition, which was overturned after a year.

I told Carl I'd soon be back in Alabama, and to stop by if he could. I gave him five dollars to receive the SCEF newsletter, the *Southern Patriot.* I walked out of that meeting buoyed up by being with like-minded people and thinking I'd enjoy reading about SCEF in the *Southern Patriot.* And that was kind of it. I thought . . .

Hop ahead to the Order of Myths Ball in Mobile, 1964. Warren Finch, a cousin on my father's side and a juvenile judge in Mobile, is twirling my sister, Patsy, around the dance floor. The Order of Myths, begun in 1868, is Mobile's oldest Mardi Gras parade society. Patsy is thrilled to have been invited. Cousin Warren takes this opportunity to whisper in my sister's ear that he has positive proof that I am a Communist. My poor sister had to live with that little pearl until her early death from breast cancer, not having the political knowledge to completely dismiss Warren. She did tell me about it, as she did most of the other strange charges about me and the movement she heard from her friends and in-laws. I tried to reassure her. But it wasn't until years after our conversation that I realized how Warren may have come across such a piece of nastiness.

Warren was a big member of the John Birch Society. Where did he get the "proof" that I was a communist? The answer can be googled at "SCEF, the Attack on the Southern Conference Educational Fund." It's from the "Student Civil Liberties Coordinating Committee."

The offices and home of three New Orleans leaders of the Southern Conference Educational Fund (SCEF) were raided by approximately one hundred city and state police and prison trusties on October 4, 1963. Arrested were SCEF's executive director, James A. Dombroski; treasurer, Benjamin Smith; and Smith's law partner and the Louisiana ACLU counsel, Bruce Waltzer. What a scene to imagine—crowded into Dombroski's house like the Marx Brothers stateroom scene in *A Night at the Opera*. Were the prison trusties allowed in or left to mill about on the sidewalk? SCEF files and mailing lists were removed from Dombroski's home and the New Orleans headquarters of the organization. Private legal files were taken from Smith and Waltzer's law office.

This occurred under the auspices of the "State Communist Propaganda Control Act." The authorization to bring SCEF to heel came from the "Louisiana Joint Legislative Committee on Un-American Activities." Nestled in all that confiscated paper was my name, address, and receipt for that five dollars I had given Carl Braden.

SCEF went to court to demand the return of its property. The case was not heard, the injunction ruled moot in that the material was no longer in Louisiana, as U.S. Senator James O. Eastland (D-Mississippi) had ordered the material transferred to chancery court in Woodville, Mississippi. From there I presume it went to Washington and into the files of Eastland's Senate Internal Security Subcommittee (SISS) and probably HUAC's files. Seven months earlier, in March 1963, Eastland had brought his committee to New Orleans to hold hearings on SCEF. Dombroski denied under oath "he was a Communist or under Communist discipline."

SCEF was early on Eastland's radar. The Louisiana Joint Legislative Committee on Un-American Activities was spawned after a television appearance on the NBC program *Today* by Alabama Governor George Wallace, who blamed SCEF for "racial agitation in Alabama." Wallace displayed photographs of Dombroski, Smith, and Waltzer at the SCEF Conference in Birmingham the previous year . . . the first integrated conference in Birmingham in twenty-five years. (The previous such conference in 1938 had been attended by none other than Eleanor Roosevelt.)

On October 25, 1963, three weeks after the New Orleans raid, charges against the three SCEF officials were dismissed. But the membership lists were out there. That had been the real goal. Now comes conjecture, not without evidence: Senator Eastland of blessed memory saw that all his cousins and friends in the John Birch Society, White Citizens' Councils, and most likely the Klan got copies of the records and sent them on to their cousins and friends. And so it came to pass that cousin Warren Finch, a member of the John Birch Society, while twirling my sister around the Order of Myths Ball, whispered in her pretty ear that he could prove that her brother was a communist.

Cousin Warren a bit later earned back some status in my eyes when, having tired of my little brother appearing before his bench, he offered David a choice: the Marines or detention. I think that last offense was running a hopped-up, muffler-less Volkswagen up and down the beaches of Gulf Shores, Alabama. David chose the Marines and did not get killed in Vietnam. Still later, Cousin Warren went on a psychic path to delusions of grandeur. He telephoned me in the 1970s when I was working with the Selma Project in Wilcox County, which by then had then gone from zero registered black voters to a heavy majority of black voters.

Warren was running for U.S. Congress, I believe it was. Wilcox was in his hoped-for district. He wanted me as his fellow advocate for all things good for black folk—two peas from the same pod—to get the news out to the black folk in Wilcox County about all the good things he, Reverend Walter's cousin, would do for them if elected. For a second I was back on a wharf at the beautiful headwaters of the Fowl River—clear and stained like strong tea, not muddy like down at the river's mouth where my folks lived. I was back on the wharf with the Finch boys: Warren, his brothers Greg, Robert, and

Inge. Inge and I were the youngest, about six years old. The boys' uncle, Eddie Luenberg, my father's first cousin, was teaching us younger boys how to swim. This riverfront property was the Finch boys' camp, bought by Eddie to give them a real place to play and swim. For Eddie, learning to swim was for Eddie to throw us overboard. I already knew how to swim, so I was not afraid to be heaved in. Inge, the youngest, was less skilled. Eddie did haul him out before he swallowed too much of Fowl River. For a second after Warren hung up, I thought, Yes, I'd help the boy I had stood with on the swimming wharf. But then, No, to the pretended friend to newly franchised blacks. So I never called him back. Not a gripping story. But think. Five hundred, a thousand slimy whispers to people like my sister Patsy, oozed by people in petty, or not so petty positions. How many of the slandered then stopped talking, stopped loving, stopped reading, stopped thinking, so as to save their jobs, their pulpits, or an office at the Rotary?

As I write this today, out in a desert somewhere west of here are vast, colorless structures owned by the National Security Administration that are using enough juice to run several mid-sized cities. The juice keeps safe, warm, dry, and available the records and chitchat our government has amassed on us. I'm sure my old SCEF membership records are secure if needed. And my FBI file. And my Alabama Bureau of Investigation file. And maybe even my Jersey City arrest record for littering. But there is nothing to worry about. Eastland and Stennis are dead. Not to worry. But thirty, forty years from now, or maybe this year, there may well be new Stennises, new Eastlands, new bogeymen to scare the people. New flavors of subversion will be "found," and our grandchildren will be in danger and our old records—the things we said, the things we didn't say, the things we did and did not do—will be used to help justify their detainment, reeducation, mental adjustments, or termination.

15. At Christ Church, Mobile, 1958

The Reverend Leigh Arsnault invited me to spend the summer of 1958 at Christ Church, exploring how the parish could engage the neighborhood of lower-income folks. Leigh had paid without being asked for an oxygen tank to ease those last days of my mother's life. My father told me this. It was the first time I ever heard him speak of money.

I lived upstairs in the old rectory—all to myself. I learned that when the staff had gone home in the evenings, when I had no other chores, I could sit on the upstairs front gallery, a gentle breeze sometimes upon my face, and see our city. Or I could take a walk to the river, where Admiral Semmes presides from his pedestal, a benign spectator to alcoholics, prostitutes, the homeless, late-night pole fishermen, off-duty sailors who made the night their own. I felt I'd died and gone to heaven to be a priest in such a time and place.

This church was truly downtown. A stone's throw away stood a lace-iron fence enclosing a small brick and mortar rectangle; all that remained of Fort Louis de la Mobile, where in 1711 the refounding of Mobile began. The habitants had tired of their 1702 colony going underwater in the spring floods, so they upped and moved down the river in 1711. Christ Church was therefore in "an old part of Mobile," a phrase that conferred prestige. The neighborhood was, however, a composite of early nineteenth-century homes both brick and wood-framed. These were spotted among later raised cottages. Then there were shotgun rental houses and four squares. Out of sight on the outskirts were developers ready to pounce, ravage, and rebuild.

Aside from the remarkable Miss Ruth Huger, who lived alone next door to the rectory on Conception Street, we had one other old lady member of the parish in the neighborhood, up a few blocks on Church Street: Miss Daisy Duvall. Because "she didn't go out," it was my privilege to call on her a few times that summer. Miss Daisy lived alone. Well, not exactly. "She won't let you in," someone in the office told me, because of the numerous cats she kept. Heading up Church Street, I thought it likely she was a crabby old lady who would close the door in my face. Not at all. Keeping people out was a courtesy; just opening the door let out a blast of cat stench. She suggested we sit on the front gallery.

Over the course of our visits, I learned that Miss Daisy was the forgotten author of a well-known Mobile photograph. On a blustery day in 1906, Miss Daisy pushed open her front door, picking her way through splintered branches of oak to a street littered with barrels and lumber from the waterfront. These were leftovers of the Storm of 1906. That storm does not have a name like Addie or James. Today hurricanes can be located in their infancies, baptized Ed or Florence or Katrina. Before this, storms gave no such warnings.

Miss Daisy was able to make her way, over and under debris, carrying

Daisy Duvall's 1906 photo of Christ Church, its bell tower blown off by a hurricane (courtesy of the University of South Alabama).

her camera, until she stopped to photograph something no longer there—the Christopher Wren Bell Tower of Christ Church. The tower had toppled straight down the center aisle. It first demolished the slave gallery (this was not rebuilt). Taking the roof with it, the spire laid itself down the aisle, splintering pews and demolishing the altar rail, and its tip came to rest just short of the altar—an unwelcome genuflection. The bell came loose and fell somewhere (because the spire was never rebuilt, the bell was bolted to the front porch of the church, where it remains). Miss Daisy made her way to the river through giant fiddlesticks of timbers. There she photographed tugs and sailing cargo vessels all jumbled together.

I was full of questions. She retreated into her house through a blast of cat gas. She returned and handed me an ancient Kodak and a small photograph album. I looked, asked questions, and made to hand them back. No, she meant me to have them. One does not say no to such gifts. Inside the album, loose, tucked in a small envelope, was the original negative of the spireless Christ

Church. Later, when I handled the camera, the rubber bulb and tube crumbled to bits. The bellows were cracked and wouldn't move, the nickel-plated levers corroded. I should have saved it. But I didn't. Where do things like that go? Or do they dematerialize because no one loves them?

That was how it had been on Miss Daisy's gallery—the cats, the smell, the rocking chairs, the 1906 storm. But it was also 1958, in a neighborhood, like the rest of the South, teetering on the lip of the Second Reconstruction.

As I walked the Christ Church neighborhood, I could see that it was mixed-race indeed, no defined black or white areas. This part of Mobile was in decline. One could faintly hear the baying of the circling developers. The Mobile Historical Society did what it could to save its spirit. Most called the saviors the Mobile Hysterical Society.

I'd visited this neighborhood once before as a kid about eight years old, escorted by my mother. She believed there would be some benefit to me to join "The Gallant Pelham Mobile Chapter of the Children of the Confederacy." An attempt to socialize me?

The house we entered back then became one of the few saved. Used often for meetings, I think it has survived even unto this day. Inside, we could see it was a mothers' meeting, children a minority presence only tagging along. Or so it looked to me, perhaps because the maternal force field made it seem a mothers' meeting. Things began officially with THE INVOCATION of great length—taking its inspiration loosely from the Book of Common Prayer. It was offered by a small boy flanked by a mother. BORING. The Gallant Pelham Chapter of the Children of the Confederacy, my prospective siblings, were docile slaves to their mothers. It was one of those organizations addicted to form: invocation, call to order, minutes, adoption of minutes, treasurer's report, adoption of same, correspondence (an invitation from another Children of the Confederacy unit to a party), old business (none), new business (none), adjourn, refreshments, dismissal.

It was clear this was a maternal training camp to prepare offspring for service in any (white) organization similarly addicted to Robert's Rules of Order and not much else. The more subtle aim was to prepare a child to stir no pot in need of attention. I was interested in the Civil War itself. About walking around the doomed earthworks surrounding Mobile, about Forts Morgan and Gaines at the mouth of the Bay. About my great-grandfather's military career and how it ended at Spanish Fort.

It was also clear these mothers didn't know a scraper from a ramrod or Grant's Pass from Fort Huger, or why to pick up a Minié ball from Fort Blakeley if they stepped on it. Indeed, thinking on the meaning of one of the earth's greatest conflicts was to be kept from the Gallant Pelham Chapter of Confederate Children. My mother and I left. She never spoke another word about my becoming a Child of the Confederacy.

Until I walked the neighborhood in 1958, thinking how Christ Church could reach out to its people, that was all I had known about the area.

How to serve the Christ Church neighborhood? In Jersey City, Grace Church's answer was to welcome children; then everything falls into place. In Mobile, my boss, Leigh, and I decided to start with a vacation church school, a tried device offered by many churches in the summer. The neighborhood children had not the foggiest notion what that big gray mossy building down by Conception Street was. The people who came to that big gray mossy building on Sunday had no idea about the children in the neighborhood, yet it was where their grandparents had been raised.

I offered to walk the neighborhood, placing posters and knocking on doors, meeting families, inviting them to send their kids to our vacation church school. The neighborhood was racially mixed but not definitively segregated. So appeared a little cloud on the horizon, no bigger than a man's hand.

I told Leigh I was not going to figure out if a house was "black" and skip it.

I don't think this possibility had occurred to him. He was a New Englander and proud of it, but he had come to Christ Church from a parish in Greensboro, Alabama, a bastion of the Black Belt. So he knew a thing or two about white churches in the South. He was a caring, loving pastor. I'd always respected him. But. He reacted to this bombshell with obvious concern but did not expressly tell me to keep our project white. He said nothing. But I could tell it had shaken him.

Today, I believe that was the end of his wanting me called as an assistant at Christ Church. If he had flat out told me not to invite black kids, I believe

I would have acceded, pleading being under the rector's authority. He communicated No, but would not say it. He was as caught as many of us white Southerners were between knowing well what was right but being unwilling to destroy a way of living that provided a tall scaffold on which we white folks hung, lived, moved, and had our being.

Reaching out to people is such a commonplace of Christian activity that it amazes me even now how clearly the Old Confederacy limited this and how the Color Line perpetuated the failing. In Jersey City, a place of rotten politics, one could still invite any kids on the block to a vacation church school or anything else and not worry about color. Not in Mobile in 1958.

Why didn't I trim my sails to accommodate this maybe mild violation of our faith that the Church was One? Or that the human species was One? I'd had my revelation. I vowed to act as if the Color Line did not apply to me. I was afraid and also a little curious to see what would happen if I lived that summer by that revelation. A fit of hubris? An adventure? Why turn back now at Christ Church's vacation church school? I also know I was and am a prideful person. Why should this be my problem at all, I'd thought. It was up to others to accept it or stay clear of me. That this would cause a hell of an uproar among parishioners, that money might evaporate, that Leigh might quell the uproar but still resign for allowing a couple of black kids into a summer program was not on my horizon—at first. I'd figured if Leigh and the vestry didn't like it, they could cancel vacation church school and not call me in the fall to be an assistant helping in a program of outreach to the neighborhood.

There was something deeper I was not aware of at the time. For one crazy white guy to act inside a spectrum which couldn't tell black from white—in the Christ Church situation, for instance—would cause him to be reviled and cursed by the whites caught up in their lies of "welcome," "family," and "inclusion." It would expose the soiled tatters of the Church. Not her robes of glory.

Truth was, back then the South was the South, the North the North. Christ Church, Mobile, not Grace Church, Jersey City.

I must have known this. If so, I paid no heed. I'd made a promise. I figured then that the effects and aftereffects on others were not exactly my business. I would explore with my own life what would happen to a child of the South who wouldn't go along. Looking back, I see my anger at white people, people I loved who did nothing to throw off this garment of shame.

No black kids appeared at the vacation church school. It had fallen out that my random walk through the neighborhood hit no black families. It was obvious that no black kids or parents would imagine that the posters on phone poles meant to include them.

Vacation church school was a great success. Some church kids came and more area kids than I'd imagined. Parishioners volunteered; food was good. We had fun. I heard later that two or three of the kids started coming to Sunday school. I especially remember identical twin boys, about ten years old. You could watch them open up daily as they soaked up adult attention.

An Excursus to Big Mound: We even had a Baptist volunteer at vacation church school, a rising sophomore from Judson College (est. 1834). Judson is located in the Black Belt town of Marion, Alabama. Here was an exotic, a creature rarely seen blooming in Anglican soil. She was a perky, beautiful, blond girl whom right off I asked for a date—to my amazement.

Daddy lent me an outboard motor. We drove up to Chastang's Landing, rented a skiff, and set off to visit Big Mound on Bottle Creek. Big Mound is in the center of what today is called "The Mobile/Tensaw River Delta," an immense, sinuous waterway, covering thousands of acres. In those days, we locals called it simply "the swamp," as in the title of Robert Leslie Smith's book about the area, *Gone to the Swamp*.

Big Mound is one of the largest prehistoric earthworks in the Southeast. At the time of our date, it showed only old scars of some small test pits dug by archaeologists. Nor were there any paths or markers to help us when we stepped ashore. I'd been there twice years before. I thought I'd landed our skiff close to the place I'd landed before. If we walked directly away from the creek, we'd come upon the mound. Never found Big Mound. Giving up, I turned back knowing we'd hit Bottle Creek sooner or later. It might take a while unless we lucked up, hitting the boat when we hit the creek. Unlikely. All we had to do then was walk along the shore left or right until we saw our skiff. I chose left; turned out left was right.

The creek, of course, allowed more sunshine to hit its banks than the woods beyond it. So we had to walk close to the creek to keep it in view. Lots of scraggly willows and Jackson vine to push through.

Then the water moccasins. Some half in the water. Some on the bank, slowly slithering or seeming to sleep. Worse, draped over, lounging, on bare willow branches at eye level—our eye level. We must have passed more than fifty as we looked for the skiff. It became a dance: stay close to the creek so as to locate the skiff, veer away from the snakes to keep them calm. I shouldn't have worried so much. I later learned how indolent moccasins are, how slow to wrath. Some herpetologists record they have picked them up, dropped them, dragged them, slung them, even manufactured a fake arm to pester them into biting it. Even with that hassling, they only struck the fake arm when mightily provoked. That's hard to believe, and I sure wouldn't have believed it then. Might not now.

Can't praise my young date enough. What a woman! Never a shriek or peep out of her, no clutching, no meltdowns. We did hold hands as we maneuvered through the brush. She never grabbed mine first. It's possible she was half paralyzed with fear. But no. I don't believe so. She might even have been enjoying our adventure . . . maybe not.

The snakes smelled. They smelled bad. Especially bad because the air had turned still, murky, and saturated. It was growing dark with a storm about to break.

I read a bit of this story last night to some friends. A naturalist among them said that indeed moccasins smell. Always gratifying to have a memory validated after fifty-seven years! Later I googled water moccasins. The great Internet revealed they possibly smelled like cucumbers. Not true. It was a funky, skunky, heavy, dead, mushroomy smell said to be related to mating.

We saw no romancing among them. Or any between us. We held hands, as said, to snake our way through the brush and *Smilax rotundifolia* bordering Bottle Creek but not for intimacy.

The moccasins thinned out. We found the skiff. The motor cranked. The storm broke. At the mouth of Bottle Creek, we turned left onto the Tensaw River. Not much wind but waving curtains of water whipping the river to froth. I broke out two authentic Spanish-American War pith helmets. My idea of fun and date impression. It worked. She laughed, putting hers on. We bailed.

I didn't need a map because I knew the way. I will name some of the waterways we traversed because they tell the story of the humans who settled here, each calling the Delta theirs: the Original People, the French, the Spanish, the Scots traders, the British, and then us Americans.

Going back, my date and I left Bottle Creek at its mouth, turning up the Tensaw, then left into Little River, then avoiding the slough into Big and Little Chippewa lakes, right into Bayou Machey. In less than a mile, we turned into Jose Creb Bayou. There is a little, unnamed branch off Jose Creb Bayou that opens into the broad, muddy Mobile River. At the Mobile and this Jose Creb branch, there used to sit a two-room tarpaper shack on poles, its small stoop facing the Mobile, the house of Chief Tallawah, the hermit. High school and college years, my buddies and I camped out with Chief, and it was he who told us how to get to Big Mound from the Mobile to Jose Creb to Little River, to the Tensaw, to Bottle Creek.

Entering the Mobile, we went upriver past Seymour's Bluff and landed at Chastang's Bluff, where the earlier mentioned John Chastang's large log house has burned only recently. There is a town named Chastang out on the highway, and Chastangs are all over the world doing useful and interesting work.

African Americans are also caught up in the names. My old, undated "Fisherman's Guide of the Mobile River Delta," copyrighted by the Powers Company, labels a lake down the Tensaw River from Big Mound "Nigger Lake." Chief told us that it was so-called because an escapee from slavery built a cabin and hid out there for many years. Mine is an old map. Newer ones record a "Negro Lake." I hope the day will not come when mapmakers will name it "African American Lake." What could one call it to honor the brave man who escaped from bondage to live, hunt, and fish on this lake? How about "Liberty Lake" or "Freedom Bayou"?

At Chastang's Landing, I helped a sopping date out of the skiff. I chucked the outboard into the trunk, pith helmets on back seat, and off we went to Mobile.

Never a complaint from my date. She seemed to enjoy it, anyway, acted like it. My estimation of this Judson rising sophomore was rising every minute. We sat close together to stay warm. You could do that in cars back then.

I thought it rude and unwise to bring her home dripping. Christ Church was on the way, its kitchen a good place to dry out. I went upstairs to bring down a book I'd been reading, *Poets in a Landscape*. I read her some of Gilbert Highet's translations of the elegiac verses of the Roman poets. I'll say it for you: What a show-off!

This is one of the few books to which I return over and over. Highet and his camera visited the haunts of these poets, sometimes recording the footprints of their houses, the springs from which they drank. And as my buddy, Henry Cole, who once traveled the swamps, might say, "A dab hand at translating Latin romantic verse."

After I'd gotten her home and she was back on the job at vacation church school, she told me that her mother had been so concerned about how late we were that she telephoned another boyfriend, telling him that we were up in the swamp somewhere and it was still raining. Her friend told her mother that if Francis Walter had her up in the swamp on a date, there was nothing to worry about.

I doubt I'll ever get an honorary doctorate, but if I do, the honor will come nowhere near that. [Editor's Note: Francis X. Walter received an honorary degree from the University of the South in January 2020.]

Leaving Christ Church: The summer of 1958 ended. Aside from that jog in the road between Leigh and myself, it was a pleasant dream. The vacation church school was a winner. The Christ Church staff was a delight. Jo Dix, the secretary, a little younger than my mother, was a dry wit. Leigh was engaging and warm and had the gift of being a caring pastor.

We had among us, as staff in an undefined job, Miss Ruth Huger. She and her sister had lived all their lives in Huger House next door to the rectory on Conception Street. Miss Ruth's sister had died. They were the Huguenot Hugers of Charleston, South Carolina. Miss Ruth, on telling where she was from often added that the Charleston family would say of the move to Mobile, "Ruth, why did you all move West?" My cousin Eugene Walter published a short story based on them: "I Love You Batty Sisters." Miss Ruth was really in the office to gain Social Security quarters to bring in some money. At her death, she left Huger House to Christ Church, a valuable piece of downtown property, stitched onto the rest of the buildings.

The old sexton, Louis Broadnax, a black man, completed the staff. Among his jobs was to ring the fallen bell that survived the 1906 storm. Mr. Broadnax and I ate breakfast together in the kitchen during the week. I had bought a hand-cranked coffee mill in a junk shop downtown and was showing it to him—a 1906 Universal Coffee Grinder (I still have it to grind beans every morning). "Do you know how to use it?" I asked.

"Oh yeah. When I was out in the woods collectin' *rosin*, coffee was the only thing I looked forward to." Mr. Broadnax and all us Gulf Coast folk said *rosin* for the unprocessed sap of the pine tree. It is called *resin* in the wider world.

As a young man in the late 1880s, Mr. Broadnax was hoodwinked into what sounded to him like the best money-making job ever. It was one of the many dupes concocted by the white man to reenslave black people, Constitution be damned. Mr. Broadnax ended up way, way out in the piney woods collecting resin—one of the world's worst jobs. There was no salary, therefore no money, only chits redeemable at the camp commissary for coffee, tobacco, and other trifles. There was one dirt road out, patrolled by armed white men on horses. Home was far away—where he didn't know.

To collect resin, you first slotted a galvanized pan into a horizontal cut in a pine tree, then you slashed a V into the tree above the pan and swabbed sulphuric acid onto the V slash. Viscous pine sap would slowly ooze into the pan. Because the ooze would always stop, you slashed a fresh V above the old cut and daubed it with more acid. Removing the pans and getting the resin into barrels kept one covered with the tarry stuff.

Mr. Broadnax told me there was no way to escape without cash. If you escaped the camp, you'd end up on a county road—where? Only money would help. He befriended one of the black men who brought in supplies and so managed to smuggle a letter to a relative, asking for money. Thank goodness he could write. The money came via the friendly supplier. One night he walked out, making it to the relative.

Mr. Broadnax and I got to talking about how you made coffee out there in the woods. "Well, we had a grinder like yours, 'cept bigger. You nailed it to a tree. Get you some green coffee beans, and I'll show you how we done it."

I did.

"Put this fryin' pan on the stove. Now put a little lard in it. That's enough. Now put some beans in. Stir 'em round. Don't let 'em burn, let 'em smoke. All right. They look roasted enough. Grind 'em in your mill. Boil some water in a pot. That's enough for the grounds you got. Boil those grounds in the water awhile. After the water's black, take the pot off the stove and settle the grounds with egg shells. Now, let's have us some coffee! That's the ticket."

I'd seen Chief Tallawah do that of a morning. Except he bought already ground coffee. Chief said if he didn't have egg shells, a little strip of dried catfish hide would do as well to settle the grounds.

By the way, the coffee—Chief's or Louis Broadnax's—was superb. Was it the process or having it from these two extraordinary survivors?

It was not easy to leave such a grace-filled place for New York City. I hoped I'd misread things, and I'd hear from Bishop Carpenter and Leigh that they wanted me there. Didn't happen. Besides that ministry to pitch into, I would have liked to stay near my family, to be of help if I could. The family was ending one way of being and skidding into dissolution after my mother's death.

Miss Ruth gave me a going-away present: an oil painting done by her. One sees a young woman seated in a chair. All diagonals. The woman has a pensive, earnest look. She and all of the elements of the painting are muted, pale grays, washed-out blues, and whites. Except for her hair of flaming red and orange.

"Who is that?!" I asked.

"A ghost," said Miss Ruth, with a look that said "No more questions."

Miss Ruth and Miss Daisy and Louis Broadnax were how it had been down there where Mobile was founded. Leigh Arsnault and I that summer were dreaming of how it might be. But I was not to be in that dream.

16. Family Grief

I came home from my first year at General Seminary in November 1957 to attend my mother's illness and subsequent death. I returned and completed the

1957–'58 school year. During that time my family in Mobile struggled with the loss of my mother, which was particularly hard on my brother, David, who was then in his early teens. David was adrift and his misery was compounded when our father began to court Gretchen, whom he eventually married. All this was conveyed to me in a series of letters from my grandmother, Bobbin.

In a September 1958 letter from Bobbin, she references "the brotherly talk." This is what happened. One night I drove up from Christ Church to visit my folks. Daddy was gone, visiting Gretchen. Bobbin was asleep. I looked in my old bedroom, which was now David's. I could see him on the top bunk. He was not asleep but said nothing as I gave him a hug.

I felt something along his side. It was a .22 rifle. I was shocked but also immediately aware that my brother was a little, frightened boy of thirteen. I slid the rifle from under the covers, removing a cartridge. I leaned it in a corner. Neither of us said anything. I was overwhelmed with sorrow, knowing that in a day or two I'd be gone. My sorrow was for us both. Standing by the top bunk, I laid my head beside his and wept. I think he finally told me he was afraid to be by himself.

Bobbin's letter reflected her anger at my innocent father for wanting to find somewhat of the love and support of my mother after her death. In Gretchen he hit pay dirt. Now my grandmother had to live with a man she felt wanted to supplant her only daughter in his affections. This led her to resent that he would not spend more time with my brother David, who was also struggling with losing his mother. When Daddy and Gretchen were married, my poor grandmother, feeling she was abandoned, became even more angry and frightened.

But before this culminated, Bobbin struggled every morning to get David up and ready for school, as she had done for me even when I was a day student at Spring Hill College. She'd sit on the edge of the bed, rubbing David's back, and when tender love did not work, she would do to David what was necessary to get him moving. She helped him with his homework, plugging on when her growing blindness made it impossible to see words in a book. His grades continued to fall, even as his elaborate excuses continued to improve.

She need not have been frightened. My sister, Patsy, had married Willie McVoy, who had graduated from Ole Miss. Patsy and Willie moved into our old house in Spring Hill and cared for Bobbin until her death. Having been the major cause of so much misery for us, as you will see, Willie's father stepped in again, buying our house from Daddy, giving my sister, Willie, and Bobbin a place to live. So my grandmother never had to move until near the end of her life when she went to a nursing home, where she died, incapacitated, cherished by my sister and Willie.

Back in the sad days, thirteen-year-old David got to go to New Orleans or Biloxi or on fishing trips with Daddy and his fishing "podner," Herbie Stein. Bobbin would have David washed behind the ears for Sunday school only to see Daddy whisk him off to go out to Middle Bay Light with Herbie for some white trout. She was truly hurt and frustrated. But I think it saved David, though like Bobbin I wished he could have hit the books as well.

Mr. Stein was well known in Mobile for his large, valuable property in Spring Hill. The acreage was littered with antique engines and other rusted machinery he had never gotten around to fixing.

Herbie's father, old Mr. Stein, came from Germany. An engineer himself, he installed and managed Mobile's first water works. His hollowed cypress logs carried water, some for more than a century. Now, although living alone, Herbie had survived a mild stroke that only affected his speech. The impairment oddly brought all his mechanical knowledge to the fore, crowding out much of what he intended to say.

It was said that at the post office, he would walk in to buy stamps.

"What kind and how many, Mr. Stein?" the postmistress would say.

"A ⅛-inch shim over that shaft after turning the end down .0005," he would answer. I assume she would give him a variety of stamps. I never heard he went away unhappy.

Herbie was good for David, exposing him to the world of mechanics. David had my father's gift of mastery over spatial and material properties.

17. A Call to Good Shepherd

During my last semester at General Seminary, word came from Mobile that Father Cole had left Church of the Good Shepherd to accept a call in Baton Rouge. What if...? Opportunity had opened up like a flower. I might have a downtown parish where I could use the lessons I'd learned in a white/black/ Hispanic parish in Jersey City. It would give me at least a faint chance of becoming the rector of a black parish in Alabama.

For my own survival in the South, where the social struggle against the Color Line and the sin of exclusion in my Church would be centered, I might not last long in a white Episcopal Church, given the present leadership in the diocese of Alabama. The Second Reconstruction was gathering steam in the South, I had promised never again to accept the privileges of my skin color, and I wanted to be there. Good Shepherd was my only chance, or so I thought.

I had four reasons for pursuing this unexpected opening.

First, Good Shepherd was located in the black business district of Mobile called Davis Avenue, surrounded by poor housing. I felt I could take all I'd learned at Grace Church in Jersey City into that setting. This would give me a fighting chance to live out my promise never to accept the Color Line which denied human equality.

Second, because the diocese had supplemented my tuition at Sewanee, I had a handshake obligation to serve at least two years in Alabama—not a burden, the only place I wanted to go.

Third, a problem hung over me because of that second reason. Even though I could be circumspect about race in my "Land of the Lost Cause," sooner or later my actions or views would get me in trouble. But this was a personal problem to be faced when it came. Being at Good Shepherd would greatly extend my survivability.

Fourth, my family was still reeling from the death of our mother. It would be good if we could all be together. My father was adrift in his grief and the strain of family circumstances brought about by her death. Gretchen Miller, a widow, entered Daddy's life; she brought with her the support he needed.

Gretchen and Daddy would soon be married. My feelings toward Gretchen can best be expressed in a saying from the black people of Wilcox County: "Ain't nothin higher than the sun and the moon 'cept [add what you want] Gretchen Miller."

As mentioned, David was doing poorly in school and was unhappy at home. He was being cared for by Bobbin, at age eighty-three, taking up where her daughter's death had left him. When Daddy talked of marrying and selling the family house, Bobbin was bereft. She wrote me, "If he marries and buys that house he talks about, I'm out of here. There's no bus service there." She enjoyed that last bit of independence, shopping downtown, not for herself but for us. "I'm out of here?" How? A sad and desperate remark. She had no resources to be anywhere else. It was hard to hear of these things while I was up in New York. I wanted to be near them.

I then began corresponding with church officials in active pursuit of a posting for Good Shepherd. Some of these letters are reproduced in the Appendix.

I got right onto setting up a meeting with Bishop Carpenter. It turned out that he was coming to New York and agreed to see me at the Seminary. I felt only the faintest chance to win him over, yet I was at peace. I remembered T. S. Eliot's words that Father Scott had written for me: *For us there is only trying. The rest is not our business.*

All I had to do was make a pitch.

I met with the Bishop and set to. He never interrupted, listening intently. His first words were, "We've had white priests at Good Shepherd before."

Not a bad beginning! Then came the not so good.

"What we do is make them an assistant to the rector over at All Saints, and then. . . ."

All Saints was the white church in white Mobile across town from Good Shepherd. I knew and admired Rector Francis Wakefield there, who was intelligent and socially aware.

"So, Bishop, I would technically be an assistant to Mr. Wakefield and answerable to him and All Saints' vestry?"

"But you'd be over at Good Shepherd. You'd be going over to Good Shepherd every day, doing everything a priest does, and you'd live over near All Saints."

In other words, the Bishop was telling me to "just go over and serve" Good Shepherd.

My response was spontaneous: "I want to live in the rectory next to the church. I want to be employed by the vestry, work with them, be answerable to them."

That was a hard one for him. He seemed to change the subject.

"Are you planning to get married?"

"Ah, no." Planning, a term subject to interpretation.

The Bishop's suggestion that I be a crosstown, visiting chaplain to a parish with no mutual contract between us staggered me. He was unaware of the humiliation he was heaping on the Good Shepherd parishioners and the men who were elected to choose, hire, and then collaborate with a priest of their choosing.

Had he dug into his psyche, it would have taken only a shovelful or two to uncover the principle governing the insult: Never Put a Black Man Over a White Man.

But yet, but yet, he did finally override that—in my case.

Then it happened. He said, "Yes," and notified the senior warden of the vestry that he was sending this young white priest down for them to interview. Why? Because he loved me. In the Appendix I have a letter in which Bishop Carpenter expresses admiration for my assignment to Good Shepherd. I believe that his sentiments expressed in that letter were what he said they were and his appraisal of me, while over the top, was genuine when he wrote it and shows a generosity of spirit.

For some sixty years, I have pondered this man's words and actions concerning the subjugation in this country of blacks by whites, concerning the exclusion of blacks from many expressions of his church's life and witness: a flat negation of the unity of the Church emphasized so often in the New Testament.

Subsequent correspondence with the vestry of Good Shepherd culminated in a unanimous vote to call me to be the rector. I then wrote to Bishop Carpenter stating my intention to travel to Mobile to meet with the vestry before accepting the call.

First thing after writing to Bishop Carpenter to tell him about the meeting with the vestry, I wrote four letters to members of my family. Thanks to my mother, we all knew what Good Shepherd was. I imagined the only unhappy response might come from Patsy. Newly married, she was getting a counter-weight to my positions from her father-in-law. My poor sister, she'd chosen to share my views with the McVoys to convince them, especially her father-in-law, that I really wasn't a tool of the communists. That was sick tennis. She'd lob Mr. McVoy's latest rant on Martin Luther King over to me. I'd smash back something for her to give him. Her struggle was not about social polity, but how to love both her brother and her new family. She didn't have the experience or the background to come to her own conclusions. She had love to spread around and was having trouble doing it.

Steeped in love, admired, spoiled, I sat in my study at General Seminary reading four letters, finding myself criticized, rebuked by my family. This had never happened. Wait. Correction. When I was seven, prompts Memoria, I refused to drink a glass of orange juice and castor oil from the hand of my mother. I can today see the cells and pulp of freshly squeezed juice suspended in the clear globules of oil. It still sickens.

Losing patience, my mother gave up but told me that when my father got home from work she would tell him to spank me. Miserable, I still wouldn't. I got a halfhearted punishment from an embarrassed father.

Now I must endure the impact of the four letters. It was paralyzing. Yet I never considered giving up. That being the only thing I was holding onto. If the family that bore and raised me cut me off, I was prepared to accept it.

Patsy was frightened, angry, and confused. Her letter included Daddy's thoughts. He never wrote anyone. Not that he couldn't—just wouldn't. Didn't I care about them? Didn't I love them anymore? Her stance was not rejection; she was still trying to understand me. What would people in Mobile think of them? How could I do this, especially to David, who'd be going to Murphy High soon? He wouldn't get any fraternity bids. Not a small thing in white Mobile. The better fraternities, Deltas and Phi Kappas, were gateways to the better fraternities at Alabama and Auburn. Their largess then opened the gates to society in Mobile.

A harsh thing she said that made me sad for her was, "I blame our mother for this." But it gave comfort to me to know she understood.

She could also blame our country. Like the Original Stain in the doctrine of original sin, racism was injected into our founding documents' craziness: that "all men are created equal" and that enslaved black humans from Africa should be counted as three-fifths of a person, thus lacking the presumption of personhood.

Immediately after the publication of the Declaration of Independence, Englishman Thomas Day wrote: "If there be an object truly ridiculous in nature it is an American patriot, signing resolutions of independence with one hand and with the other brandishing a whip over his affrighted slaves."

I have lost this letter from Patsy and Daddy. The letters from the three Pine Trees are reproduced in the Appendix. For fifty-six years they have lain, tied in packets, tucked away in a large cedar chest, what Cousin Eugene called one's "Toys and Treasures Chest." If these letters have been treasure, they have been a dragon's horde. Only twice I've read from a couple of them. Now time, the movement, and an acceptance of my sins and limitations have ground the pain away.

Bobbin was gradually losing her eyesight. I can trace the decline in the collection of letters she wrote during the seminary years. Finally she asked others to write for her.

The first fix for senility for David, Daddy, and me was mechanical or, we'd say today, environmental. When Bobbin complained of no longer being able to set the oven temperature, I drilled holes in the knob, punched in BBs at 150, 250, 300, and 350 degrees. Of course, it didn't work, because people aren't antique outboard motors. We can't fix misunderstanding, despair, loss of memory, and integrity with a screwdriver and a pair of pliers.

Letters in the Appendix are arranged chronologically. Correspondence with members of my family dealt with their deeply held conviction that I was going against rigid social norms in my determination to accept a call to a black congregation. It was painful for them, and for me, but I held my ground.

Letters to and from church officials, including the vestry at Good Shepherd, developed in a constructive manner and were a welcome antidote to those with my family.

In addition, I was greatly bolstered by the support of my lifelong friend, Louis Tonsmeire. We met the first day of first grade and traveled along together: same high school, same college, same seminary. Then I went to New York, he to marriage and a pastoral ministry in Birmingham, Alabama.

He, too, has had more than a helping hand in resolving economic, social, and health issues that racism and poverty created. So different from my ways, but so effective. We are now in our late eighties, still close. Only a couple of weeks ago, he and his wife, Sallie, were in our home. I was trying to compare our approaches. Louis said, "The final resolution has to take place between two groups sitting at a table." I thought, maybe. I said, "I've never had the patience to get to that table." Yet each in our way. . . .

I didn't think too much about being a "traitor to my people." What's the choice between being a traitor to your people or a carpetbagger?

What a letter to write. Yet I could see no other way to go. I believe I wanted it—a little bit—to call each other's bluff. Perhaps. I felt even more that it might be the last connection between Patsy, Daddy, and myself.

What pierced me most? To be told they didn't want me to do this? No. What hurt the most? To read my grandmother berate herself. As I was reading this to Faye, she interrupted, "Don't you see, it's because she loved you so much."

All letters from Bobbin used the salutation "My precious Boy." Arminnie's, "My dear Boy." Mamie's, "My dear Francis." Mamie had her own family to care about.

Arminnie's is a subtle communication. It begins as if there was no family tumult, things just as always. News of the home front as always. You could note in Arminnie's writing the bold hand and none of those newfangled ballpoint pens. Her letter begins chatty as all of hers did. Yet the clippings deal with news of the blooming racial struggle. She kept that strong hand until her death at age one hundred and four. At the Good Shepherd time she was ninety-three. I may have lost some of her letters about this crisis.

The clippings say with subtlety: My dear Boy, I know this is dangerous.

I recall the week in Mobile when we talked she said at her age she was in no position to judge or condemn me. But that did not bother her because she knew I would always do what I felt was right.

How delicate is the phrase, "You appeared so satisfied with your prospect."

Mamie's letter is blunt. It deals with the consequences of my being in Mobile in a black church. She asks if I have thought of what it would do to Daddy's business. I hadn't thought of it because I'd ruled it out.

I hope it is not just my need that sees in the letters of the three how "nice" their racism is if we can even call it racist. But nice as it may be, these nice positions did their poisonous bit to oppress a people.

An April 1959 letter from my great-aunt Mamie expressing her support for me regardless of all that transpired was a gift. These old sisters were the keepers. Where family members were, what they were doing. Mamie, the middle daughter, was then eighty-six.

Her remark "This is a stupid letter" came like a balm. Quite an admission. The old ways of keeping together had been shattered. Its pieties no longer held, so: "This is a stupid letter." Love still at the bottom of things. Didn't that help? Didn't that heal? Yes.

Revisiting these letters, it came to me that these sisters were the children of former slaveholders. Their mother, Margaret, was the daughter of Boyd Denny Simison, holder of many enslaved blacks at Mount Vernon, Alabama. I know Jacob Michael, Margaret's husband, my great-grandfather, owned at least one enslaved man because he mentions him in one of his wartime letters to Margaret. The family supposition is the slave was part of Margaret Simison's dowry. These three sisters were caught between nice parents who owned slaves and me.

At the time of the letters, I wasn't thinking so much of them as trying to get hold of myself—climb out of the sorrow and the loss of love and support—and know, with despair, that if it came to a separation from family, I was prepared to proceed and hurt them—and myself.

Why didn't I expect it? I must have believed that family love was walled off and could not be touched by the black, black wing of Jim Crow. I thought the two were separable.

18. *To Mobile*

Off I put to Mobile to meet with the vestry of Good Shepherd. I was offered and accepted two hundred dollars from a friend to help with airfare. Here is the story behind that:

In 2008 the documentary film *Traces of the Trade: A Story from the Deep North* was released. It traces the work and career of James DeWolf, our country's premier slave trader. The ambiguous words "A Story of the Deep North" is a way to introduce viewers to the complicity of our entire nation, particularly Rhode Island and the New England states, in the introduction of captured, enslaved Africans to the United States. That is, do not focus the blame for racism today on the "Deep South." The whole nation created and profited from the capture and enslavement of African people.

I doubt if film director Katrina Browne's switching "Deep North" for "Deep South" works for shock value. It is over the heads of our country's white folks.

Browne, herself a member of the DeWolf family, contacted the DeWolf descendants she could locate, asking if any would travel with her from Bristol, Rhode Island, to West Africa, to Cuba, where many kidnapped Africans were forced to work, and then back to Bristol to engage the citizens of Bristol in what they had learned. Nine DeWolf descendants agreed.

The pilgrimage was a retracing of DeWolf's version of the Triangular Trade that we had learned in grammar school. One leg of the triangle involved the capture and breaking of Africans' spirits and bodies, then transporting them into bondage, somehow so prettified that I, being taught it, was unaware of the slave leg back then. DeWolf's genius was to own all three points of the triangle. DeWolf's agents ran the West Africa business. He also owned, and his people operated, the specially crafted ships to convey Africans into slavery. At point two he owned, and one of his sons operated, sugar plantations in Cuba where many of the captured Africans were taken to work. His ships brought the molasses produced there back to Bristol, where his workers turned it into rum that made the third leg of the triangle—back to Africa either as rum or with other trade goods bought by rum, to buy more human beings.

Ms. Browne incorporates in the documentary a clip from an amateur 16mm movie of a yearly Bristol parade. The shot shows DeWolf's horse-drawn carriage lovingly preserved, celebrating the man who made Bristol immensely wealthy.

All whites in this country share with all citizens our history of one of the more cruel forms of human bondage. Most whites do what they can to forget that. What irony to feature in an Independence Day parade, celebrating our freedom, the carriage of our wealthiest enslaver of human beings. Today, the carriage is no longer paraded.

When Ms. Browne showed the documentary in Bristol, the Episcopal Church endowed by DeWolf himself invited her crew and the people of Bristol to a service of confession and repentance—a very good turnout.

One scene in the documentary shows the Dewolfe descendants seated around a table talking after a meal. Someone asked where everyone went to college. All but one attended Ivy League colleges. Then it was revealed that all their fathers graduated from Ivy League schools.

Watching this, it dawned on me where all the wealth of this family originated and how it grew under the guidance of the talented descendants of DeWolf.

James DeWolf was thus the distant source of my two hundred dollars that came from his descendant, Ledlie Laughlin, and his wife Roxanna, who at Grace Church, Jersey City, were spending their lives in service to the poor. I was flying to link my life with a church founded by free Jamaicans in 1854, in Mobile, my home, thanks to the money but certainly not the approval of James DeWolf.

The following account of my father's business is background for how his business, my sister's marriage, and my call to serve as priest of Good Shepherd were connected in what happened next when I arrived in Mobile to meet the Good Shepherd vestry.

Since the 1920s, my father and his partner, Alfred Payne, had owned and operated the Mobile Cylinder Grinding Company on the corner of Commerce and St. Francis streets, one block from the river. A monster black cylinder-grinding machine loomed to the left at the front of the shop.

By the late '40s, it had stopped, never to grind again, because there were no more steam engines propelling tugs or merchant vessels. When I came to the shop as a boy, Al, who was older than Daddy, had a few jobs on the two metal lathes. He mostly sat in the office in back at the rolltop desk. There was one path back to the office, a grease-hardened path I always admired, only one I've ever seen. It was composed of grease—yes—but grease compounded with steel and brass filings from the lathe work and dirt with sand tracked in from the street. It was unevenly laid down and almost impossible to pry up. The path was flanked by fifty—give or take—outboards: primal Evinrudes, Eltos, a Caille, Neptunes, Thors, Johnsons, and the newer Champions, Martins, and Buccaneers. My father held that if a customer did not return for his outboard, it could be he was in trouble or broke, so he never junked or sold one.

Every piece of shop machinery was driven by a big, venerable direct current motor sitting on a wooden tower. From it, by means of shafts, wheels, pulleys, and long leather belts descending, power went to machines on the floor below. The Alabama Power Company complained that it was the only DC shop motor left in Mobile so thick, energy-wasting cables still had to be run to serve it.

This calm, plodding, conservative business, so compatible with its customers, confronted expansion plans by the Alabama State Docks, which would take over the location.

Daddy and Al relocated to a lot in midtown about three blocks south of Government Street. There was room for parking. They built an adequate concrete-block structure, large enough for the sales and repair of outboard motors. They assigned the massive cylinder-grinding machine to the Marine Junk Company but took the name with them. For years this business had provided a modest living for the Walters and Paynes, and none of us could see ahead to divine how my sister's marriage would affect this.

Worse was to come. The McVoys and Walters were united in Patsy's father-in-law's desire to become Daddy's business partner in the Mobile Cylinder Grinding Company, a senescent but dependable old machine shop.

19. Meeting with Good Shepherd's Vestry

My being at home with Bobbin, Daddy, and David was more exhausting than tense. We relapsed into pretending to be as we had been five years earlier, though it felt like slogging through a swamp during high water.

I met with the Good Shepherd vestry. How healing to be welcomed with hope and excitement. They wanted me; I wanted them. The deal was sealed, and I returned home.

As already said, my sister, Patsy, was newly married to Willie McVoy, whose father was a wealthy businessman who began to develop a business plan to help his new daughter-in-law's father make more money. Not that Daddy or Al had asked him. Around the time that Patsy and Willie married, the senior Mr. McVoy moved in on my father with the idea that he and Daddy would become partners. He offered to invest a lot of money into Mobile Cylinder Grinding Company.

He and my father agreed that the aging Al Payne should be bought out. Instead of only selling and repairing outboard motors, the shop would offer fishing boats, runabouts, and trailers as well. Daddy would hire a manager to take over and improve the relaxed financial record-keeping done by Al.

I was puzzled by this. Years before, during WWII, the senior McVoys, as a young married couple starting out with nothing, came from Mississippi to Mobile along with many others to seek work in the shipyards or at the new airbase, Brookley Field. Jobs were plentiful, but McVoy took his time looking over the shipyards. He proposed to his wife that the two of them sell packaged lunches to the shipyard workers, as nobody else was doing that. Not a dinky Styrofoam box lunch with two sandwiches and a bag of potato chips, but something to satisfy a hungry welder or riveter.

I know that because in 1948, after the McVoys had prospered and left the shipyards, becoming the Mobile Paper and Container Company, I worked a summer at the Alabama State Docks building pallets to line the holds of ships. I found that the McVoys had been replaced by a small fleet of fast-moving black women who would pull up at our warehouse, fling open the trunks of their family cars, producing dripping paper plates heaped with baked chicken, fried corn, string beans, sliced tomatoes, cornbread, and ice tea—worthy successors to the hardworking Mr. McVoy, who was by this time quite wealthy in that paper-container business.

When I returned home from meeting the vestry of Good Shepherd, my father got in from work and asked to talk with me. He stood, I stood, in the living room. He began by telling me of McVoy's overture, that he and McVoy were now business partners, and that things were changing at the shop. Mr. McVoy expected Daddy to ease Al Payne out. I can easily imagine how McVoy took a look at Al's old, greasy rolltop desk with its spindles stacked with pierced papers and at Al, in an undershirt, overweight, that moist cigar stub clenched in teeth—well, he had to go. It was Daddy's job to tell him.

From McVoy's perspective, Daddy was wasted as a mechanic. He was a natural salesperson. The war was over, and people were buying. McVoy knew a man who would make an excellent business manager. Mechanics could be hired.

This was all done with money from McVoy and money from Daddy as well; he had taken out a loan based only on his good name. That all sounded workable to me. However, Daddy looked and sounded miserable.

He went on. Mr. McVoy, he said, was very angry and would not allow the brother of his daughter-in-law to become a preacher in a colored church. If Daddy did not prevent it, McVoy would call in his loan and leave the partnership. Daddy told me he would be forced to bankrupt. There was by now no way that the company could survive without McVoy's financial assistance. The bankruptcy would snowball; Daddy would lose the business and our house. At the Miller house, Gretchen was caring for her own mother. Bobbin would refuse a bed in that place, and her small income from stock could not support her. Patsy and Willie had planned to move into our house and care for Bobbin after Willie graduated. All of these plans would crumble and tumble if I accepted a call to the Good Shepherd Church.

Daddy never asked me to refuse Good Shepherd. He simply laid out the consequences. My first and most telling reaction—crowding out all others— was that for the first, the only, time in my life, I did not know if my father was telling me the truth. Or if McVoy was telling this to Daddy but only bluffing.

Or had they planned a lie together? I could not then answer that. Facing the possibility that my father was lying to me was the most sickening thing I had yet experienced.

Over the years, I have wondered why Mr. McVoy wanted to enter into such a partnership. Aside from Patsy, the McVoys had no relationship with the Walters, no social contact at all. I developed a theory: The McVoys earned their money, raised themselves up by themselves. Willie was the first McVoy to go to college. The Walters, on the other hand, were second-level Old Mobile. Patsy had been the Spring Hill Elementary School May Festival Queen. Doesn't sound like much. Not such small potatoes in Mobile. Her forebears were the Marshes and Gates from Franklin, Louisiana, and the Michaels of Demopolis and Mobile. Her grandfather, Franz Walter, an immigrant from Baden-Würtemburg, was no aristocrat but had been a well-respected owner of Walter Produce in Mobile. I suspect this second-tier respectability appealed to Mr. McVoy. He wanted to attach some money to Patsy's and her family's position and to share a little of our modest family respectability for himself.

A few years ago, I heard another theory about Mr. McVoy's offer that came from a young McVoy I got to know. I posed the question to him: Why would Mr. McVoy go to the trouble to enrich Patsy's family? He answered that Mr. McVoy was a fully developed control freak who gained great pleasure from adopting people to control.

Next day after this wrenching meeting with my father, I called at the McVoy residence, asking to see Mr. McVoy. I drove up to a brand-spanking-new Creole cottage. Mr. McVoy opened the door, and we stood face to face in the central hall. I think the only other time I'd spoken to him was at Patsy and Willie's wedding.

I extended my hand, but he would not take it. He was in a rage. We remained standing. The only words I spoke were to ask him if what my father had said about his leaving the company and Daddy's bankruptcy were true.

He repeated Daddy's words and said it was true. He was determined to keep his daughter-in-law from the shame of having a brother who pastored a colored church. My father was correct. If he pulled out of the deal, Daddy would lose home and business.

Next day I walked over to Spring Hill College to seek counsel from my former faculty advisor, the Reverend J. Franklin Murray, S.J. I would not go to a Mobile Episcopal priest. They'd bring too much baggage, and I deeply respected Father Murray.

Father Murray was the perfect guide. I brought him a confused and heartsick man. I laid on his desk a compacted snarl of fishing line. I did not know if it even had one tag end with which to begin an unraveling. My old faculty advisor was a gentle man, but best, he was a Jesuit. Unraveling was his suit and not once did he even hint at what I should do. He made sense of things, especially helping with how one deals with imponderables that affect choices.

I left Father Murray's office with several discrete balls of unraveled line, postulates, probabilities, outcomes. If an a. or b. is chosen, what are the possible results? However, it seemed to boil down to how much certainty about their intentions did I have to make a moral choice. Thanks to Father Murray, the answer was: very little. I could lay aside being certain. The crux was that the stakes were high no matter what I chose.

Before I arrived home, I knew I would not risk that happening to my family. I told Daddy I was turning down the position at Good Shepherd.

Then came a small feeling that I was like everyone else. As I was writing this, it came for the first time to me that this choice was a major violation of my promise on the brick walk. I was like everyone else.

As soon as possible, I met with the vestry. The men heard my ugly story. I told them I was morally certain McVoy would follow through. I could not take the chance. I could not accept their call. They reacted with disbelief, not that I'd withdrawn, but that my father and McVoy would do this.

I was surprised. I figured each had come up against worse from the white man, so why the disbelief? Maybe it was because they didn't know much about what white people would do to each other to keep the lid on.

There is no record of my turning them down or their response. I guess we were all too shaken for niceties. I told them I'd see Bishop Carpenter on my way back to New York.

The bond between myself and the parish did not end. It became our common resolution to work together to find a priest. [See April 13, 1959, letter in Appendix.]

I told everyone else in the family and left for General Seminary.

Mr. McVoy had one final way to mess with my family. He was investing in oil wells in Mississippi. He told Daddy it was a sure thing. The only money Daddy had was the social security payment to David after the death of my mother. He did nothing illegal because David was a minor. But he invested in an oil well, thanks to Mr. McVoy. Daddy's oil well produced saltwater; Mr. McVoy's, oil.

The Mobile Cylinder Grinding Company survived and expanded as planned. Then the business manager that Mr. McVoy had put in place embezzled funds. The company collapsed. Daddy with powers of recovery went to work as a salesperson for an automobile parts company in Mobile and seemed happy.

20. Capitulation

Sitting before the Bishop I was grateful to this unregenerate son of the South who had risen above that designation to support me. He had capitulated by consenting to allow me, a white priest in his diocese, to be under the control of a black vestry, instead of a white vestry across town, to allow me to live in a black neighborhood thirty feet from a black church, creating for me joy in my expanding world, but creating a crack in his, a small crevice in his Color Line. Now I sat before him to take it all back, to admit it had come to nothing.

I told the story of my father, my family, McVoy's threat to bankrupt my father, my report to the vestry, my capitulation.

I saw something in the Bishop I'd never seen before. Hearing of McVoy's threat to ruin my father, he leaned toward me, his mouth slightly open, a look of "He did what?!" He showed outraged disbelief, as if things like this didn't happen everyday in Dixie, except of course to black people.

You don't know, do you, I thought. You don't know that your silence is permission for those below you in power, education and social standing to flesh out your silences and unexamined beliefs with violence and murder?

You don't know, do you, that your denomination, operating as a segregated system, gives permission for worse systems, legal and illegal, to operate with your tacit blessing? Our Alabama church has a segregated summer camp, a segregated annual conference (artfully disguised so as not to be obvious to white folks), and a segregated system of clergy placement.

You don't know, do you, that just before your episcopate the lash was still laid on the backs of black convicts leased by the State of Alabama to the Big Mule owners of our coal mines? Did any of the Big Mule mine owners ever tell you what an inordinate amount of our state budget came from the leasing of convicts? You know some of them well. Did you know that the Alabama Supreme Court ruled that leased convicts could not sue when crippled by a mine accident because they were "civilly dead"?

What you do know is that dynamite will never dirty your hands; that you will never apply the lash. But it is your silence that allows others to light the fuses and lacerate the backs. Your equivocation seeps down to men like Mr. McVoy and others far worse.

But that day, seated before him, there was no force left in me to openly challenge his look of shock at what my sister's father-in-law had done. Maybe back then I felt my hubris had earned me a shellacking. So I said, "Bishop, I give up. You supported me about Good Shepherd. It didn't work. Now you find a place for me and I'll go."

Big mistake? My response cannot be cast as mistake or blessing. God, who looms over life, is a mystery. Why does God seem drawn to work among disasters and fools, molding Good from really ratty Clay? In the story of Joseph and his brothers who tried to kill him, God tells them: You meant it for evil; I made it for good (KJV Genesis 50:20). God, with a little cooperation from me, has produced good in full measure, pressed down, overflowing. Starting from my passivity and the Bishop's crazy hope that his placement would make a docile lover of the Old South out of me.

"I want you to go to Eufaula in Barbour County. You can learn a lot about Alabama that you couldn't learn in a big city." (Mobile!—a big city?) "When you get there I don't want you to say the word 'race' for six months. Then come on back here and we'll talk about it."

Leaving the Bishop's office I was questioning, "Was collapse the way to go?" I'd imagined asking if I might be posted as an assistant in one of the parishes in a Huntsville that was just leaving behind its label as "the Watercress Capital of the World" to become "Rocket City." Well, I did collapse. No way back.

For sixty years I've tried to figure out how Charles Colcock Jones Carpenter saw racism, or whether the concept was available to him. My thoughts have simmered long enough to now be served forth. My speculations have hovered like bees around one characteristic: unreflective. He very probably acted more out of feeling than thinking.

Born in 1899, thirty-four years after the Confederate Surrender, he would have known his South in its early sulk of defeat. His mother was a Jones, he was named for his great-grandfather, C. C. Jones. The Jones family was an extraordinary family of wealthy planters, owning many enslaved Africans. Living on various plantations, they stuck together by frequent letter writing, a cache of which survived and is the subject of a book, *The Children of Pride* by Robert Manson Myers. Douglas Carpenter, Bishop Carpenter's son, believes his father was acquainted with those letters and certainly oral recollections from family members during his early years in Augusta, Georgia.

The family of the Bishop's maternal great-grandfather and namesake, Charles Colcock Jones, operated plantations in coastal Georgia. Like many sons of the slave-owning planter class, Charles was sent to Princeton. While there, preparing for the Presbyterian ministry, he experienced a spiritual crisis. Set to inherit plantations and slaves, he became attracted to abolitionist thought and did an unexpected and courageous thing. He traveled alone to Philadelphia to sit at the feet of a Quaker abolitionist cobbler, Benjamin Lundy. The scion and hope of the Joneses' immense wealth in land and enslaved human beings at the feet of a cobbler!

After the Philadelphia awakening, Jones believed he had to choose between his newfound value of liberty and his home, a great patrimony, and worse, the love and hopes of his family. Or did he? Returning to Liberty (yes, that was the name of his plantation), he prayed and prayed. Slowly, I'd guess there came to him a third way. He rationalized that God, yearning that all be saved, had seen to it that Africans were captured, brought to the United States, and sold into bondage so that they could be taught to read and write, know the Bible, and be baptized. This rationalization lacked all empathy for fellow human beings as well as failure to realize that millions unable to read and write became Christians, certainly in Africa where the Coptic Church still flourishes. Of course, all are captive to the ignorance of our own era.

Jones spent himself in the years prior to the Civil War exhorting masters to teach their enslaved Africans to read and write, so as to know the Bible, and to allow them to be baptized. He was said to tell the planters that their chattel could be their brothers and sisters in Christ. Obviously, he met great resistance. Some planters evangelized by Jones hired a great nineteenth-century scientist to act as a one-man truth squad to follow behind Jones. He was Dr. Louis Agassiz (1807–73). Rejecting a part of Darwinism, Agassiz postulated that all living species, including humans, had been created by God over and over in different parts of the world. For Agassiz, while Africans were of the human species, they had been created in Africa, whites and others created in other, separate, places. No biological racist, he believed all humans were fully human but varied in intelligence. Nor did he believe in slavery. But his idea of human creation in separate places with varying intelligence was enough for the planters.

Charles Colcock Jones died, a victim of the Civil War, despairing of the fruition of his revelation, the indifference of slaveholders, and his own cussed ability, like that of all other human beings, to add tweaks and footnotes to our moral revelations.

Bishop Carpenter's foundation, built during childhood, once laid down, was not to be pulled up, pondered, or laid bare to novel constructions, and he proved that throughout his Episcopate. In the 1960s, presiding at a diocesan clergy conference, the Bishop threw out one of his favorite aphorisms (this, before women could become priests): "Boys, we're all free, white and twenty-one in here. Let's get this thing settled."

I was seated next to the venerable Father Matthew Perry, the only black man present, and thought by some of us to be the most learned priest in the diocese. Turning to Father Perry I said, "I didn't know you were white."

Father Perry replied, "He doesn't even see me." The Bishop and Father Perry had known each other for years. Mrs. Carpenter sorted out the Carpenter children's outgrown clothes to give to the Perry children.

After turning down the call to Good Shepherd, I found a white friend, Jack Thompson, who was interested and accepted the church's call. Jack, too, took note of the Bishop's lack of insight into the implications of segregation and asked if I had ever heard the lavabo bowl story. A lavabo bowl is used to catch water poured over the priest's hands before handling the bread and wine of the Communion.

The Bishop was given a modern copy of a medieval lavabo bowl used at Canterbury Cathedral. He saw the bowl as a symbol of the unity of the Anglican Communion and placed the copy in the Chapel at Camp McDowell where the most people would see it in use. He determined to preach his Lavabo Bowl Sermon in every church in the diocese, making the point that we belong to the worldwide Anglican Communion.

Jack continued, "On his annual visitation to Good Shepherd, he started in on it. I was sitting in the chancel thinking how is he going to end this because I had heard the punch line, which was, 'So if you ever go to our Mother Church, Canterbury, you can see the original bowl in use. But if you can't go you can go to Camp Mcdowell where there is a copy of the Lavabo Bowl.' The Bishop began the punch line for us, 'If you can't go to our Mother Church, you can...' Then it dawned on him where he was. 'You can, you can ask somebody who's been to Camp MacDowell about it because we have a copy there.'"

I said to Jack, "Did anyone express anger to him or say anything to him about it?"

"Nope," he said.

The Lambeth Conference is a worldwide gathering of Anglican bishops held every ten years. Bishop Carpenter attended in 1948, 1958, and 1968. It was at one of these conferences that the Archbishop of Canterbury gave him the lavabo bowl reproduction. In 1948, the bishops approved the principle that "discrimination between men (sic) on the ground of race alone is inconsistent with the principles of the Christian Religion." Not hard to enunciate. They knew the declaration of St. Paul in the New Testament: "In Christ there is no

Jew or Greek, slave or free, male or female. All are one in Christ Jesus." Growing up in Alabama, I heard white parishioners affirm the Lambeth Declaration, explaining to me, "Yes, Francis, when we get to heaven we'll all be together."

When I met with Bishop Carpenter in New York, and he approved the plan for Good Shepherd to call me, elect me, pay me, and let me live next door to the Church in a black neighborhood, he first proposed "Doing as we have always done." That would be putting me under the authority of a white church, and in effect, "lending" me to the black one. I was so keyed up in my spirited rejoinder I only later realized how insulting and demeaning this would be for those black vestrymen (vestries are the governing bodies of the Episcopal Church; at the time, women were not allowed to serve on vestries). His system assumed that blacks were too childlike or incapable of selecting their own leaders. (Childlike fits when one considers that a few years later the Bishop called the March to Montgomery from Selma "childish.")

I believe a mind formed early by tales of Emancipation and Reconstruc-

Francis X. Walter, 1960.

tion held an old rule: Never put a white man under a black man. It was his reality. He did not wish to hurt or insult anyone of any color. He lived with Color Line rules absorbed in childhood, well-defended, unexamined family values of a nice upbringing.

So why did Bishop Carpenter agree to allow me to be called by the Good Shepherd vestry with the understanding that I would live in an all-black neighborhood?

This exchange was singular for us both. He had first said in effect "Let's do it as we've done before. You serve them from a white church." And I had blurted out that I would not prostitute myself by participating in a state of white supremacy. There was no drama. He said "All right" after a small detour to inquire if a marriage was in the offing. Bishop Carpenter may have been closed off to interior moral examination, unused to seeing new realities of social injustice. I doubt that he examined the issues I raised. So why did he say yes to me? The best answer I have for that is when we came face to face, it was personal. At the moment he said Yes to me, he loved me. No calculation necessary.

21. *Misses Gladys and Victoria*

My appointment as rector of St. James Church in Eufaula was facilitated by men: priests, a bishop, six vestrymen. Only after this male curtain was withdrawn did I see Miss Gladys, the matriarch of St. James. I don't use real names in these Eufaula recollections (except when they deserve credit) and alter situations a bit, but how to cloak Miss Gladys? Old-time Eufaulans, black and white, will know just who "Miss Gladys" is should they chance to read these words.

Miss Gladys, impervious to contradiction, declarative in conversation, did not give up on me, never flagging in her effort to teach me "we are not devils, you are not an angel." I knew that in spades, but not in the way that would satisfy her. Until it was known that Betty and I were leaving Eufaula, Miss Gladys was the only white person who engaged me about race. I could not accept her premises but she did talk. She talked to me defending herself and her world. She and I knew what the issue was, and she was not afraid to raise it with me. Thank you, Miss Gladys. (The senior warden, talking to me after I had retrieved a letter off the screen door firing me, expressed for him what was the inevitability of the decision: "Miss Gladys says you should go.")

As the parish matriarch, as a Democratic Party worker (before white

Southerners had fled to the Republican Party) from a powerful political family, as a lady of "quality" by birth and marriage, and as one of that great company of old Southern white ladies, which no man can number, who don't give a damn what they say or where they say it, there was much to admire about Miss Gladys—and love. I still do. I put the word "quality" in quotes because of its Southern life as a term meaning "refined sensibility based usually, not necessarily, on breeding and lineage." Another scrappy old white lady photographed in the 1960s in front of her Wilcox County, Alabama, plantation house for Bob Adelman's searing *Down Home: Camden, Alabama*, was asked by the photographer what she meant by "quality folks." She said "People would like to buy 'The Columns.' But you don't sell things you inherit . . . it's inheritance that gives you quality. I'm scared my daughter will sell off this house when I die."

Miss Gladys's take on quality was more generous. As she went to and fro in Barbour County, she might spy a leaning dogtrot, whose sagging porch held many a rusty enamel bucket of lush canna lilies and perhaps in a swept yard a path to the front steps lined with colored bottles, neck ends down, bordering its edges. At that Miss Gladys would bestow her approval. "There's quality there."

Here she is in her sitting room in full throttle. It is early in my time at St. James.

"Mr. Walter, and I will never call you by your first name, as some do, you should have the respect your position deserves." Miss Gladys had heard that some of the ladies of St. James were calling me "Our Little Minister." She intended to put that down, much less first names. Excuse the interruption, Miss Gladys.

"Mr. Walter, my mother-in-law single-handedly ran a plantation while her husband was off during the War. She rose to the occasion. After the War, she wrote an account of how she held the place together during those terrible years. It was printed by an Episcopal publishing house that was run by a relative of ours, Mr. Morehouse. Reach around back of you. I'd like you to read something from it."

I found the faded 1899 book. Its title deserves something more than a position in the endnotes: *White and Black Under the Old Regime* by Victoria V. Clayton. She was the widow of Confederate general Henry D. Clayton, who later became a circuit judge and president of the University of Alabama.

At Miss Gladys's instruction, I read us a passage. I see myself in her sitting room reading it to her. It is one of my clearest memories. This is how I remember it:

Miss Victoria recalls how the family kept a Christmas Day with no father and husband present on one of the last bitter warring days of the Confederacy. The writer describes the family's gratitude as they are seated around the table (Victoria had lots of children). They are eating a fresh ham from a just-slaughtered hog. Outside, the enslaved Africans have come up to the Big House yelling "Chrissmuss giff!" Victoria looks into the yard, seeing smiling black faces covered with grease. She will see that they all get something, war or no war. She is overcome with gratitude toward a God who has so perfectly attuned the world for joy. Her family is happy in a warm house with a fresh ham. The enslaved Africans are also happy, engineered by God to be happy outside with neck bones.

For Miss Gladys this meant that her mother-in-law, Victoria, was kindly affectioned. Who could accuse such a woman or her daughter-in-law of hatred toward colored people? And by extension to Miss Gladys's children? And on to impute the members of St. James? So she put the question: Am I accusing them of hatred?

That Miss Gladys could drag this scene into the mid-twentieth century as an argument was a frightening look at the immediate future. She saw the opposition she sensed in me as a deeply personal attack on herself. It meant I did not approve of an essential part of her being. I did not like her and hers.

The story I read, "The Inside/Outside, Ham/Neck Bones, Family/Chattel," I've retold over the years. Miss Victoria's 1899 book was photographically reprinted in 1970 by Kessinger Legacy Reprints. Recently learning of this, I immediately ordered a copy. The UPS truck was not out of our driveway before I unwrapped it. I held in my hand a text I had last held fifty-three years earlier. I ransacked its pages. The story is not there!

I have mentioned before what a little imp—a Satan—my teenaged muse, Memoria, can be. But she'd never gone this far. The tableau! The points scoring! All false? The Big House, the ham, the prayerful family, the human chattel shivering outside gnawing neck bones. All false? I did find this pitiful reference on page 26:

The hog killing times were always glorious to us children . . . Hog killing for home use was a big time; especially to the Negroes who enjoyed the neck bones and spare ribs hugely. I can see them now with their thick greasy lips and laughing eyes.

I lit into Memoria for this over-the-top deception, using a lie to create my story. At first she sulked, not a word out of her, and then she took me on. *Francis! Wait! You didn't make it up from what you read. Miss Gladys interrupted you to tell you a story which she remembered from the book. It wasn't my fault or yours. No, better yet! Book had nothing to do with it! Her mother-in-law told that story to Miss Gladys herself and she told it to you while you were holding the book.* Howsomever, it's too good not to be repeated because it encapsulates the benevolence Victoria truly felt she bore her human chattel: a constricted personal ethic, blind to the social evil in which she and her husband existed. If truth be told, evil in which all but a handful of the white citizens in all of the United States back then lived and moved and had their being.

The sitting room encounter with Miss Gladys illustrates a failing of mine as a pastor. I sat, I listened, I nodded. I felt back then that my silence at least meant I respected and accepted her. She declared herself to me. The only white person in Eufaula to talk with me about race. I listened but did not open myself to her or begin an exchange. This is a usual pattern. Not good for a priest. I find it hard to enter into a dialogue which promises conflict. Other people just as principled as myself are good at creating spaces for exchanges on thorny issues. I am unsure of being able to exchange views without anger and judgment creeping in. Another reason, perhaps, is that I knew by then that to serve as rector of St. James in Eufaula in the '50s and '60s would be impossible for such as me. However, most of the time in Eufaula I was good at denying this. I wanted to stay. But there was my dogged resolution not to go along with a racist culture.

As we say goodbye to thoughts of Miss Victoria, let us take her out with a cherry bomb salute to her physical strength and bravery, cussedness, honesty, and her strongly held illusions. It was her memoir that Miss Gladys, her daughter-in-law, asked me to hold as she talked race with me. Victoria's memoir, so prized

St. James Episcopal Church, Eufaula, Alabama.

by Miss Gladys, caught up seven generations of Southerners, black and white, in a span of two hundred years. The white people of that time created for our country race-based slavery—the state of being a non-person—and when that died in blood, those same people created race-based debt peonage, disenfranchisement, Jim Crow, and both legal and illegal violence to keep their former bondsmen as close to slavery as possible.

When I appeared in Eufaula as the 1950s ended I felt the shaking of that edification. Its fall was inevitable. I sometimes thought the white members of St. James's I came to know—save for some blessed exceptions—were ignorant of the second Reconstruction barreling down on them. But I came to see that most white people in Eufaula did know what was coming, but like damselflies, chose to dance in the sunlight while it lasted. Not that any white person save for Miss Gladys would talk with me about it while I was rector of St. James. That generation, like their forebears, was sometimes open and generous to black folk on a personal level but not on the level of social good, social justice.

My other parishioner, Miss Helen, in her great house, made it her business to "adopt" young black men to serve as her live-in house servants. After a term of employment, she sent each off to college at her expense. But her moral horizon stopped short of changing the social order, of which she considered herself the local arbiter.

There were feeble attempts to keep the dikes from eroding. When Sammy Davis Jr. married the Nordic beauty May Britt, and they were featured in *Life* magazine, some white folks canceled their subscriptions, but I doubt that the bride and groom realized their marriage had caused that. My white informant, however, told me that those who canceled kept a subscription to *Life* running at the town's hotel so they could drop by to read it. Television was another untrustworthy medium. Some parents did their best to shield their children from interracial images. They did not know that in a few years Bear Bryant would put a black player on the Crimson Tide eleven.

Miss Victoria's views in her memoir, so typical of white Southerners of her era, are as follows:

> My father, John Linguard Hunter, was of English and Scottish descent, his ancestors belonging to the Gentry. He was a planter profession, owning at one time two large plantations in the State of South Carolina. In 1835, hearing many marvellous stories of the great productiveness of the land in the state of Alabama, he was induced to sell his plantations in his old native State and move to Alabama. Here he found everything in a crude, unsettled, condition.
>
> I was only two years old, and consequently know nothing of the country at that time except for hearing older members of the family tell about it.
>
> The little town selected for our home was merely an Indian village then. Many tribes of these natives roved over the country. Oftentimes they were very troublesome and finally became so hostile to the white settlers that they were obliged, in self-defense, to resort to some means of driving them out. This meant war, which began in February, 1836.
>
> My father and oldest brother joined the army formed for the purpose of making the red man take up his march towards the setting sun. My mother and her children were sent up into middle Georgia to remain while these hostilities, called the Indian War, lasted.
>
> When peace was restored and it was safe for us to return, we came back to our home in Irwinton, now Eufaula. A house for our occupation had been

almost finished in the village before our flight, and my mother found on our return that the soldiers had used it as a barracks, and in consequence it was injured to some extent. She cared not, though for this; she was so thankful to be free from savage faces peeping and prying around the premises. She had been very much afraid of these savages, and when the squaws visited her she used to give them anything they asked for; and in this way we were often deprived of a favorite dress or of other things which we prized greatly. Being fond of gay colors, they were always sure to want the red dresses, and, to our discomfort, carried them off.

Gently she describes the inevitable as "making the red man take up his march toward the setting sun." After describing the "removal" of the Original People, she adds these words: "My father was a slaveholder by inheritance, never having known anything else." Our thoughts, our morals, our most fixed beliefs, are consequences of our place of birth. Her quote is telling. To live is to remain the same. Imagine wired upper-middle-class parents today trying to instill that in their children! Nope. Onward and upward. Devil take the hindmost. Before it all came down in blood, these "fixed beliefs" paid their dividends to Miss Victoria's parents.

By and by the family became large both through natural increase of the Negroes, and because my husband, at the close of each year saved up money enough to invest in something to increase our income, was naturally disposed to invest in slaves being then the most available and profitable property in our section of the country.

Miss Victoria, a devout Christian, ransacked both the Old and New Testaments finding, especially in the most ancient texts, abundant justification for slavery; even as I plunder Scripture for themes to illuminate sermons of Franciscan and social justice themes.

But toward the close of the memoir she senses the darkness in her family's manner of life now thirty-four years behind her:

We never raised questions for one moment as to whether slavery was right.

> We had inherited the institution from devout Christian parents...Slave holding
> was incorporated into our laws and was regulated and protected by them. We
> read our Bible and accepted it as the true guide in faith and morals.

At the end of the memoir Victoria looks back at herself, seeing, to my
lights, another person, perhaps real, perhaps not.

> I believe now that slavery is a detriment, and if I could by any act of mine,
> reestablish it here and get back my slaves, I would not do it. But the government
> of the United States has the credit for giving the black man his freedom, while
> it was at the expense of the Southern people; and we feel the loss.

Miss Victoria had guts and stood by her man. When he set off, heading
up his militia to secure Kansas Territory as a slave state, she went with him.

Of course they lived rough in the Kansas Territory. On one marauding
expedition her husband refused to allow her to go with the war party. He gave
her the job of securing in her undergarments the gold to pay the militiamen.
She did the same thing when she followed her husband to Pensacola during
the Civil War. Enough. Enough about this iron woman whose memory, living
in Miss Gladys, now lives in me.

---

22. *Eufaula: Segregation in Moderation*

In 1992, the Reverend Douglas Carpenter, Diocesan Youth Director Peggy
Rupp, and I helped the young historian Jonathan Bass with an essay, "Bishop
CCJ Carpenter: From Segregation to Integration," that was published in the
Alabama Review.

Bass's insights were pungent and fair. He turned to us for help assigning
a defining "tag" to the Bishop. Round and round we went, finally stopping

at "Moderate Segregationist." None of us was happy about the choice but in 1992 all felt it necessary to give the Bishop a definition in regard to race. Today I don't believe a tag helps one bit in understanding racism. Better said, racism indulged, racism spoken by authority, is a force exercised on dependent people. The words segregationist and moderate do not go together. It is a nonsensical phrase. "Segregationist" does have many legitimate modifiers: Devious Segregationist; Violent; Passive; Polite; Elitist; Insane; Unreflective; Ignorant; Running for Office; View Unknown; Silent. If one separates a quart of black-eyed peas from a quart of crowder peas, one does not moderately segregate them. Peas do not assimilate. But the metaphor can be extended to human beings. Where lives touch as in integration, separation breaks down.

Bishop Carpenter was a segregationist, oblivious to the sin or immorality implied in the term.

In 1162, Henry II was King of England. He appointed his close friend Thomas Becket as Archbishop of Canterbury. Thomas began to take his consecration as Archbishop seriously. This was not what Henry expected or wanted. One evening Henry is reported as saying, "Will no one rid me of this troublesome priest?" Four thuggish knights heard it as a coded command. The rode to Canterbury Cathedral and hacked Thomas to death.

Racist jokes, minds oblivious to hurtful language, tongue-in-cheek coded words can produce action. These words can be defended as innocent but they can also be taken as permission, even orders to be carried out by subordinates.

Bishop Carpenter had influence in spades.

Another source used for Bass's article was Bishop George Murray, an assistant to Bishop Carpenter with the right to succeed him. Bishop Murray told Bass that Bishop Carpenter did not "believe in discrimination, but at the same time, felt there should be segregation." That reveals as much about Murray's confused take on racism as it does Bishop Carpenter's views. I'm sure Murray meant that Carpenter was a "nice" segregationist.

Would my Bishop in 1965 have been capable of taking in what is written above? I doubt it. By "taking in" I mean standing it alongside the world of his childhood and youth. Could he ponder and fit modern ideas into his psyche? I think not. He was a good man who lived in the past. He responded to life filtered through the past that formed him, unaware that God is also in the present.

I joined the white ministerial association after getting aholt of myself so as not to imperil the black ministers by forcing myself on them. One of the association's duties was to assign members on a rotating basis "to visit patients at the hospital." No big chore; ours was a small hospital.

But! Oh, boy! Here we go again, I thought. Just joined up and was now fixing to scandalize the white ministers. I was not going to deny my vow of nonparticipation in evil. This refusal was becoming central to my being. I felt alive in Eufaula by refusing to go along with its cast-iron caste system. Collateral damage was visited on people around me. Maybe not always damage, but perhaps an occasion of grace, a crisis. Maybe both.

"Crisis" is from a Greek word sounding about the same in English or Greek. At root it means "to separate, to discern." Another form of this word in Greek means "judgment trial." Here was a little crisis I was to lay on them.

I asked the brothers, "We're supposed to visit everyone?"

"Sure, no matter what church they belong to."

"Do we visit Negroes?"

"Well, no. They have their own preachers."

I made no reply. I could feel they knew what I was going to do. Back at the rectory, I did a thought experiment. Here's me bopping down the hospital hall. A door is ahead. I'm cocked and primed to execute the Fifth Corporal Work of Mercy, visiting the sick. I'm at the door. It's open. I have to peek around to establish skin color. If the hue is too dark, I won't go in. However, it would be rude to stand in the doorway sizing up a person's color. What if the patient saw me? So it's best for me to kneel at the door jamb and peek in to see the bed. It's also polite of me, since I'm already kneeling, to crawl past the door so as not to give offense to this black person who might be witless enough to believe a white Eufaula preacher would stop in.

So it came about after a while that a young black woman appeared in a room. We talked. Why was she there? I prayed. Before leaving I asked if there was anything I could do for her. Surprise. There was. She had left young children at home. A neighbor promised to feed and care for them. She was ashamed to ask me but it seemed the neighbor wasn't that trustworthy; so would I check on her kids, see if they had enough to eat. "Sure I will. What do they like to eat?" "White meat," she whispered. I didn't know what white meat was so I asked a parishioner. She said this woman must be really poor. White meat was salted pork fat. What my folks called "streak o' lean" or fatback. Betty and I made a bunch of sandwiches, got some fruit, and drove to the black part of town. The kids did seem to be hungry, but not starving. Adult supervision spotty, but adequate. The woman left the hospital before I could check back and that was the end of that.

Or so it seemed. A few days later, I was called up to Miss Helen's. If Miss Gladys was St. James's matriarch, Miss Helen was the ubermatriarch of both St. James and Eufaula. Not that she came to church very often, but her force field shimmered in the very aisles of the church and the streets of the town, as we shall see. I'd visited her before to introduce myself. She'd received me then in a cozy back room of her enormous old house. At that first visit with this formidable parishioner I made only one serious mistake. I was sitting in an old platform rocker. "Miss Helen, this sure is a handsome Lincoln rocker." She let me know right off it was not a Lincoln rocker but a platform rocker.

After polite chit-chat, she informed me in severe but modulated tones that I had been "seen" in the colored part of town taking food into a house. Ominous word "seen," as I had learned. Miss Helen said she was head of the board of the local Red Cross and I had trespassed on the work of the Red Cross. I should have come to her, let the Red Cross handle it.

Yes, goodness, I thought, I'll bet you're also the head of the United Daughters of the Confederacy, the Daughters of the American Revolution, and the Colonial Dames.

23. The Sexton's Father

Crossing from church to rectory I spied the sexton digging up azaleas. They looked pretty nice where they were so I asked what he was going to do with them.

This was pleasant conversation, not a management issue. It was unclear what authority, if any, I had over the sexton. Not that I wanted or expected to have any. The parishioners of this small congregation in this small community were used to being sent inexperienced, just-out-of-seminary priests by the bishop. They saw it to be their unwelcome job to break us in and keep us away from the responsibilities they had long ago claimed for their own. Not a bad system.

"Miss Gladys tole me dig 'em up, put 'em over there."

"Didun like where she had put 'em, huh?"

"She didun put 'em. Miss Rhonda gave 'em, tole me put 'em right here. Miss Gladys took a notion yesterday she didun like 'em here. Tole me move 'em over there."

"Really!"

"This not the first time I've planted, then moved. Do this. Do that. Reverend, I don't know who I'm working for. Down at the sawmill: Go up to the church. Get up here, anybody can tell me what to do. Then they send for me to go down to the sawmill."

"Who pays you? Does the church?"

"It's all together, church and sawmill. I don't know."

I knew enough to leave that alone. Even if I had wanted the sexton to do something, there was no one supervisor to ask. Just a cloud of old ladies. Well, I thought, that's my pique talking.

The sexton and I had another encounter—a bad one—in which I did involve myself. Today a niggling thought suggests I should have done more—today's pushy term is "proactive." But no. No. Unsolicited actions from the dominant class snatch dignity from the oppressed. We imagined superior persons have enough on our plate messing up ourselves.

St. James fronted Eufaula Avenue in a pleasant, white residential area. The avenue then led into our little downtown.

It was a Rah! Rah! Day for the white high school. Kids making up floats, decorating cars for a parade.

I didn't see it. Not the very first of it. But as memory pushes past fifty years, I see it. See it clear. An old black man waiting at the curb to cross Eufaula Avenue. Probably heading to the church to see his son. He comes walking down a side street. Behind him on that street a car approaches. In it are four or five excited white boys. The car turns right onto Eufaula Avenue. It makes the turn but a towed low-bed trailer does not and hops the curb. The trailer kills the old man, not immediately, but later in the town hospital.

It was after the accident, as the old man was taken away, that I crossed the street. I see the skewed trailer, the police, the scared boys, and a knot of black people off to the side. This is what they did at white catastrophes—watch, off to the side, a hushed Greek chorus. Apart, but witnesses. They tell me some of them (one of them?) saw the trailer jump the curb, fast, onto the sidewalk, striking the old man who they tell me is the father of our sexton. Now the sexton arrives. Do I take him to the hospital? Don't recall. I am at the hospital but am not allowed to visit the injured man and end up in a small corridor with as intimately involved yet separate a group as imaginable. The scared white boys are in a knot hovered over by family members, protective and defensive, waiting for the fix, which has long been their privilege. Here, too, a couple of cops. Apart in the small space are also the sexton, his family, and friends. I'm three feet from a policeman who begins to interview the boys—all together. Something like this.

"Was the man in the street when he got hit?"

"Yes, sir."

"Was the trailer in the street?"

"Yes, sir, it was."

"Did it hit him when he walked out in the street?"

"Yes, sir."

"Did all you all see him step in front of the trailer?"

"Yes, sir. All of us saw it."

This must include the driver.

Grumbling among the black folk. They repeat to me and themselves that a witness, maybe two, I don't recall, had seen the trailer hop up over the curb to the sidewalk, and fast, hitting the man.

Nobody, certainly not the police, speaks to them. I tell the sexton I would help if he wants to challenge the narrative settling over this death. Even as I say it . . . I think if he says yes it will be this that ends my ministry in Eufaula. He says no.

174 ♣ From Preaching to Meddling

24. Shaking Hands

Even if not canonically official, the notion that parishes are geographical units with boundaries, as in the Church of England, appealed to some of us in seminary. Our Protestant brethren, it was implied, only felt pastoral duties to their church members while we (me) had a responsibility to everyone within the bounds of the parish. A snooty comparison given that the very term "parochial" has come to mean a self-centered, inward perspective, the sad description of many parishes.

Eufaula, Alabama, however, fit the bill. The town's population was just seven thousand in my day, half black, half white. It was easy to think I could have obligations to such a community.

Yet a few months into my ministry in Eufaula, the only black persons I knew, the only ones I'd ever spoken to, were our sexton and Parry Lee Edwards, the one doing our housecleaning.

I was walking downtown not too long after my arrival in 1959, when I saw an old house being torn down. It was a Creole cottage, raised on brick piers, wide front steps, and a central hall with rooms on either side. Were Creole cottages lying in wait to supply turning points in my life? They seem to be the platforms for all my crises. There were stacks of lumber, siding, sashes, and shutters lying around to be bought. I noticed a neatly dressed black guy doing what I was doing, looking around. I ended up buying a hand-planed heart pine storage door and used it for a desk for many years.

As I walked through the remains of the house, I introduced myself to the neatly turned-out black man. We shook hands. I told him I was the new Episcopal minister in town, that I'd really like to meet some of the Negroes in Eufaula, especially some ministers. He said he could arrange that and telephoned the rectory to give me an address, adding that the meeting would be after dark, to leave my car several blocks away and walk to the house. By the time I set out, it was dark. When I found the address, there were no lights on. I could see it too was a Creole cottage, what we'd call antebellum. So the neighborhood had swapped races, leaving some grand houses behind. What would black people call an antebellum house? Maybe slavery-built.

I found my way up the steps onto a wide porch and was received into the central hall, which went straight through to the typical back gallery, running the width of the house. The doors to the four rooms on either side of the hall were closed. The only light in the hall was from one small lamp on a side table. In the hall were ministers and a few other men. Putting myself forward, I asked if they were aware of a problem that had occurred a few months before I'd arrived. A little black girl had been turned away from using the Carnegie Library, which sat just across the side street from St. James. She'd wanted to look up something. I said my church was across the street from the library and one of my members was the librarian. Was there anything I could do?

A little background: I'd always heard Carnegie libraries were for everyone, meaning everyone. But I'd never lived near one to check out "everyone." Turns out some white communities began to complain once it dawned on them what "everyone" meant. So Mr. Carnegie backtracked and announced that in places that complained two equal libraries would be built. Turns out this equitable, wasteful compromise was never carried through, so one of the best-appointed and most handsome nonresidential buildings in Eufaula was off limits to people of darker hue—back then.

Of course, they'd heard. I was told, No. Don't try anything. Any challenge should be reserved for a more serious problem. Pushback onto the black community would be severe if anything was done. I learned later that all the black pastors had jobs in the white community to supplement their small stipends. What were they to do?

I learned again the dogged presumption of the benevolence of the oppressing class. Here it was in myself. How eager white people are to tell others how to lift the yoke. It took some time for me to shut up, listen, then ask, "What could we do to help?"

I believed the secrecy about this meeting was to hide our goings-on from snooping white people. Not quite. It was mostly to hide from "the maids," some of whom were willing to gain favor from their mistresses by reporting untoward activities on their side of town.

After this, I gave up asking if I could be a member of the black ministerial association. There went the pleasant fantasy of belonging to both ministerial associations.

Before I left Eufaula, the man I met at the demolition of the Creole cottage caught up with me to say goodbye. He told me how frightened he had been when we shook hands, how he looked around to see if anyone was watching. It was the first time he had ever shaken the hand of a white man.

Years later in Wilcox County, Alabama, where our Selma Inter-Religious Project provided legal services and support to the black community, it was my honor to be told again that I had been the first white man to take the hand of the Reverend Frank Smith, one of the heroes of the movement in Wilcox County, a county that had not one black registered voter prior to the March from Selma to Montgomery. He was fired from the position of teacher by the all-white county school board for, well, for demanding to be registered to vote, among other things.

Reverend Frank came under the care of another hero of the movement, John Prince of Birmingham, a white priest/lawyer and a compatriot of mine. They entered into a court battle with the school board that lasted so many years I got tired of asking John how it was going. Reverend Frank had to move up North to support his family. I think it was more than ten years, but he won—big time. That Wilcox County school board was said back then to be the most civil rights-litigated school board in the United States.

How rapidly such things seemed to change back then. From telling me he'd never shaken the hand of a white man to vindication for being illegally fired, all in the space of around ten years.

I was given a privilege, a blessing, to have been allowed to have my white hand and a brother's black hand placed together for the first time—twice!

25. David Frost Jr., Eufaula Historian

How I would have lapped up the world of Eufaula hidden from me but revealed in 2010 by the gifted self-taught historian David Frost Jr. There he was, and there I was in Eufaula back then, but we never met. He wrote from what he was, a poor, hardscrabble fearless black man, always looking for a dollar and collecting stories—stories of himself, his family, the local white folks' oppression and cruelty toward his people, and sometimes the consideration people of both races showed each other.

Frost and his voluminous writings and collected genealogical data came to the attention of Louise Westling, a historian at the University of Oregon in the 1990s. She edited Frost's book, *Witness to Injustice*. There is Eufaula laid out. Some of the whites I knew, some at St. James appear—but not as I knew them. A previous chapter in my writing, "Not All the Sick," tells of a woman I called in my writing "Miss Helen." I call her an ubermatriarch of the town. Here is David Frost's take on her humiliation of "City Police Irby." He is, of course, a white man.

City Police Irby used to loan money for twenty-five cents on the dollar and every Saturday he would be on the street collecting his money. When they did not have his money he would beat them right on the street with his club. When he was collecting he would carry his teenage cousin along with him. One Saturday a man that used to drive a cab named Mackie Charles owed him some money and while he [Irby] was beating him on the butt with his club his teenage cousin was beating him in the face with his fist until his nose bled.

Mr. Lannie Fountain, who was a deacon at Mt. Level Church and my Sunday school teacher, owed Mr. Irby some money. Mr. Irby forgot to carry his cousin with him and he went to Mr. Fountain's home to collect.

He had forgot that Mr. Fountain was half white and did not take his beating and he set out to beat Mr. Fountain right in front of his children but Mr. Fountain beat him. Mr. Fountain sent for me [Frost] and he got me to take him down below Clayton where he stayed a few days before he came back. Everybody was afraid that Mr. Irby was going to get a mob and lynch Mr. Fountain but Mr. Fountain was not afraid. I think that Mr. Irby was afraid because he never bothered Mr. Fountain again. I think that was the only time that Mr. Irby had ever been hit by a black man.

J. D. Webb and Willie Grant were my playmates and my schoolmates. After we had finished gathering our small crops a man came around from below town getting people to go with him and pick cotton. They would have to stay down there all week. My parents would not let me go but J. D. and Willie Grant went and they picked cotton all the week. The man paid them off and they caught the bus and came back that Saturday. When they got to Eufaula and started home Police Irby arrested them and charged them with loitering and took their money and put them in jail. When J. D.'s mother Mrs. Lizzie Webb Dickerson heard that the boys were in jail she started to the jail. But she went by [Miss Helen's] home, the white lady that she was working for, and told her. [Miss Helen] called the jailhouse and told them that they had better turn those boys out at once. Before Mrs. Dickerson got to the jailhouse she met the boys and they told her that Mr. Irby had taken their money. She went back by [Miss Helen's] home and told her. [Miss Helen] called back to the jail and told Mr. Irby that she would give him thirty minutes to give those boys their money back. By the time those boys got home Mr. Irby was there with their money, telling them that he was sorry.

26. Ditches to Die In or Avoid

Color Line comes up; I do not see it. However, I did apply the "ditch to die in" test. Here is a ditch not to die in:

At one of my first vestry meetings at St. James, Dr. Ed Comer, the senior warden, said, "Francis, we always bought Ray's liquor (my predecessor). We'd like to do the same for you. Y'all drink, don't you?"

I allowed we did, blundered on to say that they paid me enough, and needn't do me this favor. There was a pause. Then Ed said, "No, not that. You give us a list and the money. Our preacher shouldn't be seen going into the State Store. You know how the Baptists would talk." He got a chuckle about how those same hypocritical Baptist men out on the golf course used to stash their bourbon in the rough so they could share a friendly drink with the "whiskeypalians."

After the vestry offered to buy our liquor and I declined, I became curious about Eufaula's State Store (at that time in Alabama, the state government controlled all liquor stores). I think I wanted to imagine the effect of my going in. I had another reason to look. My one vestry defender in the liquor deal said he didn't see any reason I shouldn't buy my own booze in town. I learned he worked behind the counter of our State Store. I think he felt put down by the fake morality of the more well-off members. The store was a modest building set among the line of storefronts on Main Street.

Like all State Stores the front was painted dark green. Two doors were set door jamb to door jamb, two signs set over them, "White" and "Colored." Once inside would spirits seekers mix and mingle? I looked. No. A large-diameter galvanized pipe ran from the doors down the middle to the counter. The pipe was a glossy gray, smoothed by countless eager black and white hands easing up to the counter. There was no way I was going in that store. Walking home I did try a thought experiment to see if I could go in and keep my pledge to ignore segregation. OK: I'm heading downtown toward the closer door of the "White" sign. I go in that side. It's closest. I buy a bottle of sherry and head home. Another day I'm on the sidewalk approaching the "Colored" sign. As I get closer I realize we need a bottle of red vermouth. Going in that closest door may get me arrested if I refuse to change lanes. Two days later readers of the *Montgomery Advertiser* could see "Episcopal Priest Arrested in Eufaula Liquor Store." But I can easily avoid that by thinking I'm in a hurry. Some other day. So I join the duplicity of the vestry, minus the State Store clerk. I took the out provided by the vestry, and at the next vestry meeting told them I appreciated their offer, but would buy needed wine and liquor in Phenix City just up the road.

I will speak only of ditches that pockmarked the paths of Episcopal clergy. There they lay, had we the eyes to see them. They beckoned, "Hop in, Father, I am the one. I am serious. Dying would be worth it down here."

"Dying" meant, in ascending order:

1. Cryptic but unpleasant warnings from powerful parishioners.

2. Machinery set running to discreetly move the offender to another parish, bearing recommendations of ecclesiastical authorities.

3. In the worst case, where the ditch was deep and obvious and there was no way to get the guy out, the vestry and bishop would be direct and clear that race was the reason and he was welcome on his own to seek employment outside the diocese.

Our ditches after ordination began as seeming scratches in the soil. Who wouldn't hop over them? For example, Willie the sexton needs a letter from the church. The rector tells the secretary to use courtesy titles, e.g., Mr. William Pettaway, an employee of Trinity Church. The aging secretary's grandfather was a pro-slavery raider in Bloody Kansas. The rector backs off. No, don't make a fuss. Why risk upsetting Miss Delia? Just leave off the offending courtesy title.

As the ditches get deeper and more compelling, if we get accustomed to hopping over, soon we do not see them, wide as they may. Just float over.

However! Thank God for my being open to However! I did not want to die in the State Store.

Living in the rectory before Betty arrived, I knew we needed a housekeeper. Women parishioners suggested Parry Lee Edwards, whom I hired. I asked the same women the going rate of pay for domestic workers. The rate of pay was so low that I offered Parry Lee a considerably higher amount. Those women also told me that Parry Lee was a Jehovah's Witness. I had been reading about Jehovah's Witnesses' treatment under Nazi Germany. Many died at the hands of the Nazi SA (Sturmabteilung) or in concentration camps. The Witnesses refused to perform the Heil Hitler salute or pledge loyalty to the Third Reich and earned the hatred of fellow prisoners and both the joy and hatred of their persecutors by telling the truth, if interrogated. The small band of Witnesses to which Parry Lee belonged might be a Southern anomaly to Jim Crow, so I asked if Eufaula's Witnesses included blacks and whites. She told me that there were two separate bands of Jehovah's Witnesses in our town.

One day I was walking downtown when a white woman stopped me to ask if I was the new preacher in town. I said yes, and, her color changing, she let me have it. She and her friends knew I was paying Parry Lee above the Eufaula rate and asked if I knew what that meant and just who did I think I was and so on.

Later I was in Blooms's Florist Shop a couple of blocks from St. James. The Blooms were Jewish. Like a good Jewish mother, Mrs. Bloom took me under her wing and told me it was all over town that I was paying my maid too much. Although it was probably too late now, but I could do what Eufaula Jews did. They knew the rate was unjust but to keep peace and for the Blooms to stay in business they supplemented the going rate by payment in kind. She said, "Give Parry Lee food, Reverend Walter; give her shoes and clothes. People will not have to know what you are doing if you do it that way."

---

27. Dining Room and Kitchen

Early days in Eufaula, Betty and I were invited to a holiday family meal. The setting was a large, gracious, nineteenth-century home; the host, one of my vestrymen. It was a large and happy gathering. We were pleased to be invited and included. Toward the end of the meal, the adults began to take stock of the ages of the children at the table. There were groans about where the money would come from to get them through college. Some jokey poor-mouthing going around the table. Our surroundings didn't look poor to me. I recall being faintly intimidated by the wealth and standing of that family and their imposing home.

Social inferiority was a common subsurface feeling of mine in younger days, harkening back to the family's move to Spring Hill in 1939. Our niche was to be relatively poor but socially lodged among the respectable old Mobile families. I don't recall us Walters poor-mouthing.

In later years after I had been a guest in houses with clay chimneys and tarpaper siding, I found that poor people don't poor-mouth. People of the upper-middle classes sometimes do. Are we defensive of what we have? It seems the super-rich don't poor-mouth either. Something in common with the poor! Maybe a flicker of shame that also danced around the table that day had its basis in how the wealth was accumulated. By slavery, by sharecropping, by removal of the vote after 1901, by the hundred means of squeezing two bits here, six bits there from people with few defenses against a brutal system. Not that the people of the table, most members of St. James, had necessarily done those things themselves, but the ancestors had and produced the wealth being poor-mouthed. "Property is theft" said St. Basil of Cappadocia around 360 A.D. (Or something very like it in his "Sermon to the Rich.") The way out is to admit the darkness in what we have, then use it for communal good.

As the meal wound up, Betty helped clear the table and tarried in the kitchen behind the swinging door. Back at the rectory, she told me of the contrast between the kitchen and the dining room. She and the "colored" cook started talking. You know: Do you have children? How many? How old? Any still at home? The cook's were all grown but one, she said. Just one at home now. She and her husband had had lots of kids. All had college degrees. She rattled off some of their professions.

"How did you get all those children through college?" Betty asked. The cook said she and her husband got the first through by themselves, wasn't easy. Then that one had to get a job and put the next one through. All the children knew that was the deal. Apparently each one had done his or her part. Just one more to get through college.

That was the kitchen talk. No jovial whining. Had the cook heard the table talk and wanted to nail home a contrast? Most probably. The help always hear more than we imagine. As this kitchen talk went on, I sat at this gorgeous table hearing how these folks might go broke putting their kids through Auburn or Alabama.

But this is small beer against a thousand trespasses once called the Color Line.

28. Confirmation Class, 1959, Eufaula

Before the 1982 Prayer Book revision the discipline of the Episcopal Church required that children baptized as infants be instructed and receive Confirmation from the bishop before receiving Communion. Confirmation happened around age twelve. I told those who asked that twelve was considered the age of reason. Roman Catholics were confirmed at age seven with the same rationale, but five years ahead of little Anglicans.

That was swept away by the revised 1982 Book of Common Prayer, which also provided language attacking racism as contravening the oneness of humankind. This support was not available to me in Eufaula. I was stuck with the 1928 Catechism and Offices of Instruction. As I began Confirmation classes in late fall 1959, six or seven kids were in attendance. The Catechism's creaky medieval heritage was showing. It saw kids living under the reign of Henry VIII, chimney sweeps or children of tenant farmers.

Question. What is your duty toward your neighbor?

Answer: To honour and obey the civil authority; to submit myself to all my governors, teachers, spiritual pastors, and masters. And to order myself in that lowliness and reverence which becometh a servant of God. To keep my hands from picking and stealing; not to covet nor desire other men's goods; but to learn and labor truly to earn mine own living, and to do my duty in that state of life which it shall please God to call me.

Out the door with the American Dream if anyone still took these words seriously.

So I improvised with something provocative, woke 'em up. We examined the distinctions among blasphemy, swearing, cursing, insulting, and plain old dirty words. I suggested that "Go to Hell" and "God damn you," if seen for what they meant, were prayers, and if you believed in God, were far worse than words about sex or excrement. Those terms did not hold a candle to appeals to God to consign someone to eternal suffering. They woke up—somewhat.

Then things took off in a direction I had planned. I told them that words have meaning and can hurt people. I knew that they and their parents used the word "nigger" casually. I suggested that many colored people were hurt when whites used the word "nigger." It was news to them that there were any other words.

Later when we got to a section on the mechanics of receiving Communion I laid out the chalice and paten with unconsecrated bread and wine. As they tasted wine for the first time there were a few "Ewwws" of disgust. I went back to what was so lacking them: the unity of all people in that sacrament of the world, the Church.

I said, "Can you imagine this? You are kneeling at the rail, your family and church members are kneeling with you. Can you imagine being so repulsed by a fellow member of Christ's Body that you would leave the rail if that person knelt there?"

The kids were not flippant. They were thinking. No. They could not imagine that.

I said, "I'm not so sure. I'll bet someone who is a Christian will walk past that window before we finish—someone that you might not wish to receive Communion with."

No, could not be. They started looking. After a bit a black man walked past. Silence. They kept looking. They had not seen this invisible black person. I said, "One just walked by."

One kid said, in all innocence, "You mean niggers?"

"Yeah. Lots of colored people are Christians."

They got interested, grappling with it. Most said they would leave, but they were not happy about it. One girl said she would remain.

"OK," I said. "When you receive Communion, distance does not matter; whether black Anglicans in South Africa are at an altar there or someone black is at St. James next to you, it is all the same—we are one in Christ Jesus. This is a decision you have to make. Do you want to be confirmed? Do you want to say Yes to this body of believers? It includes all sorts of people. You can always wait and think about it some more."

What a burden to lay on them! Well, if not then, when? I knew no one could defer. Think of the mothers, fathers, aunts, uncles, and grandmothers preparing to come to church. The Confirmation gifts they bought: Prayer

Books, Bibles, the three-ribbon page markers with the precious little silver bobs, the anchor for hope, the heart for love, the cross for faith. At my Confirmation I thank God that my aged friends at St. Paul's, Gladys and Warren Fields, gave me a pocketknife. How that hit me! Faith has to do with the life a twelve-year-old boy leads.

By the way, I said, "Negroes find the word 'nigger' hurtful when whites use it. Remember those hurtful insults we were talking about?"

"But Mr. Walter, we just talk that way among ourselves."

A carnival was then in Eufaula. "OK, suppose you are at the fair waiting in line to get on the Ferris wheel and this colored kid is standing in front of you and the two of you started talking. Would you say 'nigger' to him?"

Devoid of sarcasm came, "What would I talk to one about?"

A second kid said helpfully, "Mr. Walter, colored people have their own day to go to the fair."

Bishop Carpenter came, and laid his hands in blessing on all of them. Who among them now alive remembers the man walking past the window, the Ferris wheel, the challenge not to be confirmed? Did anything in our weeks together contribute to their integrity in years to come?

Something must have stuck and been taken home because shortly before I was asked to leave, the senior warden came to me. Wanting to be nice, in a jocular tone he explained why I had to go.

Your sermons are respectful, not in our face even though we know what you're getting at. We can sit there and take it. But when you start in on our kids, that's different. We only have so many years to train 'em before they're off to Auburn or Alabama. Can't have you interferin' with that. It's gettin' harder and harder. Now we have to be careful what my daughter sees on television. Some black guys are on a football team. We had to cancel *Life* magazine.

People had shared that with me, making fun of themselves. Yes, canceling *Life* but making sure there was a copy in the lobby of the Eufaula Hotel.

Two parishioners openly supported me and wrote the vestry. One told me of her sorrow in passing her black half-sister on the street frequently but being unable to speak to or even acknowledge her—for fear of losing her business in town.

The walls were solid, protected. So how did all that sperm manage to leak over the Color Line?

We never had couple friends in Eufaula. I could, for myself, drive west to Greenville to visit the Reverend Ed Holtam, a Birmingham native with whom I served as a fellow and tutor at General Seminary. We shared similar views on race and the looming struggle. Or I could go north to Auburn where the Reverend Merrill Stevens with his wife, Wallie, served students at the university. After mutual spiritual direction and confession, Merrill and I would drink their home brew with Wallie. Students, too, enjoyed it. "One batch brewing under the house, one batch bottled, one batch being drunk," was the Stevenses' recipe for inexpensive hospitality.

One Sunday we actually had a newcomer at St. James! She was the wife of a military guy serving south of us. Probably at our domed radar station south of Eufaula. Thanks to the Cold War, Betty found herself a fellow artist. They ended up sharing a large studio over one of the old shops on the main drag. When the U.S. decided Mutual Assured Destruction wasn't such a hot topic and rockets were far better than aircraft, this base was turned over to the Mental Retardation Division of the State Mental Health Department as a facility to house the mentally disabled. Fancy that! In a later life I operated residential homes for such persons and a couple of times went to pick up people to come live in ordinary houses in Birmingham. One time I asked a staffer at the state's converted mental health facility what they used the big windowless former radar dome for. "Recreation," I was told.

So with happy anticipation we received an invite to come up for drinks with two couples our age. One couple were members of St. James. Drinks were poured and we settled into Stage One: "Where y'all from? Have kids? School? Work?" Stage Two was more our turn: "Tell us about Eufaula. Been here all your lives?" Then we moved to Stage Three: THE HELP. Finding Help, keeping Help, rebuking Help, accusing Help, losing Help, finding new Help, training Help, then admit defeat and put up with Help. We did not have to bad mouth our Help. There was nothing to bad mouth. I could say I had hired Parry Lee Edwards. She was a pleasant, useful person whose only oddity was that she belonged to a segregated Jehovah's Witness Church and she had done something bad and was under some discipline. Not that we asked her about this, we heard it from other white people. We didn't, if I recall, share this with the two local couples. We had little to add to the topic except that we liked Parry Lee. Drinks were freshened. Turned out the two Eufaula wives shared, or I should say managed, the same "yard boy." "Oh, so he comes to you, too?" Etc. It turned out that in this case he was chronologically a young man. Generic "yard boys" could be any age. One wife said something like "He's real cute." The other agreed.

With that the two husbands shot to their feet like angry Jack-in-the-Boxes. We are talking some sort of mood change! The wives got it, they knew. Those women! Their faces! Abashed, not because the new preacher and his wife were present, but because they had crossed the Color Line and insulted their husbands. The temperature in the room plunged. After a seemly delay we excused ourselves, thanked them, and walked the short distance down Eufaula Avenue to the rectory.

29. Carl and Anne, Eufaula, 1959

In 1959, when I came to the parish in Eufaula, Carl Braden was an occasional guest in the rectory. By then there was nobody in Eufaula, black or white, with whom Betty and I could talk about the pall of racial mores which hung over our town, choking everything. Push a little bit and there it was, not to be spoken of, the hem of it not to be lifted, for God's sake. Carl provided relief. Carl during those visits became another mentor. I set before him my vow not to participate in the culture of segregation, racial distinction, or whatever it might be called. It was becoming more nitpicking, as I tried to live it out in Eufaula. "You could," he said, "ask for the gift of a sheet. Throw your clothes away, sit by the side of the road, and hope people will feed you from time to time. Stay there, then you will die, and what good would you have done?" He added that even my free sheet would probably come from underpaid workers breathing clouds of lint choking their lungs. I got it. An absolute goal was impossible, but as a virtue it could enlighten my, life showing me which fights to pick, which to avoid.

The last time Carl stopped by Eufaula, I'd heard of some sort of meeting to be held in a black church. Looking back to that evening now I think I felt a coming release from the tension of keeping my guard up. The freedom to think and talk with Carl became perhaps a foretaste of things to come. I thought something like, "Why the hell shouldn't I go to a meeting of Eufaula citizens? If this ends it for me in Eufaula, so be it."

Carl and I went. In those days, it was hard to know right off at a black meeting if you were at a church service or not. Or at something we white folks might call a "secular" or "political" event. The black culture then in those places didn't make the distinction between a gathering of God's people and a gathering to do some kind of business. The deacon prayed, a hymn was sung, the scripture was read, the minister said a few words; then the principal speaker was escorted to the pulpit. Out of their fine-tuned manners no one in the church took looks at the two white guys seated among them. Turned out it was a business meeting of a Negro burial association. After the speaker concluded the business meeting he invited the two guests to speak. Carl went first. Then I told them who I was, what church in town I served, then at a loss for what else to say, spoke of my admiration for Martin Luther King Jr. and his message of nonviolent resistance. That was the effective end of my two years in Eufaula though it took a few more months to play out.

But before leaving memories of Carl, SCEF, and Mrs. Roosevelt, I'd like to say something about Anne Braden. I read her book. I met her a few times. When she died in 2013, amongst the flurry of obituaries and recollections of her friends, one of them lamented that Anne in her later writings and interviews never acknowledged she had once been a member of the American Communist Party. It's possible to toss off a remark like that today, but I wonder why the friend didn't realize how dangerous it had once been to admit membership, even association, with the Communist Party. How hard it might be to give up protective reticence for one's self-preservation. Didn't this friend remember that in 1961–'62 Carl was imprisoned for not taking the Fifth during a HUAC meeting? For refusing to respond to the mantra: "Are you now or have you ever been a member of the Communist Party?" In the liturgy of these show trials, the proper response was to take the Fifth. Carl didn't. He told Francis E. Walter and the Committee it had no legal or moral right to question his associations. He would not demean himself by rehearsing the Fifth. For that he went to prison for his unprotected silence.

I knew Anne to be a Christian and a communicant of the Episcopal Church in Louisville. There she was a member of the altar guild. Altar guilds are by custom female, the members given to wearing little black or white lace doilies as head gear (not so much today) so as to go reverently into the chancel, once a male preserve, to collect, wash, starch, and iron linens, clean and polish silver and brass. The writer Hilaire Belloc, a Roman Catholic, had himself a time gently ridiculing Anglicans in his "Anglican Alphabet." Of lectern stands for holding Holy Bibles, he is said to have written: "E is for eagle, brass and absurd. F for the females who polish this bird." I treasure the incongruity. I once found it funny: a Communist altar guild member! It was only incongruous because I'd bought the lie. Just who would have said it was morally impossible to be a member of the American Communist Party and an altar guild member in the '30s, '40s, and '50s? My sound-alike Francis E. Walter, that's who. That congressional triad, McCarthy, Stennis, and Eastland. *Life* magazine, *Reader's Digest*, that's who.

30. *Charity vs. Social Justice*

In Eufaula in October 1960, the "First churches"—Baptists, Episcopalians, Methodists, and Presbyterians—were electrified by television news reporting of the "Kneel-in Demonstrations." They immediately laid plans to keep such upsetters of timeless decency out of their churches.

The laws of the Episcopal Church gave me as rector oversight of worship, so I added this to our weekly mail-out:

KNEEL-INS AND CHRISTIANS

Your Parson was at Camp McDowell when the first of the "Kneel-ins" began in Atlanta. We certainly talked about them as many did, all over the world. The power of God worked in our discussions for we were led to a deeper look at ourselves. This is always Jesus's way. He directs the interest that situations and other persons create into a look at one's self.

We began by saying, "Their motives are wrong," "They don't really want to worship," "They etc." Then someone said, "Who checks our motives at the door?" As we thought of ourselves things got easier to talk about—more practical. "Should anyone check motives at a church door?" "Can a church be a church and keep people out?"

The Church is one form the Kingdom of God takes on earth—perhaps the most official form. The King has shown His love for all. He does not wait, but goes out to bring in the blind, the lame, and the profitless. The Church is His agency on earth to accomplish this in-gathering and to create this absolutely non-exclusive fellowship. There are no signs by St. James's, or St Stephen's or St. Matthew's reading:

"WELCOME: Negroes, Whites, Republicans, sex perverts, alcoholics, employees of the Fed. Gov't, mill hands and bankers."

Why aren't these signs there? Because we don't need them. Of course those people are welcome. It's obvious.

Yes, it is truly obvious. And so, dear brethren, we live in fearsome tension as the White Southerner in us tangles with the Christian in us.

It is not painless to be a member of Christ's Body; so you must not expect me, your pastor to delude you or cry peace when there is not peace. We must trust and love one another beseeching God for the grace to do so.

As you ponder what God is calling you to say, and do, and be in this time of racial crisis, you might well read the Gospel for Trinity Eleven and use for your prayers the ones for "Unity" and "Guidance" (P. B. pp 37, 595).

This caused an uproar among members, mostly because they realized my posting would get all over town. The senior warden of the vestry wrote an angry letter to Bishop Carpenter about my message.

In his response Bishop Carpenter looked back to slavery times to placate the senior warden: faithful house slaves weeping for Ol' Miss in the slave gallery where they sat.

Now in 1960: ". . . be sure that the ushers are on the alert . . . have them seat the colored people properly . . . in this way no difficulty will arise and this is what many of our places are intending to do if this situation should arise." Everyone in Alabama knew that "properly" meant "in the back."

Then the Bishop used the argument that the demonstrators were "childish." "For as long as any of us can remember colored people have from time to time come to the 'white folks' church,' and been properly seated by the ushers when they wanted to see what the white folks did, for a wedding or a burial or something of that sort." So the Bishop wrote.

In these sentiments above Bishop Carpenter stretched the old, supposedly infantile, curiosity of "colored people" to include 1960s' nonviolent black people who will soon risk their lives to say, "We are Somebody!"—and want recognition as such.

The Bishop could not escape his fully internalized nineteenth-century paternalism of black folk and enter the light of their equality as adult human beings. Later he will be calling the march from Selma to Montgomery "foolish" and "childish." Bishop Carpenter was a particular kind of racist—the kind who expected of himself and other whites a certain kind of generosity, of charity, that meant to help folks who could not help themselves. Such "charity" does not reach the level of Love because it lacks the ballast of social justice.

The organist at St. James was a member of one of Eufaula's first families, older than I and confident of her opinions. She and I usually worked well together selecting hymns, matching hymns with the church seasons and weekly Scripture readings. As with many small congregations it was the Devil's own to introduce new hymns from the Episcopal Hymnal. At our meetings I would mention some appropriate hymn, and she would often respond with the 1959 version of "No Way." We compromised on inserting a new hymn every couple of months and warning parishioners beforehand.

At one of our sessions, I suggested Hymn 263. I did this with forethought. My approach to racism at St. James was to use titration (a drop at a time), see what happened, and decide when to add more. Hymn 263, "In Christ There Is No East or West," fit the theme of an upcoming service, and no one could say it was arbitrary. The rest of the verse is even more scandalous:

> In Him, no South or North.
> But one great fellowship of love
> throughout the whole wide earth.

It gets worse:

> Join hands then, brothers of the faith,
> Whate'er your race may be!
> Who serves my Father as a son
> Is surely kin to me.

We were at the organ when I mentioned Hymn 263.

"I can't play that," she said.

I was surprised at her answer. She was a member of St. James, a volunteer organist. I assumed that perhaps she privately accepted the message of the hymn, but believed fellow parishioners of this tight-knit community would strongly object.

I said, "Why not?"

She pointed to the title line, right-hand corner, where the words "Negro Melody" were added. She was refusing to play a Negro melody in our church.

In small communities with strong denominational loyalties, one cannot shop churches if one becomes miffed. In such instances there is forgiveness and sufferance aplenty. If a parishioner fell out with people at St. James, there was no other Episcopal church to attend. I could sympathize.

Glancing at Hymn 263 again I saw that a "2nd tune" was offered on the next page. Even I saw that it was not a "Negro Melody." Why not press on?

Before I could say anything, she said, "I could play that."

I was surprised and gratified. I had thought it was the words.

Eufaula proved Bishop Carpenter right when he promised that sending me there would teach me the real Alabama, something he said the urbanity of Mobile had denied me. When I arrived, parishioners and other white towns-people graciously showed me around or had me over for a meal. Betty had not yet arrived.

One man, related to a well-known Alabama politician, asked if I'd like to see a historic building he'd bought. I think he told me he planned to fix it up and create a restaurant. It was in the oldest part of town on a bluff overlooking the Chattahoochee River. As we drove over, I sensed he was unusually keyed up over this acquisition and eager to show it to me. Is this a make-or-break opportunity for him, I wondered, and why does my approval mean so much to him? Anyway, there was a tension as we headed for the front door. He reached for the door knob but it fell off. "Damn niggers!" This blip soured everything. He was deflated and listless for the rest of the tour. Looking around I saw no evidence that African Americans or any other low-rated people had been do-ing anything around the place.

This taught me that some white people had a use for black people that I hadn't known about in Mobile. It's their fault! What would some white folks do if they couldn't blame THEM? I later learned that one's ancestors could also step up to excuse behavior and relieve one of changing. The ancestor excuse is dying out today. It only works in small communities where people stay put and know each other's forebears two or three generations back. This way of keeping and conserving also did much to preserve the Color Line that took the place of slavery.

Examples of blaming ancestors:

"Suicide runs in that family."

"All the Stuart men drink."

"Bad nerves goes way back with our family."

"What do you expect? Their people were common as pig's tracks."

"Those sorry Smiths. None of 'em ever hit a lick at a snake."

Someone in town was being treated for breast cancer. I offered to drive her and her mother to Montgomery for a session with cobalt radiation. A brutal process. None too stable at best, she reacted with hysteria; left in a cold room, strapped to a stretcher with an enormous machine circling her body. Driving back she was still weeping, seated alone in the back seat. Her mother looked over at me, "The _____'s have always been allergic to cobalt."

During the first Advent/Christmas in Eufaula, parents agreed with me it would be good for our youth group to go caroling in the back of a straw-filled pickup truck. Betty offered to have them to the rectory afterwards. I found myself in a truck bed of prickly hay. She was in the rectory fine-tuning spiced hot cider and home-baked cookies.

So there I was in the truck, in the hay, with the carolers. "Let's go to Parry Lee's house." A lot of the kids knew her because she'd worked for their families. I didn't do things like that in Eufaula like a Russian holy fool. I knew I was pushing. Not too much, just enough to creep up alongside people's race-settled views. A nudge. However, the reaction floored me. There was loud, nervous laughter. "She's our maid! Screech!"

I had banged on the cab telling the driver to take us by Parry Lee Edwards's. Now I had to bang again, "Don't."

We finished up at the rectory. This too was a bust. It wouldn't have been so hard if the Parry Lee teaching moment had challenged a smidgen of their white exclusionary lives. The kids looked at the fragrant, steaming silver bowl of cider like it was a witch's brew. "Eww! What's that?! Don't you have any Cokes?"

The president of St. James' Women's Auxiliary caught up with me one day in the parish hall.

"Mr. Walter, every year the women from all the churches have an annual program on World Mission. We meet in different churches and this year it's to be at St. James. We need you to be there because we begin with a worship service and a program. This year the purpose is to raise money for missions in Africa and the Orient."

This sounded better and better, and I would certainly help. World Mission had to reference people of color, and she said it was a program of the National Council of Churches of Christ which provided the materials. That would be good for everybody. This was in the happier days of 1957–58; the John Birch Society, the National States' Rights Party, and Lord knows who else had not yet proclaimed the NCCC a Communist front sworn to destroy Christianity and our Republic. She continued, this year the women were planning for some to dress in various native costumes to create a colorful procession into the church as the service began.

Uh oh. A shadow passed between us and I knew trouble was at hand. She was innocent; no, not exactly innocent, but one who had never been helped to, or been adventurous enough to, examine her life and values, or question racism in the South, over against the values of the Gospel.

"Do all the churches in Eufaula that belong to the National Council of Christ churches participate?" I asked.

"Oh, yes," she replied.

"What about the African Methodist Episcopal Church?"

"What! What do you mean?"

Ignoring her question, out of my mouth came, "Unless all the women of the NCCC churches are invited I won't allow the program to be at St. James." And our conversation was over.

But on getting to the rectory, the sarcastic thought came to mind how much more authentic-looking black AME women would be in native dress processing into the church than the white ladies of Eufaula.

Today I see how little I offered my parishioner. I simply threw my refusal in her face and withdrew. I could have said, it was my obligation to say, "Let's get a cup of coffee tomorrow and talk about it." That would have cast off the mantle of prophet on the mountaintop and taken on the role of pastor/shepherd. I was unable to bear reproach, maybe even too angry, to reach out to her.

Here a wall between us went up, my life so long ago as unexamined as hers.

"And the Lord God called unto Adam and said unto him, Where art thou? And he said, I heard thy voice in the garden and I was afraid, because I was naked; and I hid myself." (KJV Genesis 2:9,10).

From the beginning enmity surrounding racial justice in the church defined my ministry. Acting as priest and rector of St. James was daunting. On the one hand I saw clearly the Mountain of Truth revealed through Martin Luther King against members of St. James living within a construct of separation, acted out in ways running from a code of etiquette toward blacks made up of petty insults putting them continually on a lower plane all the way to violence and death. St. James was united in racial superiority and determined to remain segregated from the black race, never having known anything else. As priest of my first parish, my own determination was to lead them out of segregation. As young and inexperienced as I was and without support from my bishop, my acts of nonparticipation presented an insoluble dilemma for me and parishioners at St. James.

31. Leaving Eufaula

When Betty and I returned from the conference which founded the Episcopal Society for Cultural and Racial Unity (ESCRU), it was evening. There had been a negative article about it in the *Birmingham News*. As well there should have been. The Committee on Memorials (Petitions) to our Bishops asked the House of Bishops to advise our new organization whether persons of a different color could be married by the church. This was no joke. It was only a few weeks before that I had asked the same of Alabama's Bishop Murray. He said no. Some on our committee thought such a bomb was starting off a little too explosively. I said it was at root about miscegenation. Might as well get that over early. Arriving at home we found an envelope stuck in the screen door, with a letter informing me that I was fired as rector of St. James and was not to preside at the next Sunday services and would receive a month's severance pay.

I notified Bishop Carpenter who then communicated with the vestry, I presume through Dr. Ed Comer, the senior warden. The Bishop told the vestrymen that they could not bar me from presiding at the service before I left and that there must be a final vestry meeting for termination at which I would be present.

I appreciated and respected that support. At the vestry meeting, I was told not to contact any vestryman individually and that my firing had been a unanimous decision. That last service expressed nothing of what was roiling our hearts. A visitor would have noted nothing amiss. Episcopalians are genteel.

One vestry member broke ranks to visit me. One evening we sat in his car by the rectory. He expressed his sorrow at having to join the vote of the vestry to make it unanimous.

Just before leaving Eufaula I was blessed three times. After the vestryman broke the rule that no vestryman was to contact me privately after I was fired, two more people, one a parishioner, the one who created an awkward moment by remarking that the "yard boy was cute," met me in the parish hall to tell me a story. The third, a future mayor of Eufaula.

Her story reconstructed:

"Don't you think you're the only one in Eufaula with your ideas about colored people! Let me tell you! I married a Eufaula man. I want to live here! I have my family here! You don't have to talk about things like that. I don't! My husband was in the Army when we first married. We were posted to _____. I was pregnant then. We talked about where I would have the baby. Doctors off base were expensive, and back then we were poor. The base had two free doctors, but one was colored and one was white. It wasn't allowed for patients to demand the white doctor. We had a fifty-fifty chance of getting him and decided to use the free base doctors and hope for the best. My labor was long and, finally, I asked the nurses for something to knock me out. I had not seen the doctor yet. I came to during the delivery and when I looked between my legs, there was the biggest, blackest face I'd ever seen. I'd never been so happy to see his face in my life! That has stuck with me ever since and changed the way I think about the races.

"But do you think I'd ever tell anyone here about that? But you had to go talking about colored people. Now you have to leave. If you ever tell anyone about this I'll say you're lying."

The third time was just before we left. It was very late, and I was sitting by myself in the kitchen. The doorbell rang, which was scary but I decided to go to the door.

In this I will use the man's real name. He was not a member of St. James, but I knew who Hamp Graves was.

"Do you have a church key?" were his first words.

"Sure, in the kitchen, come on in."

I thought the remark funny because of my being in the church business. We sat at the kitchen table. It was my first time to see sixteen-ounce beer cans. I inherited my mother's sensitivity to alcohol. Could I get through sixteen ounces?

"You've been talkin' big about colored people. Now you got to go. Let me tell you something about me. When I was in the Army, my barracks had a big bathroom attached. There must have been fifteen washstands on one wall. I was washing my face after shavin'. Damn! I'd forgot my toothbrush. I looked at the feller next to me. 'May I borrow your toothbrush?'

"'Sure.'

"He handed it over. He was black as the Ace of Spades. I brushed and handed it back. Do you think it mattered to me? But we don't talk about things like that here. You had to go talkin'. Now you got to go!"

Hamp Graves was elected mayor of Eufaula after that and was reelected many times until he died in office.

We pulled out of Eufaula in the blue Volkswagen, with Harry the cat, headed for Mobile. We were not at an emotional bottom but buoyed up by the $1,800 grant from the National Council of Churches, a fund set up for the likes of Southern pastors like me when fired for dabbling in social justice. There were two more bright spots. First, we had a glorious place to stay in the Mobile area: a log house fronting Dog River, set amongst wisteria, azaleas, camellias, and longleaf pines. Next door lived the owners, Clarendon and Venetia McClure, folks of my parents' generation.

I had learned in racial catch-up lessons after I left Mobile that Clarendon was a member of a biracial group which met quietly and anonymously to temper, when it could, white outrages locally.

Clarendon was also my mother's friend through music. When her swollen arm ended her piano playing, Clarendon coached her in voice lessons. When my mother died, we gave him her Mason & Hamlin parlor grand. For years its keyboard had protruded across the doorway to my bedroom. It took a while for me to stop twisting sideways to enter my room after we gave it to him. Clarendon and Venetia were the only people I could think of to ask about housing and BINGO! They immediately offered the log house just up Dog River from their own. We had another comfort in store as we headed southwest. Nelle Harper Lee, the author of *To Kill a Mockingbird*, had a sister living in Eufaula. When the book came out Eufaula was up a stump. The book ought to be in the library because one of our own wrote it. The book ought not to be in the library because—well, you know what it is about. However, pride won over. That being settled, Nelle was invited to a reception given by her sister. Her sister was not a member of St. James, but we got an invitation.

I pondered this at the time. Word was getting out about me and I was already not welcome in many settings. I figured Nelle's sister wanted to temper the event with one or two people who approved of the message of the book and not just the fame. Memoria has refused to return my e-mails asking her to ratify that I actually went to the reception. Must have, because I felt at ease telephoning Nelle in Monroeville asking if we could stop by to say hello on our way to Mobile. No need to say why we were going to Mobile. Dame Rumor took that off our hands. Nelle said to come for lunch and meet her at a downtown hotel—a healing, gracious hour, one of the best I have ever floated through: no complaining, no explaining, no blaming.

We drove south-southwest, no interstates: Eufaula, Clayton, Laverne, Evergreen, Bermuda to Monroeville. Then dropping south with one desperate cat. VW's of that era had mouse-fur cloth headliners. Harry, mad with fear and long of claw, paced from floorboards to seats, up sides and across the headliner upside-down. Pit stops after throttling him with a collar were unproductive. ("Look, Harry, I'm peeing. Sure feels good.") This was in the olden days before cat tranquilizers. On the Bay Bridge Causeway into Mobile, Harry made a claw-extended trip up my trouser leg and into my lap to release all the pent-up cat pee since Eufaula. We were headed to the McClures' in Mobile to check in. I decided to tell them the truth about my sopping pants' front, but l doubted they believed me.

32. *Breitling Cousins Dissed by Miss Amelia*

Taylor Branch in his three-volume work *America in the King Years* lists in its indices many references to Mrs. Amelia Boynton of Selma, Alabama. Mr. Branch calls her "the founder of the Dallas County Voters' League" and reports that she was called "the Mother of the Voting Rights Movement." Who has not seen the footage from January 1965 of Sheriff Jim Clark seizing Miss Amelia by the collar of her attractive winter dress coat, shoving her onto the pavement? She was part of a group peacefully protesting in front of the Dallas County Courthouse for the right of black citizens to register to vote.

The joke in this image, which did so much to advance the enfranchisement of black people, was that Jim Clark, more given to violence than thought, seeing that news cameras were present, ordered the cattle prods to be laid aside and used his beefy hands to throttle Miss Amelia. Taylor Branch records that Ralph Abernathy that night offered the name of Jim Clark as an honorary member of the Dallas County Voters' League for his role in advancing the voting rights sttruggle.

Miss Amelia and her husband owned and operated an insurance company in Selma. In their office was a framed display of seventy-five prominent Selma blacks denied the right to vote from 1952 to 1962. It is said that the sight of this picture tipped the balance of King's mind to come to Selma.

I knew nothing of Miss Amelia back when I had breakfast with her at the Demopolis Inn on July 9, 1965. Back then Betty and I were still living with her Aunt Wanda Harris in Decatur, Alabama, and I was in Demopolis looking for a job. I was determined to live and work in the South. My ideal job would have been as a field representative for the Episcopal Church or for the National Council of Churches to discover how such bodies could assist the movement in the South.

My ideals were forced to face necessity. I had a white Methodist friend on the staff of the U.S. Civil Rights Commission. He had about guaranteed I could get a job with the commission. I was far from keen about working for the government but was in no position to reject offers out of hand. My friend called me at Aunt Wanda's to say that he and other staffers were to meet with members of the Alabama Advisory Committee to the U. S. Civil Rights Commission in Demopolis. Why not come down?

I had never been to Demopolis but from childhood had a mental map of it, peopled by forebears on my mother's side. This was thanks to my great-aunt Minnie, who kept up with all relatives, living and dead. I must have mentioned the job search to either Arminnie or Bobbin because when I arrived to check into the Demopolis Inn where the feds were to stay, I was newly aware that I was related to the Breitlings who owned the hotel. The inn is long-gone. Even in 1965, it was out of fashion, a well-kept but tired old tan brick building downtown, awaiting the construction of some plastic motel on the edge of town to take its place.

On checking in, I said to the female Brietling desk clerk, "I'm Francis Walter; Miss Minnie Michael is my great-aunt." Since Arminnie "kept up," of course she and the clerk knew each other, and the clerk's Brietling face lit up. Then she sobered a little and asked, "So, you're not one of those civil righters are you?"

I didn't go to a Jesuit college for nothing, so I said, "No, ma'am," meaning, "I'm not a staff member of the U. S. Civil Rights Commission"—leaving off "but I'd like to be." However, next morning sitting at breakfast with Miss Amelia and my government friend blew my cover.

When a white teenaged waitress appeared to take our order, she was obviously nervous at the situation of her white servant self waiting on a black customer with a hat on. Miss Amelia ordered "Eggs Benedict." The girl was stupefied as to what "Eggs Benedict" meant. She said, "I'll go see," and left.

She soon returned and said, "We don't have any."

Miss Amelia ordered scrambled eggs.

The waitress left. Miss Amelia looked at us and said, "Small town, small mind." Demopolis was much smaller than Selma.

Maria Katherine (Breitling) Michael (born 1816 in Doffingen, Germany; died 1910 in Demopolis, Alabama) was my great-great-grandmother. She was caught up in a scheme by some exiled Bonapartists from the Alsace-Lorraine who had fled to Philadelphia. From there they came to Demopolis, Alabama, with a plan to establish a fanciful utopian refuge for Bonapartists in a warmer climate. They named it the Vine and Olive Colony. As Albert James Pickett wrote in his 1851 *History of Alabama*:

> An ordinance of Louis XVIII had forced them from France on account of their attachment to Napoleon . . . the refugees [in Philadelphia] dispatched Nicholas S. Parmanter to the Federal City to obtain from Congress a tract of land in the wild domain of the West . . .

No one in Philadelphia came to inspect the land in Alabama. Wine grapes and olives would not grow there. Incompetent surveyors more than once mislocated tracts of land.

Many of the refugees were titled gentry who had never grown anything (but not the Michaels or Breitlings). Pickett politely said of those gentry, "Having been accustomed to Parisian life, these people were indifferent pioneers."

The first town was called "the City of the People," Demopolis. The county, when established, was called Marengo; other small settlements were Aigleville and Linden. Would Napoleon have been amused?

Pickett: "The French were less calculated than any other people upon earth, to bring a forest into cultivation."

---

33. Bishop C. C. J. Carpenter Tries to Cope

Below is a clipping from one of the Birmingham newspapers in March 1965, printed just before the Selma to Montgomery March. The clipping was copied into a mailing of the Episcopal Society for Cultural and Racial Unity.

BISHOP ASKS ALL TO RETURN HOME
The presiding (sic) bishop of one Episcopal Diocese of Alabama asked all

out-of-state Episcopalians today participating in Alabama racial demonstrations to return to their homes.

The Rt. Rev. C. C. J. Carpenter, bishop of Alabama, issued a statement which closely paralleled an appeal made Thursday by Archbishop Thomas J. Toolen of the Mobile-Birmingham Diocese of the Roman Catholic Church.

The bishop said that as far as he knows Alabama Episcopalians have "not participated, but have continued to go about their normal activities.

"As bishop of the diocese of Alabama, I earnestly hope that none of our Episcopalians will take part in the demonstrations that are causing much ill will and unnecessary unhappiness in our state, nor in the proposed 'march' from Selma to Montgomery which can serve no good purpose, but to the contrary can be detrimental to progress and serve only as a very costly public nuisance.

"This 'march' is a foolish business and a sad waste of time in which the childish instinct to parade at great cost to our state will be indulged.

"So far as I know, our Alabama Episcopalians have not participated, but have continued to go about their normal activities.

"I cannot be responsible for some Episcopalians from other parts of the country who have their home work so well organized that they can spend time telling us what to do in Alabama, but I hope they will soon go home and let us get on with the progress we are trying to make in this part of our country for which we feel a special responsibility."

The photocopy was flanked on the left by a church news release and on the right by a canon (law) of the National Episcopal Church.

March 21, 1965 — Seven Churchmen, including four clergy, were turned away by vestrymen at St. Paul's. The clergy and white laity would have been admitted, after "registering" (using the Newcomers card reproduced in this flyer), but Negro laity would not have been allowed in. None entered. Behind the cordon of vestrymen was a stained glass window of Christ: "Come unto me, all ye that labor. . . ." One vestryman stated that he felt if Negro Episcopalians moved to town, they should start a new congregation.

Canon 16, Section 4: "Every communicant or baptized member of this

Church shall be entitled to equal rights and status in any parish or mission thereof. He shall not be excluded from the worship or sacraments of the Church, and not from parochial membership, because of his race, color, etc."

The Bishop is angry, and some bedrock assumptions are exposed in this outburst: ". . . I earnestly hope that none of our Episcopalians will take part in the demonstrations that are causing much ill will . . . unnecessary unhappiness . . . proposed 'march' . . . detrimental to progress . . . public nuisance . . . a foolish business . . . a sad waste of time . . . childish instinct to parade . . . at great cost to our state . . . will be indulged. . . ."

In the newspaper article, Carpenter used favorite phrases: "which can serve no good purpose but to the contrary be detrimental to progress." The word "progress" was one of the Bishop's old saws: "We're making progress!" A term used by him to point out glacial social improvement visible only to him.

So what to him are these persons with darker skin than his? A foolish race with childish instincts who want to be indulged at great costs to the state, so as to parade around. Not march with fife and drum in even tread, moving as one, but shuckin' and jivin' down the road.

Every white person from Zip City to Dauphin Island knew exactly what these coded words meant: Colored folks, God bless 'em, can be a sad waste of our time. Their childish instincts move them to parade around. Looks like once again we white folks will have to indulge them with our tax money. But we shouldn't have to do this. What can we do to stop stuff like this? Normally, we can tolerate what these foolish people do, but this is too much; this time it is too much to indulge this childish race.

We see inside a man who has lost his temper and let loose a tirade. We also see the spirit of C. C. Jones, his great-grandfather, at work, normally kind, wishing the best for these people. The Bishop has helped them and is ready to help them again with time, talent, and money to build their own separate institutions. He will, at times like this, allow the thought to enter his mind that his model will help to keep them lovingly in a restricted place, never to be exactly equal to white people. He is saying this: We have been decent white people who have cared for colored people, who, when educated, can build their own society with our benevolent white help.

Another missive but from the Birmingham Jail again embroiled the Bishop in controversy. It began during the Birmingham demonstrations. A group of prominent white religious leaders issued a public call for a return to law and order, on the very day Dr. King was jailed for protesting. This was the second of their calls for restraint. According to historian Jonathan Bass, Bishop Carpenter delivered the clergy letter personally to the press, to protect it, as he said, from any alterations before it was printed.

One of King's aides smuggled a copy of the April 13 article by the clergy to King in jail. So on the margins of the article and on odd scraps of paper was born "Letter from Birmingham Jail." Through the convention of alphabetizing, Carpenter's name headed the list of ministers. So he was the only one initially to receive the letter from King.

What a trick of chance: From next door to the location of a church where C. C. Jones preached incorporation of Africans into the church but never their freedom from bondage, his great-grandson C. C. J. preached his whole life a blurry racial trope.

Bass records that in the aftermath of the demonstrations, Mayor Albert Boutwell of Birmingham appointed Carpenter chair of the Group Relations Committee of the Citizens Advisory Committee—sixteen whites, fourteen blacks. A principal goal of the committee was to have blacks appointed to the all-white police force and to end segregation in public places. The Bishop invited the committee to meet at Carpenter House, the diocesan office.

Those who wish to give Carpenter a pass on "race relations" point out that this was one of the first, if not the first, efforts by cities to address this exclusion from the police forces. They do not add that Birmingham was one of the last in the nation to achieve that goal.

My favorite quote to nail my former Bishop as ... as what? Will the hackneyed phrase please step forward: "Not a part of the solution."

As Birmingham's policy of racial exclusion and intimidation of blacks tottered to a slow reduction, we hear Carpenter, the chair of the Group Relations Committee, say to the members: "Come on, fellows, let's get in here and kick the ball around a little bit, but I don't want any of you picking it up and running with it." This from a Bass interview with Doug Carpenter, the Bishop's son.

34. Beginning of the Selma Project

What was to become the Selma Inter-Religious Project (SIP) began to crystal-lize in early August 1965, out of the glorious confusion of Martin Luther King's call: "Come to Selma." Much credit goes to the Reverend Bruce Hanson of the Commission on Religion and Race of the National Council of Churches of Christ in the USA for bringing the Selma Project to fruition.

In March 1965, after the beating death in Selma of the Unitarian Univer-salist minister James Reeb, the Selma to Montgomery March, and the Klan execution on Highway 80 of the courageous housewife Viola Liuzzo, it was no longer a moral option for the faith groups to "Come to Selma," only to fade away. The term "ministry of presence" began to be used.

When the fall term began, Jonathan Daniels and Judith Upham, on leave from the Episcopal Theological Seminary in Cambridge, Massachusetts, were paid a small stipend by the Episcopal Society for Cultural and Racial Unity. Contributions for this stipend came from various faith groups and individuals. One should remember that ESCRU was neither legally nor canonically part of the Episcopal Church, but a separate tax-exempt nonprofit. It was bitterly opposed by some of our Southern bishops.

The Unitarian Universalists also wished to have a more permanent representative. The informal Episcopal presence of Jonathan Daniels, sup-ported by ESCRU, would end when he returned to seminary in Cambridge, Massachusetts.

So it was Bruce Hanson who began to pull these threads together to make a strong cord—truly inter-faith: two Jewish groups, Roman Catholics, Episcopalians, Unitarian Universalists, and some that wished to support it without being on the letterhead.

I told Bruce, when the job was offered to me, that I could hardly imagine not accepting, but I did first want to drive down to Selma to do a bit of going around with Jonathan, learning what he did and did not do.

Henri Stines and I joined up in one car, idling down the main street to avoid a speeding ticket, and were stopped anyway by a Selma city policeman. Not, fortunately, by a deputy of Sheriff Jim Clark of Dallas County. We were asked who we were and our business in Selma, then asked to follow him to the Selma police station. There we were politely asked the same things all over again and sent on our way.

We next visited the SNCC office, which, like in the setting of a novel, was across the street from Selma's police station. SNCC was on the second story of a building in the small black part of downtown; the local black funeral home was on the ground floor. SNCC workers had the perfect perch to see who came and went from police headquarters. They could not have foreseen what would happen to Jonathan Daniels.

Congress passed the Voting Rights Act; President Lyndon Johnson signed it on Friday, August 6, 1965. On the following Monday, August 9, U.S. Attorney General Nicholas Katzenbach announced he was sending federal voting registrars to nine Southern counties. On Tuesday, August 10, three federal examiners arrived in Lowndes County, where only 3.8 percent of blacks of voting age were registered. Later it was found that over 100 percent of eligible white citizens were registered, some of whom had been resting quietly in their graves except to get up to vote.

On Friday the 13th, August 1965, Jon Daniels, with Richard Morrisroe, spent the night in Selma. On Saturday, then the largest business day in any Southern rural town, SNCC was assisting young local blacks to hold a demonstration in Fort Deposit, Lowndes County.

Morrisroe, a young Catholic priest, had met Daniels at a conference in Birmingham. He was slated to be a parish priest in Chicago but knew he would personally be active in the struggle for equality. Feeling unprepared, Morrisroe wanted to experience being with black people in their heartland. He had been to Selma four months earlier for the march to Montgomery. Now he was returning to learn more. He hitched a ride to Selma with Jon. Both spent that Friday night with Daniels's second family, the Wests, at Carver Homes, a black segregated apartment complex owned by the Selma Housing Authority.

Saturday following, August 14th, the two left for Lowndes County, arriving in Fort Deposit, the county's largest town, population about 1,400.

Jon wished to be there because he had become associated with the Lowndes County SNCC workers. SNCC had been approached by black young people local to the Fort Deposit area. They wished SNCC to train them in staging a demonstration against the white merchants in Fort Deposit who imposed particularly humiliating rigmaroles on their black customers.

The young people had been inspired by following racial protests on television and in hearing firsthand of Selma's protests. Now they wanted to do their part. Jon was eager to be there to help in nonviolent training. Neither Jon nor SNCC members planned to join the demonstration. When they saw white male youths with baseball bats and firearms milling about the stores and noted how few the black kids were, they decided to join in. Scenes of this and much more can be seen in documentary films.

Morrisroe, who was getting a fast education in the Southern struggle, also joined the local young people. FBI agents were also present. Ostensibly, they were observing the newly arrived federal registrars who had set up at the Fort Deposit post office to register blacks. The loose mass of whites anticipating the youth demonstration also tried to intimidate blacks lined up to register.

The FBI agents walked to a Methodist church north of town, trying to get the SNCC/black youth group assembled there not to demonstrate, explaining that they would not protect them as they were only to observe. Older blacks, planning to register, also asked the group not to act.

The "F.B.I.s" were our enemy. Their informers were everywhere. Certainly not to protect black folk. Need I speak of Hoover. I still get the willies if agents want anything to do with me.

The group began to decide what to do.

One young woman said of the FBI: "They're trying to intimidate us—that's all they're doing." A man declared, "I don't want to scare the older people away from voter registration, but I think we need this."

According to historian Charles W. Eagles in *Outside Agitator: Jon Daniels and the Civil Rights Movement in Alabama,* in the end, the demonstrators rejected any suggestion that they cancel the protest but agreed to proceed nonviolently.

The local police arrested a number of demonstrators against segregation, including Daniels and Morrisroe, but none of the armed white males. The

FBI only watched. The prisoners were placed in an open garbage truck, taken to the jail in Hayneville, the county seat, and booked. The booking records for the whites show names garbled and incorrect. Eagles suggests that these aliases were given to allow the local prosecuting attorney fodder to prove the two planned illegal activities.

Eighteen young black males and females and two young white males were arrested. They were witnesses to what transpired. Centuries ago someone called these witnesses "spiritual athletes." This is one of the things saints are. We can't all be Albert Schweitzer or Oscar Romero, but with their witness some of us will get off our butts to serve our resplendent planet and the people, other than ourselves, who are suffering.

The SNCC workers were agitated and on high alert. Stokely Carmichael had been arrested separately from the demonstrators and had just been released from the jail in Hayneville and was en route somewhere; most of the staff thought he was searching for bail money.

The SNCC people were not happy to see my white face. Henri's Haitian hue made it easy for him to be the one to learn that Jonathan had been arrested and jailed in Hayneville. I knew I had every reason to be disrespected. SNCC was then semiofficially ousting its own white people. This was on the belief, which I endorsed, that it was a gruesome mixed message for white folks to be freeing black folks from white oppression. I later worked hard to keep the Selma Inter-Religious Project (SIP) ancillary to the black movement.

While we were in the SNCC office, this idea was firmly cemented in me when a young black woman came up right in my face to say, "Give me twenty-five cents for a Coke." I handed her two bits. I thought of all the shuffling ways in which I could have been asked in the past. I was happy to enter a new day. A little shock was a small price to pay to be trampled under the feet of a righteous young black woman.

I did see one other white person in a corner working a mimeograph machine. He had on a crisp white dress shirt, no rolled-up sleeves.

"Who's that guy?" I asked.

"Oh, he's the FBI plant. We give him all the shit work."

That was the way it was then with the FBI. A waste of time to insult agents or try to get rid of them, whether they were trying to be undercover or "out there," asking questions.

The SNCC workers gave a short tutorial when they learned we intended to go to Hayneville to see Jonathan and the other prisoners.

"Take anything metal or shiny, like a spoon, out of the car. Don't carry pocketknives. Drive with the windows rolled up. Reflections on glass will make it harder to hit you. See, if they shoot you, the first thing they'll say is, 'He come at me with somethin' shiny in his hand. I thought it was a knife. Yeah, there it is over on the ground.'"

With this advice, Henri and I set out for Hayneville, over the Pettus Bridge to "Bloody Lowndes." I was not particularly scared. My feeling was, "This is what you have to do because this is what you want to do. You don't want to do anything else."

We found the shabby little jail and knocked on a wing of it, at that time the sleeping quarters for the trusties. Two black trusties told us the sheriff was over by the courthouse eating lunch. (If you went there in later years and stood in front of the courthouse, you would see a brick storefront to your right, across the street. It had become a kind of doodad gift shop—what a comedown.)

Henri and I walked into a restaurant full of white guys, every one of whom looked up at us but as if looking was hardly worth their time. Someone told us that Sheriff Frank Ryals was over at the courthouse. I was relieved. I felt it would be harder to concoct that we had attacked the sheriff in the courthouse than jumped him in the electric atmosphere of a restaurant full of good ole boys.

On its ground floor, the courthouse has a hall in the middle, from one end to the other, offices on either side. Back in 1965, as I recall, the hall had no exterior doors and was a sort of tunnel with a dirt floor. We met Sheriff Ryals in the middle of that passage. He seemed more wary than we did.

We were focused on Jonathan because Father Stines had $200 for bail, and Jonathan had been technically working for ESCRU. For myself, I was there to see him, in jail or out, to help me take his place and also because he was one of ours. I hope you will read the account in *Outside Agitator*, which gives more twists and turns on this meeting.

Sheriff Ryals relented, giving us permission to visit Jonathan. We walked back to the jail through a deserted town. The trusties showed us to a staircase leading to second-story cells. It occurred to me years later that the black trustees did not even pat us down or had any way of knowing if it was true that the High Sheriff had OK'd the visit. Simpler days!

The cell we wanted was near the end of this narrow passage. Even before we got there, we were walking through paper plates, cups, and some of the worst-prepared Southern food I'd ever stepped on: dry cornbread, congealed and half-cooked pinto beans, dried-up baloney, and stale white bread. Few of the prisoners would eat the food, pushing it out into the corridor, where it was kicked along to the staircase as the law came and went.

Nothing had been done about the toilets overflowing; their filth remained on the floor. Water for drinking and washing was randomly turned off. Jonathan walked to the bars to greet us. The others stayed toward the back, including Morrisroe, though others say he was in another cell at the time. We told Jonathan of the money available. Jonathan said unless everyone, which included the women downstairs, were bailed out, he wasn't leaving.

At the time, and I stress at the time, I thought him too buoyant, even giddy. Or maybe playacting, but for a good cause, to keep up the spirits of the younger demonstrators. What I was thinking initially was: *You're from New Hampshire, buddy. You're in the South. Your life is on the line. This is not a game. I know this, Jonathan. I was born here.*

How blinded I was to his person. Two years later, I had only to read the first paragraph of William Schneider's record of Jon's letters and papers, *The Jon Daniels Story,* to know I had been standing, facing, through bars, the most fully realized and free human being I will ever be honored to know. Charles Eagles adds to my appreciation when he writes of another reason for Jon to surmount the harsh conditions of arrest and imprisonment. He had of his own volition chosen to leave New Hampshire to attend the Virginia Military Institute. As Eagles wrote, "Being locked in an isolated jail in bloody Lowndes appeared not to bother the seminarian, the inhumanity and cruelty experienced at V.M.I. apparently had prepared him to deal with the jail's discomforts."

I am not ashamed I misjudged him. The minutes allowed did not allow me to review my own prejudices. The squalor masked the man. His kind comes rarely.

35. *Jonathan Daniels Is Murdered*

Leaving the jail, Henri and I eased out of Hayneville, neither arrested nor followed. Henri returned to Atlanta, where John Morris and other ESCRU people discussed what to do next. I stayed in Selma that night, Thursday, August 19, at the Torch Motel, Selma's only motel for blacks. Next day, I caught up early with Mew Soong Li, of the National Council of Churches of Christ, whose work was resolving community crises. Mew and I wound up with a Unitarian minister, John Ruskin Clark, in the office of the Reverend T. Franklin Mathews, rector of St. Paul's Episcopal Church, then all-white and the nexus of Selma leaders defending at full throttle Southern-style racism.

The Reverend Mr. Clark was one of the Unitarian ministers replacing on a rotating basis the murdered Mr. Reeb. Clark was in Frank's office to assess "Where to go from here?" Mew Soong was there to see if Frank might help start a biracial group to address the crisis in Selma. In part I was there to tell Frank of the job I was taking in Selma and the Black Belt counties and what all of us might do to get Jon and the others out of jail. Frank and I knew each other well from serving together in the Episcopal diocese of Alabama.

Frank had the gift of hail-fellow-well-met good humor. Bishop Carpenter liked Frank. In clergy conferences, Carpenter allowed Frank to make quips and comments as the Bishop was presiding. Something none of the rest of us would do, either out of fear or knowledge of how inappropriate it was. These gifts helped Frank not a whit in his attempt to straddle the likes of us and the racist power brokers who sat in St. Paul's pews. His straddle leaned heavily to the right.

In Frank's office, we clumsily began to talk. The telephone rang. Frank listened, hung up, and, speaking across his desk, said, "Jonathan has been killed and so has a Catholic priest. The bodies are being brought to (the black funeral home under the SNCC office)." We all stood, held hands, and prayed. Then I said, "Frank, let's go to the funeral home for prayers for the dead."

I had another concern. A rumor from Mississippi had it that a civil rights activist shot in the back would be blasted in the front by a shotgun and turned over to the killers. All that was left was to drop a knife or pistol by the body: "Judge, he was comin' at me with a knife, or it coulda been a pistol." Clumsy defense, but with tens of thousands ready to believe. Or could it be that the vehicle transporting the bodies had been waylaid by the killers? The time to commend their souls to God and secure the bodies was at the Selma funeral home.

In Frank's office, we did not yet know that Father Morrisroe was still alive, and the ambulance was on its way to Montgomery with Daniels's body and the injured Morrisroe.

Frank reached across his desk, handing me a *Book of Common Prayer*. He said quietly, "I can't go with you." Jon had worshipped with the people of St. Paul's every Sunday he was in Selma. He spent time talking with Frank and people in the congregation—some who hated him, some who deeply respected him.

I left alone and drove to the funeral home. In seconds I learned that Jon's body and the still-living Morrisroe were on their way to a morgue and a hospital in Montgomery.

That night at the Torch Motel, I inscribed something like this in the frontispiece of that Prayer Book:

> This was given to me by Frank Mathews when we learned Jonathan Daniels had just been murdered and were incorrectly told that the bodies of Jonathan Daniels and Richard Morrisroe were coming to Selma's black funeral home. I asked him to go with me to the funeral home for prayers for the dead. He refused.

I wrote the above in a spasm of anger at a fellow priest who would not do his duty. Both St. Paul and St. Augustine of Hippo had some counsel for me: Don't let the sun set on your wrath. Wrath nursed turns to hate. I knew that, but it took about thirty-five years for me to act on their counsel. It was then that I destroyed that Prayer Book.

Now, dear reader, have I invalidated my action by writing this?

I spent the next week or so communicating with people about the memorial service to be at Brown Chapel AME Church in Selma. My wife drove down from Decatur. We stayed at the Torch. She and I worked the phones, contacting and advising people who wanted to come to a memorial service and inviting others who were suggested by the church. Many black churches in Alabama also had special memorial services to honor Jon.

Years later, two old guys, myself and John Morris, the founder and once director of ESCRU, organized a Friends of Jon Task Force to petition the Triennial Convention of the Episcopal Church to recognize Jon as a saint and martyr of the Church Universal. Our Episcopal catalogue of spiritual athletes is much easier to get into than the Roman Catholic calendar. This is new for our denomination, and we are still a bit shy to call them "saints." They are catalogued for us in a book called *Holy Women, Holy Men*.

So John Morris and friends mounted a campaign. I drafted a letter to all the delegates. It was mailed before the Convention. John set up a booth in the convention's auditorium hall, cheek to jowl with folks selling vestments, books, and incense. I, with others, operated the booth. We prevailed; it wasn't hard. We had briefed the bishops of Alabama and New Hampshire, and they presented the motion jointly. The extraordinary thing was the number of people who stopped by the booth to tell us where they were when they heard Jon had been killed and how their lives had changed from that moment.

Our Church hadn't been ordaining women for very long back then. At a later time, a middle-aged white woman stopped by to tell us her story. She was in her car when she heard the news. She was just an ordinary woman on her way to a women's prayer group at her church in Texas. She was deeply moved and glad to be going to a group that would pray with her for Jon, his family, and the nation. She immediately told her sisters in the prayer group about Jon's death, who he was, and how he came to be in Selma as a volunteer activist. She told the group that she felt moved to be more active in the cause herself.

She said to us, "Do you know what they told me?! 'You'll have to go somewhere else to do that.'" She said she wasn't angry; she felt this peace that said, "Yes, you have to go somewhere else."

"I walked out," she said. "I went to seminary. I was ordained and have a small church in Texas. We don't have many resources, but we have black, white, and Hispanic members and some gays."

She looked happy.

Mrs. McElroy once prepared this dinner for Jonathan Daniels and white friends in Selma: baked chicken and dressing, green beans, fried corn, sweet potatoes, crushed pineapple/shredded carrots/mayonnaise, lemon congealed salad, pickles, dinner rolls, banana pudding, iced tea.

Sounds nice doesn't it? No. It was brave. It was dangerous. In those days in Selma it was dangerous for blacks to invite whites into their homes. Some years after Jonathan's death, Mrs. McElroy prepared and brought the same dinner in boxes by bus from Selma to Birmingham where her son, the brilliant and celebrated organist Quentin Lane, lived, and where she, Quentin, and other friends and supporters of Jonathan enjoyed the feast and celebrated his life.

---

36. *Twelve Tons of Books and Miss Lilly Walker*

So I became the director and sole employee of the Selma Inter-Religious Project (SIP) officially on October 1, 1965. I began commuting to Selma from Aunt Wanda's in Decatur. It was a long commute, about two hundred miles.

The first thing to do, though the "firsts" tumbled thick and fast, was to address twelve tons of books sitting in a Selma trucking warehouse. A Selma Project board member had called to let me know they were a gift to the black children of Selma and surrounds from a group I will not mention. The donors from up North heard, or believed, that the black children of Selma and surrounding areas needed books. This was true. But no one asked anyone down here what kinds of books. The donated books were mostly old college textbooks. I truly believe there was not one children's storybook among them. No books about black history for children or adults.

It's a saying among charitable organizations that one never turns down an unsolicited gift that is useless. It comes in the front door with thanks and out the back with a sigh. Even so, I called the board member. Upon hearing me out he agreed they were useless. He felt it would be a great waste to truck them back even if the money to do so were available. I then had to remove them before the Selma Project had to pay for storage. Then figure out what to do with them.

The trucking warehouse was in a small business district on the other side of the Alabama River, so I crossed the Pettus Bridge with only books on my mind. I was not comfortable going there. However, the white guys at the warehouse were only cool toward me, nothing worse. The manager, it turned out, was very helpful. I climbed up a stack to see what we had. Well, I've told you, reader, what we had. I had to get the books—useless or not—out of the warehouse.

A young activist familiar with the black part of Selma volunteered to help. He knew of an old black lady who owned an abandoned house in that part of town. She agreed to let us use it for free. The Selma Project paid to have the books trucked over. The young man and I tossed and lugged books. They piled up in two rooms. The front door had no lock.

An advantage perhaps? We could hope. No luck.

I found a waste paper company in the area that would buy them for chump change if the hard covers were torn off. Every book had a hardback cover. My friend and I pulled the covers off.

In a way, I enjoyed this mindless labor. There we sat on top of the pile, ripping and chucking covers, which was not physically difficult. Nor was it humiliating. It was humbling, a virtue for someone just starting an exciting and worthwhile job by doing something dull but necessary. It was not standing face-to-face with a line of state troopers, singing, *I luv Gov–ner Wal–lace, I luv Sher–riff Cla–ark, I luv ev–ry body in my HEART!*, hoping not to get hit upside my head by a trooper who had lost patience with the singing.

It was soon clear I needed to stay over sometimes in Selma to get things done. The trip from Selma to Decatur was taking too long. My first hosts were the Fathers and Brothers of St. Edmund, who staffed a black parish in Selma and a hospital that obviously welcomed black folk. The Edmundites' mission was to serve parishes in poor areas, they performed it well in Selma, and they were fully engaged in the movement. Well, until their bishop came down on them.

I felt, however, I ought to spend my nights in the black side of town. Alonzo and Alice West, with whom Jonathan had lived, suggested if I wanted to stay nights in the black part of town, I should walk to the other end of Carver Homes to knock on the door of Miss Lilly Walker's apartment. She was very old and very brave and never missed a mass meeting at Brown Chapel AME Church.

The door was opened by a tiny, spry woman, a bit in manner and dress like my grandmother. She would be delighted to have me stay any time. No! She didn't care if she got "throwed out" of her apartment. And that was exactly what the local white masters of Carver Homes had told the renters would happen. Though I don't think it ever did.

Miss Lilly and I became instant friends. More than friends. I hadn't been there but a couple of times when she called me "my chile." I said, "Yes, ma'am" and "No, ma'am." She had only a young nephew whom she wished to coddle and leave all her furniture to when she died. He had become a great disappointment to her. I came along very timely. And I was beginning to think: "Now I have four old ladies to love, three white, one black."

"Come on up and see your room. Will you be staying the night today? What would you like for supper?"

Her living room was chock-full of overstuffed maroon furniture—really bulbous. You sort of had to twist to get by some of it. She cooked for me. All delicious, wouldn't accept a dime. Memoria comes by to remind me that all I did do to repay her was to bring her home-canned pears and fig preserves from Aunt Wanda's larder. One morning to my extreme embarrassment she brought me breakfast in bed.

The day came when I told her Betty and I were about to buy a house to be closer to Selma, and I probably wouldn't be spending as many nights at her place.

Later in our friendship, she told me that she had worked most of her life for a kind Jewish family. But now she didn't work anymore. It was this kind Jewish family who had given her the elephantine furniture. Lucky the black folk who worked for Jews in the Black Belt. They respected those who worked for them. They were no strangers to oppression.

Miss Lilly said she'd been fixin' to tell me she wanted me to have all the overstuffed furniture in the house. Her employers had given it to her over the years, and sadly her nephew wanted nothing to do with it.

That was a pickle. I had to get out of that without hurting her.

"Miss Lilly, it would be hard for me to get all of this to our new house. I don't have a truck. How 'bout I look around and if I see something else, I'll ask you if I could have it instead?"

That was fine with her.

I'd already admired—to myself—a mule-ear straight chair with what she told me was a hickory-bark bottom. The bottom was old and cracked in places. I'd never seen anything but white oak splits for this sort of straight-chair bottom.

"This, Reverend, goes back to slavery times. It was my mother's [or grandmother's; I've lost the note I made about that]. It's a baby chair, was what we called it."

She grabbed the mule-ear finials and rocked the chair because the spokes on the bottom were loose on purpose, a rocking chair with no rockers.

"How do you fix hickory strips to weave the bottom, Miss Lilly?"

"Find you a young hickory and peel the bark off. Make strips to weave. Then soak the strips in water till you can work 'em. Then weave 'em."

The beauty of a hickory-bark bottom is that because of the bark being on top of the chair bottom, it takes on a sheen like waxed mahogany. Can't find a soul who knows how to do it. So it has a white oak bottom for now, a regular weave.

Then with many a hug, Miss Lilly and I took our leave.

In the Birmingham Museum of Art, there is on display a mule-ear chair exactly like mine/Miss Lilly's. It could have been made by the same craftsperson.

37. Settling into Life in Tuscaloosa

Tearing book covers gives one time to think. Uppermost for me was where we should live. In Selma? I ruled that out. Betty could not be more supportive of my work. But she was an artist, not a foot soldier in the army of the Lord.

Unlike the shock troops of the Student Nonviolent Coordinating Committee (SNCC), the Southern Christian Leadership Conference (SCLC), and young adventurers, God bless 'em, we were older.

We didn't want to sleep on floors and be wary of being shot all the time. Overarching those considerations was that we wanted to adopt a child. That meant doing business with the Alabama Department of Pensions and Security (DPS) and a final hearing before a probate judge of our county of residence. Our chances would plummet below zero if we lived in Selma.

Living in Tuscaloosa, a university town, in a home we owned, would up the adoption chances. Betty could pursue a master's degree in art from the University of Alabama, which she eventually did, as well as getting a job managing the University Art Gallery. Selma was seventy miles from Tuscaloosa. When necessary, I could stay with Miss Lilly or the Society of St. Edmund.

Thanks to new friends in the UA art department and old friends at Canterbury, the Episcopal College Center, we were quickly directed to a house for sale, at 76 Brookhaven. Mr. Rosen, a lawyer, had lived there and was handling the sale. The development of modest houses was built in the '50s and '60s. As I walked around the yard with Mr. Rosen, I told him enough about my work to tip him off. He never missed a beat. He was on the side of the angels, and being Jewish didn't hurt either.

He unlocked the kitchen door. In we went. We had passed into the living room before he stepped into the kitchen, carrying two twitchy midget dogs. He set them on the kitchen tiles and joined us in the living room. Except for the kitchen and bathroom, the entire house was wall-to-wall brown carpet. Squatting in the living room doorway, Mr. Rosen started begging the midget dogs to join us. They exploded into a frenzy of nervous tics, twitches, and trembles, running to the passage to the living room, looking at Mr. Rosen, then shying away in confusion. Still squatting and calling, Mr. Rosen beamed at us while their tiny claws clattered tickety, tickety, tickety—to the doorway and away.

"You'll never find any dog hair in this house! They're trained never to set foot on the carpet."

What a guy, I thought. We're not going to have any trouble buying this house. We did have trouble but not from Mr. Rosen, who became our advocate. Mr. Rosen gave me an FHA (Federal Housing Authority) loan application.

We paid a deposit to him and moved in. Mr. Rosen did all the paperwork.

One of our first telephone calls to this new address came from Dun & Bradstreet. All I knew about Dun & Bradstreet was that they did money. They wanted to know about me and money. I told them I'd call them back. Being in the business of happily hopping back and forth over the Color Line, I was suspicious of any untoward requests for information.

I called John Morris for advice: "I know it has to do with money, John, but why would they call me?"

"Maybe a relative has died and left you some money."

"Nope."

John advised me to cooperate. He considered Dun & Bradstreet harmless. I cooperated. Today I believe local whites had asked D&B to call. They were building a dossier to keep me from an FHA loan.

Some time after Mr. Rosen and I shook hands, Betty and I contacted the Tuscaloosa welfare office, which operated under the Department of Pensions and Security, to let them know we wanted to adopt a baby. There were papers to fill out. The DPS wanted to know lots of information about our physical appearances and heritage: hair color, eye color, height, weight, and, I think, our parents' and grandparents' national origins, as well as other questions that made it more than clear that the DPS thought it critical to the welfare of the baby that it should grow up to look just like us.

Be advised, neither the DPS or we ever mentioned a child of a different skin color. We figured we were in enough trouble already. Our psyches didn't need any more grief or anger.

We tried to fill out the application as generically as possible without lying so as to up the percentages of getting a baby. We were told they could not tell us when—sometimes they said "soon" and sometimes "in three years."

I pushed on to getting an Alabama license plate in the Tuscaloosa Alabama state troopers' office. I didn't need to be told the waiting room would be segregated. Determined to sit in the chair closest to me, I didn't try to think of what could happen. The segregated waiting room was vacant, and the white section was closest to the entrance. Got the license plate on the same day.

October 2, 1965, was the day after I was on the payroll as director of the Selma

Inter-Religious Project. On October the second, we bought a house, signed up for a baby, and changed to Alabama license plates. Not too bad.

Memoria just floated in. "Francis, are you senile? This happened over a period of a couple of weeks!"

A hitch occurred weeks later, and it was scary. The Birmingham office of the FHA wrote, denying our application for a mortgage loan. We reapplied and were refused again. I called Mr. Rosen. He was outraged and immediately offered to go with me to Birmingham to meet the director.

Mr. Rosen told the FHA director that he considered the rejection indefensible. It took only one Walter/Rosen visit. The loan was approved. I believe I know which movers and shakers of Tuscaloosa were behind these shenanigans.

38. Selma Project's Evolving Office Space

Our first SIP office was in a garage previously housing the hearses of the Druid City Funeral Home, locating us in the black part of Tuscaloosa. It was spare but did not leak. The only amenity was a tiny partitioned space for a sink and toilet.

In the office we could see out our back windows a dilapidated shack, dirt yard, leaning outhouse, old tires, the usual junk, and lots of kids in the yard. We had not been there long before these kids started peeking in our screen door. Louise Moody brought scissors, manila paper, crayons, and coloring books, and laid them on the floor. No instructions, just offering what the marketing industry redundantly calls "a free gift."

One day the writer Paul Good sat across from me at my plywood desktop in SIP's office. Somebody up North had referred him to us for source material. When asked where he might go in central Alabama to record real poverty, I said, "Look under my desk." He did, and found two little black girls on their tummies busy with colors and coloring books. So it was that Good got to know the kids, their mother, grandmother, and grandfather. One day he heard two of the children squabbling. One said, "I'm going to tell my daddy on you!" The other one said, "He may be your daddy, but he ain't no daddy of mine." Good's time spent with the family enabled him to write the wrenching chapter, "He's No Daddy of Mine," in *The American Serfs: A Report on Poverty in the Rural South.* An older son, "Junior," once set our office ablaze. A fly speck to the wider world, he ended up in Alabama juvenile detention.

One last view from our office window of this ground-down family: At times a family member would appear and place a wooden straight chair in the yard. Then he or she would lead the grandfather, who was blind, out to the chair to sit in the sun. The grandfather carried a peach tree switch in his hand.

The grandkids played a game of running up to the chair, trying to poke their grandfather and run away without getting a lick with a switch. I watched as the old man struck out at them in anger, as the children enjoyed the game.

SIP's second office was semi-covert. A friend at the university directed us to some two-story surplus Second World War buildings belonging to the university over near Bear Bryant's football field. They had been abandoned and were to be torn down "sometime." The friend wanted to say as little as possible about the matter. We had lights, electricity, telephone hookups, and gas heaters, but no bills ever arrived. We were there for a couple of years. On reflection, we were suing the university for allowing a segregated white elementary school to use similar surplus buildings across town. But no one ever sued the university for sheltering workers for racial equality and integration. I guess no one in authority knew.

In our roomy quarters, no longer being within hailing distance of each other, we needed a telephone system for the secretary to buzz when we got a call. Feeling that the phone company offer was too pricey, I rigged up a system to refer calls on the cheap. While on a sojourn to the Gulf Coast on Mobile Point, I had salvaged hundreds of yards of telephone cable used during World War II to alert Fort Morgan if sentries saw a German submarine. Occasionally lengths of the cable would be exposed after a storm. The cable had two copper strands, so by screwing buzzers into our desks, the secretary was able to push doorbell buzzers installed on her desk to alert us to our phone calls.

Francis Walter, c. 1965, in the Selma Project office, which was located in the unused garage of a black funeral home in Tuscaloosa, Alabama. Next door was a black barbershop, which Walter "integrated" to get his haircuts.

After we left that space, when the buildings finally were being torn down, we acquired an old boarding house that helped define the looseness of association within SIP. It provided conference rooms and a kitchen; bedrooms upstairs were turned into office space or stayed as bedrooms. I stayed in one for a while.

The house had a small backyard with two large, productive fig trees. I think the house fit the need for some order and community, but also allowed staff members and associates a place to meet and plan—some staff lived in the counties they served.

We did have to evict some tenants after purchasing the house. Someone said, "I smell something bad." I tracked it down—bats in the attic. From the depth of the droppings they had been tenants for many years. I was extremely sorry to evict them. I lit sulfur candles in the attic (safely contained in large tin cans) for a few days. Bats left. Droppings I removed and put some on the azalea bushes out front. They died. Bat droppings are extremely concentrated manure. Be warned.

39. Another Way to Steal from the Poor—1965

Money danced like sugarplums before the eyes of the just and the unjust: it was the butter of President Lyndon Johnson's promise of "Guns and Butter" during the Vietnam War. The "butter" was money for "the War on Poverty." This was to pacify opponents of the "guns" who knew the overseas war siphoned off resources that could address the poverty of a large section of the American people. To give Johnson his due, the butter would go a ways to effect his New Deal ideal of social justice.

The promise of this butter had mixed effects on the organized black populations in the South newly registered to vote. I would like to address something I learned about it in the Alabama Black Belt.

The Student Nonviolent Coordinating Committee along with the blacks in Lowndes County spurned "War on Poverty" money, as did the movement folks in Greene County. Both saw going after it as a diversion from gaining political control. So those two counties were early to elect blacks to local county offices.

When I spoke with Vernon Jordan of the NAACP and Southern Regional Council in October 1965, he offered a more nuanced approach: blacks should go for small local OEO (Office of Economic Opportunity) grants. Stay away from trying to control the umbrella groups called Community Action Agencies, which called for more balanced black/white boards and more support from local (white) governing bodies.

The following parable shows why Mr. Jordan was correct. Memoria has dimmed my recollection of a climactic meeting at which I was not present but heard about. It had to do with the creation of a Community Action Agency (CAA) for Selma/Dallas County. Lots of OEO money available. Here is the gist:

The white mayor, Joseph Smitherman, slippery as an eel, so skilled at changes as to draw the respect of a chameleon, was behind the adoption of a Community Action Agency for Selma/Dallas County. He and the educated black teachers and preachers had made a common cause to create a CAA under their control.

Smitherman was not trusted by the rural blacks of Dallas County. And if he was not present at this meeting, his fingers were. Organizers in Selma/Dallas County fondly called these black folk in the county the "rurals"; in these micro politics, they were looked down on by the black teachers and preachers of Selma.

Black folk called a meeting to consider war on poverty money. On the podium sat the teachers and preachers of Selma. On the floor were the rurals who had driven in to represent their interests, which were literacy, food, healthcare, what became Head Start, housing, and jobs.

During a presentation from the podium, a rural black man rose to ask a question. A teacher or preacher said, "If you can't speak proper English, sit down." This exposed, in a few words, the social divide between the small group of educated blacks in Selma, the City Mice, and a class they looked down on and were used to bossing around, the Country Mice, out picking cotton. The rurals, it was said, got up as one and left the meeting. A moral victory, which still gives me goosebumps to recall, but they lost a chance to use Johnson's butter to address their needs and gain some control of their lives in Dallas County.

At a meeting on November 9, 1965, which I did attend, I made the following notes in my journal:

Attended big OEO meeting at Green Street Baptist Church to consider whether the group should accept the Mayor's demand that this group subsume itself to whatever plans the Mayor wants to emanate from his office. Motion to accept was tabled. Much debate, many more prosperous Negroes [I guessed] wanted to accept. From the acknowledged accurate report of the meeting between Mayor & a committee of this group I don't see how anybody could accept his proposal, as follows:

1. join his OEO group.

2. select 11 Negroes to pick 50 Negroes to join 50 whites (no mention of how whites will be picked).

3. mayor will have power to disqualify "objectionable" Negroes on this committee, also whites "like KKK members."

4. committee of 100 will only have advisory power.

5. from them 35 persons will be "selected" by the mayor to make up a group that admittedly will represent all government & social service organizations (over 20). This group of 35—the victorious City Mice and some Dallas County rural black people, now under the control of the big cat of a small town, Mayor Smitherman. I don't know when this gimmick first appeared—Athenian democracy?—will have hiring & firing power & be the incorporated group. No promises about Negroes here.

In Smitherman's proposal, some people (black?) select 11, who pick "50 Negroes" to join 50 whites. Doesn't say how the 50 whites got picked. This sounds so fair, 50/50, black and white together. Then the mayor alone can disqualify whom he will from the 100, who by this time have only advisory power. Then the squeeze narrows it down to 35, "who represent all government and social service organizations (over 20)." These are the state and county agencies set up at varying times after the Yankees got tired of Reconstruction around 1900 and went home. The twenty social agencies are all under the control of Mayor Smitherman.

I wonder whether there was ever a tiny OEO office back then unknown to Sargent Shriver, the head of it all, where politicos could get blueprints like that.

Things settled down in Selma; it got itself a Community Action Agency.

40. Retaining Control After the War

An uninitiated traveler, passing through Lowndes or other Black Belt counties in 1965, seeing tarpaper shacks with clay-and-stick chimneys and leaning outhouses, would not think the people living there contributed a penny to the area's economy. But white folks after the Surrender and Emancipation came up with many a way to squeeze a dollar here, six bits there, from the children and grandchildren of their former chattel.

For example, in Lowndes County, its cultured whites were charming and yet sometimes cruel, depending. They kept, as their patrimony, the right to impose violence, subjugation, contempt, and, at times, condescending charity on people of color. This was justified because their forebears had lost a great war that ravaged their land and property. The children of their former vassals were close at hand for retribution.

Every spring white furnish merchants extended credit for grits and white meat for hungry black folks and cotton seed for planting or, if need be, a new plow or hay for the mule.

Come fall at the gin, Sam, who could only write his name, was handed cash and a piece of paper by the gin operator, who said, "Sam, bad luck again. The bales you made was almost enough to pay off your last advance. Seein' as how long we been knowin' each other, here's $150 I'm loanin' you. Maybe you can clear your debt next year."

Sam has no way to know his "debt" is over $3,000—five times? ten times? his annual income.

A China Grove is a thick stand of Chinaberry trees that give a deep shade. In Alabama, there is at least one "China Grove Baptist Church" affording such shade for many a Sunday dinner on the grounds. Mingo—Old Miz China Grove—went to pick her some blackberries down at the far east end of her pasture. "Lord have mussy! Somebody done moved my fence over 'bout ten feet into the pasture!" She sinks into despair. Even if she had the money, no lawyer or surveyor in Wilcox County would take her case. There were no black lawyers and surveyors she'd ever heard of.

Young Mr. Rutledge will begin paying taxes on that little acre he stole, and in two shakes of a sheep's tail, no folks, white or black (for different reasons), will talk about what he did. When Miz China Grove is too old or sick to go down there, he'll fence in a bigger chunk.

Miz China Grove has long since been dead—without a will. Who would agree to write one for her? No, sir! The law says if you die intestate, your land becomes "heir land." Unless all heirs agree to sell the land for a stipulated price, it cannot be sold. At least that is what everybody believes. Her ten children and grandchildren who live all around—Mobile, Detroit, New York, even Los Angeles—have probably heard the term; all it means is they can't sell the land unless they all agree on a buyer and a price.

Even though most of her children come to the funeral, they go home, disorganized, with no idea how to do anything with the acreage of the old place. One more problem, best left alone. So they pay no taxes. On the day the land goes for auction on the block at the courthouse for nonpayment of taxes, Mr. Rutledge, by common consent of his peers, is the only bidder.

He has him a duck pond and a little huntin' lodge for him and his buddies on Miz China Grove's old place.

Loans and Land Theft: There were loans, loans, loans. A handful of well-off white men in the Black Belt held chits a'plenty backed by the debtor's acreage, plow, mule, cow, cook stove, wash pot, chicken, and so on. Another piece of devilment about loans: In her time, Aolar Young had a white man she could always go to for a little loan when things got tight. It was Judge Hamp, always had been. Her daddy went to him. But one time when things got too hard for her and her children, she owed him too much for sure for the judge to lend her anything.

So she went rappin' on old Doctor Morrisette's kitchen door. Hardly had time to snatch off her bonnet when he answered, and she asked for a loan.

"Aolar," Doctor Morrisette said, "you know damn well Judge Hamp's the one y'all borrow from. Now git off my back steps," he said with a laugh, "'fore I take a switch to you." Lucky for Miss Aolar, Dr. Morrisette didn't tell Judge Hamp on her.

Then came changing times. When in 1965, exactly one hundred years after the Surrender, President Lyndon Johnson signed the Voting Rights Bill, which he had rammed through Congress as mercilessly as (to compare the great with the little) on August 5, 1864, the federal monitor USS *Tecumseh* cinched the Naval Battle of Mobile Bay by running out her fifteen-inch gun, at that time the largest naval gun in the world, firing it directly at the already stricken ram *Tennessee*, the Confederate flagship. As Lieutenant Wharton of the *Tennessee* reported,

> A moment after a thunderous report shook us all while a blast of dense sulphurous smoke covered our port-holes, and 440 pounds of iron, impelled by sixty pounds of powder, admitted daylight through our side, where before it struck us, there had been two feet of solid wood, covered with five inches of solid iron. . . .

So fell the value of blacks to white folks from zero to a positive threat in those counties with majority-black populations.

When federally appointed registrars invaded, giving blacks the vote, the old ways of extracting value from them, even by dribs and drabs, disappeared. A large hole admitted daylight into the practices of the former rulers.

"Let's get those ungrateful niggers up North. If they get to votin' they will

230 • From Preaching to Meddling

put in judges and high sheriffs. Shoot, they'll be doin' to us what we been doin' to them."

So debts were called in; evictions began. No credit was available. Even if some poor soul had been living free in her shack on the white man's land, too old to plow and sew, but her nephew was said to have registered, off she went.

Things were at a boil in late summer 1965 in counties I knew about, Dallas, Lowndes, and Wilcox, and put the fear of God into white folks who had once lived in a stable, if grossly unfair, relationship with their black neighbors. A tent city for evictees with no relatives to help grew up on Highway 80. The Freedom Quilting Bee sold at token prices three (I recall) lots on its nine-acre site for evictees.

So those ways and worse it had been for a hundred years. Yes, exactly a hundred years when President Lyndon Johnson rammed the Voting Rights Bill through. Then the old ways of extracting wealth in dribs and drabs weren't worth it anymore.

You can sense the urgency from the Selma Inter-Religious Project's second newsletter, which I sent out in February 1966:

> Many of the religious groups joining in the Selma to Montgomery March in April 1965 united in a common program beginning in October 1965. The purpose is to continue the relationship established between these groups and the people in the civil rights movement in Selma and the Black Belt, to bring resources to bear where needed, and to serve where-ever bridges are being established between white and Negroes. While there are a dozen members, four major religious organizations act as sponsors:
>
> The National Catholic Conference for Inter-Racial Justice
> The National Council of Churches of Christ
> The Union of American Hebrew Congregations
> The Unitarian-Universalist Association
> [The Synagogue Council of America joined soon after the newsletter was mailed.]
>
> Much of my time since December has been spent working with the Wilcox Co. S.C.L.C., Inc. The biggest problem was intimidation of registered voters. It was jointly decided that one way to stop intimidation would be to send updated,

signed and witnessed accounts of intimidation to the Justice Dep't. We would demand that the Justice Dep't stop landowners and banks from interfering with persons attempting to exercise constitutional rights. We would demand an injunction to stop such persons immediately.

Everett Wenrick, an Episcopal seminary student, and I interviewed and recorded accounts from 25 families. These 25 cases were sent to the Justice Dep't through Mr. Charles Morgan, attorney for the American Civil Liberties Union in Atlanta. Mr. Morgan added these cases to others he was reporting from the Black Belt. Sixty other cases were sent directly to the Justice Dep't by the Wilcox County S.C.L.C., Inc.

Incentive was added to this as we read [what] the Justice Dep't had done in West Feliciana Parish, Louisiana, just what we were asking in Wilcox. On Jan. 2, a man from Wilcox County and I were able to make these demands directly to Attorney General Katzenbach and his aides. We were allowed to meet with him a few moments when he came to Mobile to deliver a speech. He assured us investigating agents were already in the county. He reminded us of the West Feliciana case. During his speech the mention of agents in Wilcox drew applause. There were no agents then in Wilcox.

So far there has been no federal action against this form of harassment in any Southern county except West Feliciana. Wilcox is not the only place or worst place where this is happening. An A.P. dispatch, dated Jan. 18, reports 20 Lowndes county citizens (not the Justice Dep't) have asked U.S. District Judge Frank M. Johnson Jr. to enjoin landowners in Lowndes from evicting sharecroppers because they registered to vote. Judge Johnson has ordered the Justice Dep't to be named as a party to the suit.

All our documentation, even our little interview with the Attorney General, has helped the 85 families not a whit. My own feeling now is that we could have better used our energies standing beside these people in some dramatic form of direct action. But the crisis is over; hindsight can not return to their homes those who have journeyed to already overburdened relatives in Chicago, Birmingham, Mobile, Atmore, and Pensacola.

The notices the tenant farmers received, usually by registered mail, may interest students of the Southern way of life.

Here is a reconstruction with names changed.

Beauregard, Cathcart, and Mims, Inc. Investments and Securities

Montgomery, Alabama

Willy:

Because of ill health I am turning my land over to another agent. You will move off by Jan. 15, 1966.

Sincerely yours,

Miss Addie Mae

Mr. Willy Hobbs has lived on Miss Addie Mae Cathcart's land about 25 years. He is 69 years old. Miss Cathcart is the same age. She lives in a big house in Montgomery. A few days later Mr. Hobbs receives this notice from the Camden Farmers and Confederate Bank:

Willy:

Your note for $3,106.00 is due in its entirety February 1, 1966. You must sell your two cows and pigs to pay this loan.

Mr. Charley Wallace

Loan Dep't.

Mr. Hobbs makes 400 a year. He pays what he can, about $150, on his loan every year. He has owed money to the bank as long as he can remember.

Last week I heard that Mr. Hobbs had been to the bank to inform them that he was moving to Birmingham to live with his eldest son. Mr. Charley Wallace told his friend "Uncle Billy" that since he was moving the bank would work something out about the loan. Mr. Hobbs' youngest boy will move with him. He has been active in the Movement and is a member of the first common laborers union to establish a local in the county.

Apparently, his removal to Birmingham is worth $3000.

There has been little emergency relief. "Operation Freedom" run by the Reverend Maurice McCrackin contributed food, clothing, and $1,400. Part of this went to spring the only man jailed so far for nonpayment of debts. A Negro church has bought land for one family. One newsletter reader has offered to send emergency food. Several families have been able to get FHA or conventional loans to build on Negro owned property. It is significant that the mere report of federal investigators loose [in] Wilcox has made at least two landowners change their minds about evicting tenants. This demonstrates the practical and immediate effect an injunction would have. Injunction may yet come. But deliberate speed will not bring back the families, known and unknown, who have been driven away.

Something not in this February 1966 newsletter was my impression of U.S. Attorney General Nicholas Katzenbach. In the newsletter, you read that a Wilcox County man and I were able to speak directly to the attorney general.

It went this way: We heard, but we were not informed, that he was coming directly to Wilcox County to address the eighty-five cases of eviction, physical threats, recalling of loans, and seizure of personal property for registering to vote or just going to a meeting to learn how to register. Or in some cases, getting an eviction notice for having a relative registering.

So eight-five cases from Wilcox sent to the Justice Department, and we'd not heard pea turkey back. Suddenly, the overkill. We hear, secondhand, the attorney general himself is coming to Wilcox County to address the eighty-five cases. The familiar case of nothing, nothing, nothing, nothing. Then the head himself is on the move.

If Memoria serves, Dan Harrell, the SCLC director in Wilcox, placed black folk, some of them evictees, along the highways into Wilcox to stop the A.G., saving him the trouble of a prepared speech. Nothing. Then we heard he was actually going to speak in Mobile at the Brookley Air Force Base, a federal property much safer than Wilcox.

Memoria swears it was the Reverend Dan Harrell himself who accompanied me. We barreled down to Mobile, getting to Brookley Field just before Katzenbach was to speak. Today it amazes me that Dan and I drove through the gates of this facility, as though we had some kind of invitation for the address, walked into the vast auditorium, walked backstage, right up to the A.G., who was waiting for the curtain to be drawn. Nobody stopped us. We joined two or three folks standing by Katzenbach. Informal days! Where was security?

I was struck by how he looked: perspiring, florid face, and very fidgety. But he listened to us. We said we'd been expecting him in Wilcox County. We told him of the evictions and how many. I said I had personal knowledge of twenty-five cases that had received no attention from the Justice Department.

He went onstage to tell the crowd that even as he spoke, federal agents were in Wilcox, dealing with evictions. Wild applause!

There were no federal agents in Wilcox County then. Was he lying, or was he lied to by his staff? Deluded audience—clapping in the auditorium so vigorously on hearing that feds were swarming over Wilcox as the A.G. spoke!

As far as I know, no owner in Wilcox was ever punished, however lightly, for breaking this federal law. Mr. Katzenbach was a busy man, but he was our servant. We never heard a mumbling word from him after his speech.

41. The Freedom Quilting Bee

Much of my work in 1965 involved the effort to bring relief to the black residents of Dallas, Lowndes, and Wilcox counties who were under increasing threat due to the voter registration drive. As noted earlier, forcing folks from land they had lived on for generations was a common tactic of the white power structure.

In December 1965, I was driving through Wilcox County with Everett Wenrick, an Episcopal seminarian and civil rights colleague, and took a wrong turn and ended up on a dead end at the Alabama River. As we took stock of the situation, we saw a trail that led to a cabin situated back from the road a ways. Near the cabin was a clothesline on which hung three gorgeous quilts with bold colors and intricate designs. I was struck by this beautiful handiwork and immediately wanted to meet the skilled artisan who had created them.

After opening a barbed-wire fence gap (a kind of gate) and going through, I saw a woman who looked as though she had urgent business in the back-property wood lot. I yelled and she just went on about her business, so when I got halfway up to the house, there wasn't anybody there.

Three weeks later I returned with Ella Saulsbury, a black woman from Camden, the Wilcox county seat, who was a field worker with the Wilcox

County SCLC. Ella was able to make the introduction to the quilt maker, Mrs. Ora McDaniels.

According to the author Nancy Callahan, Mrs. McDaniels said "she had run into the woods, a white man was coming to see her and she didn't know him. She was afraid so she had run away." But because she knew my black associate it was okay for us to sit down and talk. I asked her if she would be interested in selling some quilts.

Ella and I had earlier stopped at another lady's house to discuss quilt making and marketing. We learned that this woman's charge for quilts was three quilts for five dollars if the buyer supplied the cloth scraps and the thread. From what we learned from this visit, Ella and I began to develop a plan to purchase and resell quilts as a means of creating steady income for the quilt makers. We figured that we could dramatically raise the women's income by buying quilts for ten dollars each and reselling them in New York.

To develop a market, I contacted Tom Screven, a friend from Alabama who had a New York background in theater, antiques, carpet, and home furnishings. Tom was eager to help market the quilts because he was appalled by the conditions in which the poor black people of his home state lived. When I broached the idea of sending quilts to him in New York, he said to "send them up." He showed the two quilts around and found that his New York friends were intrigued by the quilts themselves but also by how they were made and by the prospect of bettering the lives of the women who made the quilts. As a result, Tom began to develop plans for a New York quilt auction and I began to explore ways to get more quilts.

I borrowed $700 from the Jonathan Daniels Memorial Fund and bought seventy quilts at $10 each and shipped them to New York. As I was going about Wilcox County meeting quilt makers and buying quilts, I began to hear that a number of women in the community of Gees Bend were particularly good quilt makers. Gees Bend was not far from Camden as the crow flies but was on the other side of the Alabama River and therefore was about fifty miles away by road (segregationist Wilcox officials had shut down the local ferry to frustrate black voter registration). In Gees Bend I met a remarkable woman named Minder Coleman who had been a community leader since Roosevelt's New Deal days. Mrs. Coleman and several other women in the area were

Handmade quilts hanging on a clothesline in Wilcox County, 1965.

highly skilled quilt makers. There was real excitement in the group when the opportunity to sell quilts in New York was raised.

Less than two months from the day that I saw the quilts on Ora McDaniels's clothesline, I had accumulated the quilts for a New York auction. Some were made specifically for shipment to New York; others were taken from trunks or directly off beds. Tom and a couple of his friends put together a brochure which provided background on the Black Belt of Alabama and the poor black families who lived there. At the same time, Tom was talking up the auction and also collecting surplus fabric from firms in New York to ship to Alabama for future quilts.

I had begun discussing ways to put together a formal organization for marketing the quilts with the Reverend Dan Harrell, who was a regional representative of the SCLC working in Wilcox County. Early on we had the idea that the quilt makers would continue to receive ten dollars each for the quilts and that any amount above that would go into the operating budget of the SCLC. It didn't take long, however, for Reverend Harrell and I to conclude that all proceeds should go to the quilters themselves by way of a formal cooperative. A large meeting was arranged for Saturday, March 26, at the Camden Antioch Baptist Church. More than sixty quilters attended. The name Freedom Quilting Bee was adopted for the new cooperative and officers were elected.

The very next evening, Sunday, March 27, the first quilt auction was held in New York and forty-two quilts were sold. The average selling price of these quilts was $27; a second auction was held on May 24 and the average price paid was $28. (They sell now for thousands of dollars.)

I had received a letter in early March from Estelle Witherspoon from the community of Alberta, which is near Gees Bend. Mrs. Witherspoon had heard of the quilting endeavor and wanted to be involved. She and her husband were the most esteemed couple in the black community and she was a fourth-generation quilter. Mrs. Witherspoon was a natural leader, became a major force in sustaining the Freedom Quilting Bee, and would eventually be involved in the American co-op movement. On April 2, 1966, the Freedom Quilting Bee was legally incorporated and Estelle Witherspoon was listed as president and Minder Coleman as vice president. In 1968, the Bee bought a small house and dedicated it as their headquarters, the Martin Luther King Sewing Center.

Update: I am jumping ahead chronologically, but as director of the Selma Project, the Freedom Quilting Bee took up most of my time. My center of interest and activity was its promotion and growth from its inception to its end, its glory days to its decline. All this is covered in Nancy Callahan's *The Freedom Quilting Bee*. She, bless her, lists almost everyone I have left out of the account. (An author, cultural historian, and mental health counselor, she died in 2020.)

Years later came a bigger than life speculator in folk art, who also took an interest in the Freedom Quilting Bee, but unlike Callahan, his interest was exploitation of the quilters. It is said he kept an enemies list, and I hope I'm on it.

However, as my grandmother used to say, "Give the devil his due." His association with quilters in the Alabama Black Belt gave their quilts and us

The first Freedom Quilting Bee house, Wilcox County, Alabama, 1966.

stunning gallery exhibitions in major museums and art galleries.

True friends of the Freedom Quilting Bee included the decorating firm Parrish and Hadley, which played a major part in propelling the Bee into the national consciousness. One day in the late '60s Mr. Hadley gave me this advice: "We are a business. The quilts have been a great success. When the interest gets to Chicago, it is over. To stay in business we have to move on to something else."

I was grateful to Mr. Hadley, who was telling me the truth. Shortly after that in one of the fashion magazines, I saw how one of the trendsetters was gluing exquisite fabrics to the walls of her dining room.

The next blow was our nation's Bicentennial, 1976. Kmart was featuring expensive quilts to celebrate our heritage. I learned their quilts were machine-quilted in Ireland. Then when Ireland got good at it, off production went to the orient. What crap! Truly it was over.

Our prominent friends gave countless hours—free of their star power to promote the quilts, among them: Stanley Selengut, Doris O'Donnel, Mrs. Parrish, Aerojet General head Sally Victor, Lee Krasner, the artist Sara Stine who came to Wilcox County with her two young children when it was dangerous, the DuPont Corporation which commissioned "the largest quilt in the world." Sears Roebuck's endless appetite for corduroy pillow shams led to corduroy scraps emerging as glorious quilts.

So the Bee peaked with the help of what one old Alabama pulpwooder called "your higher-type people." Among them were Joyce and Bob Menschel—she a Wall Street security analyst, he a partner in Goldman Sachs. They gave countless hours and sage advice on the marketing of art: how to remain sensitive to authenticity while taking into account practical matters such as uniformity of size and preventing dyes from running.

As of this writing in the new century, the Bee's Sewing Center stands empty. But, oh, we had us a time.

Jeri Richardson, a friend of ours, was studying at the University of Alabama in 1966. She asked if she might do her doctoral thesis in art education on the Freedom Quilting Bee. The Co-op Board was delighted to cooperate. Jeri asked members if they would write their life stories including why they were members of FQB. She offered a small honorarium for their participation. Though called an appendix in her *The Freedom Quilting Bee Cooperative of Alabama: An Art Education Institution*, to me it is the most gripping and historically valuable part of the thesis. I have included in my Appendix what Jeri Richardson wrote.

The FQB gets a visitor, John Hyman, from the New York foundation.

FREEDOM QUILTING BEE
GROUNDBREAKING,
March 8, 1969
10:00 AM

GROUNDBREAKING AT THE BUILDING SITE

Welcome by the Master of Ceremonies .... The Rev. Lonnie Brown
Alberta, Ala.

Flute and Drum Music .... Messrs: Ed Young, Lonny
Young, G.D. Young
Memphis, Tenn.

Freedom Songs, Folk Songs .... Mrs. Berniece Reagon
Atlanta, Ga.

Procession to Building Site

(Everyone led by the Youngs)

Lesson from Holy Scripture: Haggai 2:1-9

Song .... Tuskegee Choral Group
Tuskegee Institute, Ala.

(During the singing everyone but the choir will process around the
outline of the building.)

Dedication .... The Rev. Francis X.
Walter
Tuscaloosa, Ala.

MINISTER: "Forasmuch ... Amen."

(After these words, the President, Vice President, Manager, and Board

Above, a crowd gathered for a groundbreaking ceremony to build the FBC a new home, the Martin Luther King Sewing Center, below.

An excerpt from the March 1969 program is inset above.

42. Cahaba

One day in 1966, during my work in Selma, I needed to flip, to forget about the movement by making a little visit to the deluded innocence of my youthful Alabama. I needed to get away.

I was in Selma. I could take a break, so I'd go to Cahaba, the abandoned ruins of Alabama's first capital, just a few miles from Selma. Some ruined houses still standing—a black family apparently lived in one of them, the ruined walls of St. Luke's Episcopal Church, the outline of a Confederate prison compound where, like Andersonville, the boys in blue starved to death.

Before leaving Selma, I was over at the Wests', the family who, at great risk to themselves, gave Jonathan Daniels not a place to crash, but a home, a black mother, father, and sister. Lonzie West, the father, hearing I was going to Cahaba, asked to hitch a ride. He had some business in the area. Of course.

He joined me on the front seat, white man, black man. Worth the risk to affirm our humanity, to throw it into the teeth of anyone who disagreed.

However, Lonzie's presence postponed my escape to gentler, misinformed times. He did get out before I turned into the dirt road to Cahaba. I'd last been there when I was around sixteen years old.

Then click! I was a kid interested in "Southern history" or a man of 1859 visiting the pleasant town of Cahaba, a place of artesian springs. I'd read of one plantation house in Cahaba that was air-conditioned. The water bubbling up is around 50 degrees Fahrenheit. One planter had rigged an open-ended chamber hung with Spanish moss. Atop the chamber, which looked like a cabinet, was a funnel delivering cool water to dribble through the moss. In front of this cabinet was a fan. Amazing creativity wafting cooled air to the house. The engine propelling this nineteenth-century AC was a human being without agency or legal standing.

Refreshed, I left that time and place to return to Selma and the struggle.

43. *Me and the Bishop, Licensed in Alabama*

In 1967, Betty and I were trying to adopt, she was working on her art education master's degree, I was traveling across the Black Belt working with the Selma Inter-Religious Project, and Bishop Carpenter had still not granted my license in the diocese of Alabama. These were intertwined issues.

On January 21, I got up early and drove to Birmingham to meet with the Bishop. He was polite, but it was not a great meeting. I made notes immediately afterwards in my diary that he was ". . . wanting to know how much longer I was to be involved in my [SIP] work. Suggesting I get 'stabilized' as a curate [a lowly assistant in a parish church] somewhere for a 'few years'—not in Alabama."

Then I gave "a long recitation of my work at Bp's request: co-ops, end of movement, Black power, Black Belt white-black relations, anti-poverty maneuverings [meaning projects funded by LBJ's War on Poverty]."

The Bishop "listened intently, asked couple of intelligent questions but received this strange terminology & report as if hearing about a flying saucer landing in the Church of the Advent's meditation garden. Also . . . a bemused look. As I looked back, I recall feeling he was not only hearing of a world he didn't know but was kind of approving of it and my place in it."

I asked why he couldn't grant my license, and he cited "objection of clergy (in Alabama). Too many bosses for SIP especially Jewish & Unitarian support."

Then I raised the issue of his not answering letters from the adoption agency. And he "said he could not in conscience recommend we raise a child. That shook me. We agreed he would write agency just declining any observation about us since I was not in his jurisdiction." He never did.

I drove to Florence. News of the interview was shared with Betty and her family because they were all concerned about adoption and realized Bishop held one of the keys. Betty and I drove back to Tuscaloosa and arrived home too tired to go to the office for any mail. We were sorry to say goodbye to Ernst and Eola Seeman, our best friends in Tuscaloosa; he was leaving to become head of the University of Miami Press. Then Betty was doubly depressed when she got a "B" in a course where she expected an "A." Meanwhile, the Bishop's rejection of our adoption effort also sank in on arriving home. It was an unhappy evening.

Ernst Seeman was born in Germany into a family long in the publishing business. Eola was an Alabamian, the child of a man who had moved from the North, buying a languishing property near or on the Alabama River. It was he who threatened an old black woman that if she didn't clear out of the shack on his property—because she had registered to vote—he and his son "would take the roof off the place" the next day, which it was said they did.

To verify this report so it could be added to the depositions going to Attorney General Katzenbach I decided to drive to Eola's father's place to check it out. First, I walked two houses over from our house to tell Eola what I was going to do. This with a very heavy heart.

Eola was beautiful, imposing in her quiet and her measured movements. And almost a head taller than me. I told her what I must do, and her calm acceptance was a great relief. She even gave directions to her father's place. We managed a spontaneous hug with tears.

When I drove down a day or two later to discover what had become of the threatened woman and offer help, I met Eola's father in his vehicle on a dirt road just before the entrance to his spread. We greeted one another. The way you did it back then one finger lifted off the steering wheel in a sparse but accepting "wave" of acknowledgment.

I relaxed. He didn't know who I was. I was later told by a Selma white man (who tolerated me) that my old 190D Mercedes was recognized by black and white as I "tootled" around Dallas, Wilcox, and Lowndes counties. But Eola's father probably didn't recognize me.

I could not find a shack or an old lady. If I found her and she needed help, I could have contacted the Reverend Maurice McCrackin of Operation Freedom, which could provide food and shelter in such emergencies.

It felt a bit too dangerous to be looking around his place, so I headed home.

Next day to my shock I received a one-sentence letter from Bishop Carpenter stating that I was now a licensed priest in the diocese of Alabama. Within a day or so I learned that Bishop Claiborne in the diocese of Atlanta had also licensed John Morris. The Reverend Emmet Gribbin came over to express pleasure and invite me to celebrate Communion at his church the following Tuesday because he would be out of town. Our spirits were rather raised.

My diary entries show that over Sunday, January 29, and Monday the 30th, I drove to Camden in Wilcox County and attended the board meeting of an antipoverty group. I was appointed chairman of the committee to prepare a meeting for a Washington representative of the OEO who would explain a health program for which Wilcox and Dallas counties were eligible. I also made announcements to key persons of my being licensed. And I went cloth-buying at Hancock's, perplexing the store manager about who I was, why I was buying so much—$92.80. Then there was more office work.

In 2016 I added this:

This instant, one-line licensing of a priest not thought capable of raising a child was a mystery. All the Bishop's intransigence gone. Had there been love and respect between us during that strange meeting? I think so. On his part, was it the polite pressure from fellow Northern bishops? I suspect both; that it may have been that the old Confederacy got a cautionary word from the Yankee, victorious part of our church up North, 102 years and seven months after the Surrender. But love was there, too. Love born out of our personal struggle.

It is easier to act with love in a situation in which pressure to act lovingly is being applied. I believe he cared for me because I stood up to him. One of his old sayings, his most frequent, was, "This is not a problem. It's an opportunity."

In the middle of one of our struggles in his office, I could not resist saying, "Bishop, this is a problem, not an opportunity." Pause.

"Yes, this is a problem."

But it was our problem.

There are a couple more diary entries to share:

February 8, 1967. Celebrated my first public Eucharist in Alabama since June 1965 at Canterbury [the Episcopal Student Center]. An embarrassing yet so gratifying bunch of dear friends showed up, twenty-five in all while usually only about five come to this 5 p.m. mass. Afterward dear wife had asked everyone on over for drinks, so about everybody in the chapel came, and the celebration continued at our house. It was quite an event. The end of a long struggle on my part. John Morris was licensed in the Diocese of Atlanta at the same time.

July 8, 2016: The founder and first director of the Episcopal Society for Cultural and Racial Unity, the Rev. John Morris, operated from Atlanta. Different diocese, same problem, no permission to act as a priest. Bishop Randolph Royall Claiborne had perhaps more reason to exclude John than for Bishop Carpenter to exclude me. Claiborne's cathedral in Atlanta sponsored an elite, white, segregated school, effectively picketed by ESCRU members from all over the United States. Even a child of the Kings who wanted to attend the cathedral school was rejected.

John Morris and I had joined forces to be licensed, but I will not bore you with the politicking with clerics who indicated they would talk to (I would say "put the squeeze on") Carpenter and Claiborne, those two defenders of the embers of Dixie. And yes, they still lie glowing beneath the ashes today.

Since John and I got our licenses in two jurisdictions at about the same time, it seemed reasonable to believe that there was pressure from the North to both those prelates of the Old Confederacy.

Bishop Carpenter died in 1969. He worked on until the end. The assistant, Bishop George Murray, told me that toward the end he would go, surreptitiously, into Carpenter's office to answer correspondence. I asked him to write Alabama welfare to say neither he nor Carpenter had jurisdiction over me. He said, "No."

To wind up this licensing struggle, I was right off asked to conduct services or preach in a number of Alabama Episcopal parishes. A little bump. Bishop Carpenter at first wanted me to celebrate the Sacraments but not preach if I was at any Alabama Episcopal church. I said, "No, not acceptable."

He backed off. The local Tuscaloosa clergy said they'd be delighted if I took over a service at Bryce Hospital (for the insane). A delicious spot for me. I enjoyed letting the Bishop know I had found a home among the insane. There were maybe five or six competent Episcopalians at Bryce, and we soon began enjoying each other. The custom was for elected official folk in Alabama to dump a grandmother or great-aunt or great-uncle in Bryce at bargain prices.

A darker side of this ease of committal at Bryce was the ease by which persons who rocked the racial boat got sent to Bryce. More on that down the line.

44. Adoption and Revelation

While much was going on with the work of the Selma Project, I would like to continue the story of the adoption. Settled in our house in Tuscaloosa, we asked the Department of Pensions and Security to start the interview process for adoption as soon as possible. We were assigned "a social worker," though we later learned she had no degree in social work; she had needed a job to help put her husband through law school.

In our early meetings, we were so pleasant and followed the old adage: "The best way to get what you want is to hold your mouth right." We were disgustingly eager to please.

I will give our interrogator a false name similar to her own. Let's call her Nonie Nevers, suggesting: "You're never getting a baby from us."

She started with the basic: "Mr. Walter, what do you do?"

"I'm a priest in the Episcopal Church."

"Where do you pastor?"

"Well, I don't have a church. I work to assist poor people in the Black Belt."

By the next meeting, she had been coached by the boss, who I was pretty sure was a Tuscaloosa Episcopalian. Miss Nevers, as weeks went by, never was able to grasp the inner workings of the Episcopal Church, or pretended not to, but she had notes to help with her interviews.

"Do you work for the bishop in Alabama?"

I did not yet have my license from Bishop Carpenter, so, "No, Miss Nevers. I am answerable to the bishop of the diocese of Newark, Leland Stark. The laws of our church allow this sort of ministry."

We were frequently told by DPS that it often took three or more years to adopt. Why? "Well, we have to find a child just right for you and parents just right for the child. It can take time."

After a couple of meetings, Betty told Miss Nevers that she was going to begin a master's in art degree at the University of Alabama.

"Mrs. Walter," said Miss Nevers, "You really should not do that. The department wouldn't give a baby to a working mother."

"For heaven's sake, Miss Nevers, the minute you tell us you have a child available, I'll drop out of school."

"Well," she said, "I don't know if we can approve of your going to school."

As the meeting went on, Nonnie Nevers read the script more and more, which I was certain had come from the director.

One day Miss Nevers said, "It's time for you all to prepare a room for the baby—all the furniture, linens, diapers, changing table. Then we'll make a home visit to approve of the room."

I got a little, just a little feisty: "Miss Nevers, there's no baby in sight. You say it often takes years. Why can't you tell us there's a chance in six months or a year down the road? Then we'll fix the room and call you."

But we capitulated. Some months later, when we were talking with Miss Nevers in her office, I said, "Seeing that empty room all ready for a baby sure makes us sad." It didn't, though; it made us angry.

Then Miss Nevers said, "We have written to your bishop, Bishop Carpenter, asking if he would write a letter of recommendation for adoption, but he has not answered our request."

"Miss Nevers, I've told you already: He is not my bishop. Bishop Stark of the diocese of Newark is my bishop."

We could never engage Miss Nevers. She just sat, reading from the notes on her lap. Finally, the big day came. We never would have imagined it. In her same unflappable tone, she said (and I truly remember the exact words), "Mr. Walter, would you all ever use your child to integrate a school?"

"Miss Nevers, the child, if we get one, would have to be what? Five or six years old? If the state of Alabama hasn't integrated the school system in five years, we will be long gone from Alabama."

She was not finished. One more question to read out to us: "Mr. Walter, do you believe in nonviolence?" Never a smile nor a smirk from our young mentor. My guess was she had not the foggiest what "nonviolence" meant.

A moment of silence on my part to gather my wits and leave anger aside. "Let me ask you a question, Miss Nevers. Have you all ever given a baby to a policeman and his wife?"

"Oh, I suppose so," she said.

"How about a soldier? One ever get a child from you all?"

"Of course," she said.

"Well, they are trained to kill people and rewarded for killing people. Are you saying you'd not give us a baby if I wouldn't kill people? Miss Nevers, you probably mean 'nonviolence' as taught by Martin Luther King and the Southern Christian Leadership Conference. I believe in that form of nonviolence. I would like to follow its path completely. But so far, I can't, not completely. If someone attacked my wife and I knew they wanted to harm her, No. I would not just stand by. I would do what I could to save her. Even if I had to hurt the attacker. Other than that, I will hope to be nonviolent."

Before facing our next fruitless meeting, Betty and I had a talk. We realized that our reputation was that of wimps. We had, without a word to each other, decided not to confront, not to fight the system, not to push. Be sweet. "Hold our mouths right." Hoping to get whatever we wanted from whomever had it. Never use pressure. Be nice.

It came to me that my compatriots in the struggle in the Alabama Black Belt had tried "Nice" since 1865, had "held their mouths right," and paid for it with more oppression. We decided to go on the attack.

Yes, we were passive when asked if we had ever participated in a demonstration and similar questions. Then after the two questions read to us by Miss Nevers about using one of their babies to integrate a school, and a senseless question about nonviolence, we resolved to change tactics. Being agreeable—making no demands and answering questions politely—was not working. I realized how this equated to the "Yessuh, boss" rejected by the movement. I saw how difficult it was to be assertive when the stakes are as high as adopting a child in Alabama. The only thing we gained from being passive was that they had dropped their demand that Betty immediately discontinue her plans to enroll in the Master of Fine Arts program at the University of Alabama. It was quietly forgotten. At least as long as we remained passive, she was able to continue in school until a real baby was in the offing.

First step in the new tactic was making a call to the supervisor of the Tuscaloosa Department of Pensions and Security (DPS). I'll call her Mary Davis.

"Mrs. Davis, this is Francis Walter. My wife and I have made tactical mistakes in our efforts to adopt a child. We believed that if we cooperated, did what you wanted us to do, you would allow us to adopt a child. We were wrong, and will now go on the offensive, but continue to follow the way of Mahatma Gandhi when opposing injustice. Gandhi said he had no enemies, only opponents. You are now our opponent because it is clear that you are blocking our application to adopt. Another tactic of Gandhi was that as far as possible he informed his opponents as to what he would do to achieve his goals. We will also do that from now on."

Unused to such client behavior, Mrs. Davis was in unknown territory. She was flustered, and did not know how to respond.

DPS and Mrs. Davis chanted a mantra we had grown sick of hearing. A couple would advance some plea, and DPS would chant: "You have to understand. Our only concern is for the welfare of the child." To laugh, cry, or scream was the only honest response to that. When still in the cowed, trying-to-please role, we accepted it without reacting.

Our new strategy was as strange to us as to her. We now felt in control—at least of ourselves. We turned to others for support. I shared this turn-around with John Morris of ESCRU, who immediately offered to collaborate. John was connected to an official in the federal Health, Education, and Welfare Department, whose job it was to work with his state counterparts to determine if their state agency was in compliance with the federal executive regulations being developed from the civil rights legislation. They were familiarly known as compliance officers. If enough non-compliance was found, a cut in federal money could be made to the state agency. This was usually done with one fed sitting down with one state representative. Bargaining ensued.

John said, "Let me talk to this guy about Alabama keeping you all from getting a baby."

Time passed with no word from John. Then the telephone rang, and the caller asked if we were the Walters who were trying to adopt a baby in Alabama and being refused. "Yes, we are. Who are you?"

"You don't need to know. I think you all will be adopting a baby soon. I doubt I'll ever call you again." Click.

The next call was from the head of Tuscaloosa DPS, Mary Davis, herself. I am sorry I cannot reproduce her accent on this page. It was an Alabama, upper-middle class, plummy dialect, soothing if things were going as she wished. But now her voice, though still Southern, was agitated; still soft in tone, but with a touch of grievance, "How could you do this to us!" I heard fear in it too.

"Mr. Walter! The *New York Times* desk called us from Atlanta. They say they're going to print a story about us not letting you and Mrs. Walter have a baby! You promised, Mr. Walter, you'd let us know about anything you did!"

"Mrs. Davis, I did promise. This is the first I've heard about it, you calling me. Honestly, I have no idea who is calling you. But we talk about you all the time, everywhere. When we go to Mobile to visit my family we talk. In Birmingham, we talk."

Raising her voice Mrs. Davis said, "You did talk to the *New York Times*!"

"No I did not."

"Well, who did you talk to?"

"I told you. Everybody. Everybody but the *New York Times*."

Time passed, but not too much time compared to our interminable struggle. Being called in for more interviews stopped. Miss Nevers faded from our lives, never to read another question from her lap.

One day the phone rang. It was Mrs. Davis! Exuding fake joy, she drawled, and I remember it word for word, "Mr. Walter! A miracle has happened! You all can go anywhere in the country to adopt a child! We'll approve the paperwork. We'll stand with you in the probate judge's office, and he'll approve the adoption!"

The last wall fell. You see what going on the offensive can do? Sometimes. "Mrs. Davis, Volunteers of America in New Orleans is waiting to hear this. We visited them a long time ago and saw the facility. They know us. They've been waiting on you to approve us. They are also waiting for your file on us."

"Don't you worry about that, Mr. Walter!"

When I told Betty, we immediately began packing. After resting in a charming French Quarter hotel for the night, we went to the office of a Volunteers of America social worker—a relaxed, smiling social worker, holding our file. We asked if we could see it. No, we could not. "I'll tell you two things about it," the social worker said. "Number 1, it's the thickest file we have ever received. Number 2, if you ever thought you were being denied a baby because of your political and social beliefs, you were right."

The rest went like greased lighting. We walked from there to a room where this soon-to-be-our baby lay in a bassinet. Then we were on Highway 90 headed for Mobile, where Bobbin, her great-grandmother, held Margaret Elizabeth. Arminnie held Margaret Elizabeth, and unless Memoria fails me Mamie that same day down on Rickarby Street held Margaret Elizabeth. The mother of these Three Old Pine Trees had been named Margaret; Mamie's first child was Margaret; the second one Elizabeth. Then that Elizabeth had two daughters; the first Ann; the second called Betsy, short for Elizabeth; Betty was baptized Elizabeth.

Then on to our house in Tuscaloosa where Aunt Wanda, Betty's mother, Hilda, and I don't know who all came from Florence to Tuscaloosa to hold Margaret Elizabeth in her new home.

Miss Nevers and Mrs. Mary Davis held true to their promise to influence the probate judge of Tuscaloosa to approve the Alabama part of the adoption. After another house inspection, all went as well as bruised bureaucratic egos could allow.

On February 5, 1970, four years and thirty-five days after we told the Tuscaloosa DPS office we wanted to adopt, a judge in New Orleans signed final papers making Margaret Elizabeth our daughter. Not very long after that we adopted, from the same Tuscaloosa office, our son Andrew William Francis Walter—lickety-split.

45. Excursus on Two Bishops: No Baby

Back during the midst of the adoption struggle, every so often Miss Nevers brought up the we-wrote-your-bishop issue, and I would again attempt to make clear the role of bishops in our Communion. Again I told her that C. C. J. Carpenter was not my bishop; Leland Stark was.

"But why doesn't Reverend Carpenter just write a letter of support for you all?"

Why not, indeed? He did not like black folk or whites in Alabama challenging his views on how "the races" should get along. But I would not say that to Miss Nevers. I only shrugged.

Father J. Barry Vaughn's *Bishops, Bourbons and Big Mules: A History of the Episcopal Church in Alabama* gives a pungent example of this. It goes back to 1939, and shows Carpenter's set views that I was traducing. Vaughn writes:

> In April 1939, Martha Jane Gibson, a native of Connecticut and member of Christ Church, New Haven, who taught at Talladega College, went to St. Peter's [Talladega]. What occurred there created the paradigm that Carpenter would follow when dealing with racial incidents for the rest of his life.
>
> In a letter to the bishop, Gibson charged that St. Peter's rector, Robert C. Clingman, had told her that the church was "reserved for the use of white persons only, at all the regular service hours." Gibson stated that Clingman thus summarily excommunicated these twenty or more Negro communicants. She graciously noted, however, that she liked the priest ("a very pleasing young man") and that she believed St. Peter's vestry had intimidated him. "I felt very sorry for him, as he was evidently fighting hard to rationalize his conduct as a concern only for the welfare of the parish."
>
> Hilda Davis, the dean of women at the college had also "been denied the privilege of participating in the church services at St. Peter's Church, Talladega. The priest thought it was unlikely that the vestry would allow him to have a separate 'colored' service, but he insisted that he was willing to stand his ground … "forbidding the church to the negro completely is a little more than I can

stomach." The point was moot, however, because he believed that "the negroes will not come at all unless they can have absolute equality with the white people," a position Clingman attributed to Dr. Gibson and the philosophy of the school. Clingman says that he went personally to Gibson, to Dean Davis, and to the president of the college to explain his situation. "I was born and brought up in the South. But somehow along the way I have arrived at a viewpoint absolutely contradictory to that traditional Southern, inbred, caste-conscious attitude."

Carpenter tried to smooth things over with Gibson. He claimed that "the Episcopal Church [was] doing as much as it [could] for the Negro communicants, and I would assure you that the Negro is very much in our hearts . . . we try our best to justify St. Peter's exclusion of the Talladega College students. In some parts of the state, due to forces which you probably do not understand, it is not advisable to attempt to mix the two races, and it is not for the good of the Negro that this attempt should be made."

The tone of Carpenter's letter to Gibson was condescending. In effect, he told her that she simply did not understand the "Southern way of life." Carpenter's solution to the problem created by the visit of Gibson's students to St. Peter's was essentially the one Clingman offered—a separate service for the students at a location other than the church. He even asked if the college could "provide a room which may be used as a chapel."

During efforts to help Miss Nevers understand that Bishop Carpenter had no role in this matter, I brought the subject up with Bishop Murray to see if he could prevail on his superior to write the recommendation or say why he would not. There was a ledge outside the dining hall of our Episcopal summer camp that was just the right height to sit on while waiting for the bell to ring for a meal. That is where I found Bishop Murray, sitting alone waiting. I sat down beside him, and asked if he would ask Bishop Carpenter to write DPS to say that I was not under his jurisdiction, adding that there was no need therefore for Bishop Carpenter to reply. Murray's answer amazed me even as it revealed something of his limited understanding of Alabama white society.

"I couldn't do that," he said.

"Why not?"

"You and Betty can never have friends."

That was a shock. "Bishop, we have plenty of friends, many of them from the University Art Department faculty, and we have friends at Canterbury (the Episcopal Student Center); our neighbors, Eola and Ernst Seeman are close friends. Tell you what, we'll have a party, invite you to meet our friends."

He was silent.

Bishop Murray was a puzzle to me, I suppose because he was so different from me. He was all over the place in feelings about what to do about the undergirding of racism in this country. He was brave enough after the Daniels murder to accept an invitation to Jonathan's seminary and allow Jonathan's fellow students to engage him for several days. But he went to no observances of Jonathan's death in Alabama.

One of my minor sins is to sometimes look in another person's medicine cabinet when visiting the bathroom. Bishop Murray's office had a small private bathroom. In his medicine cabinet I saw an array of antacids. That's what he has to do to straddle the fence, I thought. This amalgam of conflicting attitudes took a toll on him. I suppose I stayed healthy by taking a toll on others.

When Bishop Carpenter banished me from St. James, Eufaula, and the diocese of Alabama, I went across the hall to tell Bishop Murray about it. His secretary and I were buddies but had never used our friendship to talk about her boss.

Years later she said to me, "Do you remember when you went in to tell Bishop Murray that Bishop Carpenter had fired you?"

"Sure."

"You're the only priest who ever made him throw up after you left his office."

For a short while I reveled in that. How long it was before I felt compassion for him I don't recall, but I did. Someone told me later—when the nation had inched into the 1980s—that Murray had remarked that I had been right "back in the day."

46. Newsletter Report of Selma Project's Activities

One of the ways SIP communicated was through a periodical newsletter intended to explain our mission and report on our activities. How well it worked is open to question. One reader told us, "I like you people, but I can't figure out what you are doing." The Selma Project was designed to support, not lead or initiate in the racial struggle. Supporters and staff were primarily white, who understood their work was to aid blacks in freeing themselves from the control and domination of white people in the Black Belt counties of Alabama. Our newsletter introduced our activities to as many people as we could reach. We also attended meetings and programs in the counties.

I vividly recall attending a meeting of the Greene County Board of Education just before black folk took over the county electoral offices (due to their majority in the population). I was the only attendee other than the board members. Lord have mercy! Black cloth covered the walls making it resemble a movie theatre. The board sat at a table in front arranged like da Vinci's *Last Supper*. In the center of the room was a camera; bright lights shone on the table. When addressing the board, a speaker would stand in a designated spot so cameras could record his voice and every facial expression. Every action of the board was recorded and stored away. "No lyin', cheatin' colored people with their communist lawyers are going to outsmart us," they seemed to be saying.

After the meeting I asked where the money came from to equip this paranoid fantasy. "Oh, that's what they used the Title I money for," said a black activist with a shrug.

Other misuses of federal Title I funds, given states to advance poor children's learning at that time in the South, were just as revolting, including an endless train of football uniforms, new gym floors, and on and on. As far as I know, no one was ever convicted of this theft of millions, an unheard of and appalling development.

I was the director of the Selma Project. From my diaries, some of my activities at the time were:

a) assisting the Cooperative League Fund of America to analyze and offer technical assistance to the sewing operation of the Freedom Quilting Bee.

b) planning a weekend work party of black and white Alabama kids (the ones who went to the youth conference in Taize, France). These young people had been given a $4,000 grant by the Episcopal Church to repair and equip a community-owned black day care center in Aliceville, Pickens County. We scrubbed floors, removed asphalt tile, scraped flaky paint, tore out walls and doors in preparation for remodeling and licensing.

c) proposal writing and fundraising assistance to three projects.

d) helping with the transition of the 1970–71 Mennonite couple leaving the Freedom Quilting Bee and the arrival of the new couple, Paul and Linda Swenger. Paul was a conscientious objector doing his alternate service under FQB and Selma Project supervision. The previous couple, Bob and Joann Plank, helped clear land, planted corn, remodeled two rooms in the sewing center for licensing as a day care center, stopped leaks in the sewing center roof, built a whole house for an incapacitated FQB neighbor, raised hogs, established good hog breeding stock in the area, cooked in the day care center kitchen, hauled people to the doctor and to the hospital, trained a local man to operate a tractor donated by the Mennonites, thus getting more than two hundred more acres in production for local people, taught Sunday school, and fixed up the house the FQB let them live in.

e) gave information to three visiting feds—two HEW people investigating the use of ESAP funds by public schools, one Justice Department man who alleged he was investigating that the University of Alabama was renting property to a segregated white "Academy" in Tuscaloosa. Since the Justice Department had received repeated complaints about this from black students at the University of Alabama for way more than a year and had done zero, it was hard to give this fresh-scrubbed person the time of day. One always wondered in these cases who was really being investigated. Everyone, I guess. Louise Moody worked on that case for the Selma Project and worked with black Tuscaloosans to expose and attack a similar arrangement in which the City Board of Education rented a school to a segregated white "Academy" operated by a Baptist Church.

f) assisted young people in the Episcopal Church in Alabama plan a

*Below and overleaf: three scrapbook pages
from the SIP newsletter of the early 1970s.*

Begun as a one-man interfaith ministry in the Black Belt after the Selma to Montgomery March, the **Selma Project** now has seven staff members serving in places all over Alabama where people are oppressed.

Our inability to stop joining up with Alabamians who are being victimized has taken us beyond the classic Civil Rights Movement/Church response from which we come.

Things began in 1965 with an Episcopal priest, Francis Walter, working with civil rights and grass roots groups in the rural Black Belt. He was sponsored by the Churches and Jewish groups that had marched in Selma. Today the seven staff members still work with these people but also with folks trying to improve the schools, with students in college and high school, and with civilians, and soldiers struggling against the military system.

The priest is still with the Project. We still get some financial help from churches. Since 1968 we have been an Alabama non-profit corporation with a board representing the groups and issues with which we deal.

Within the staff personal politics goes from radical to liberal, religious convictions from very to none. As we look back five years we don't think the Project has stopped doing anything good it was doing in 1965. We still support the same people in Selma and the Black Belt; those who once shook the nation under Martin Luther King.

We still work with the Freedom Quilting Bee Handcraft Co-op, which we helped start. We are, as always, open to minister to Whites in Alabama who begin the long inner struggle against the racism in themselves.

Now we are certainly bigger and we have changed. We have a legal program that won't stop growing.

The two lawyers and the legal researcher on the staff practice the kind of law that protects and exposes. This takes an enormous amount of time. We help protect the fundamental rights of our client groups. We attempt to expose the root inequities of a society designed to negate those rights. This is our way of teaching people things they were never taught in school.

SELMA PROJECT

P. O. BOX 2628 • TUSCALOOSA, ALA. 35401

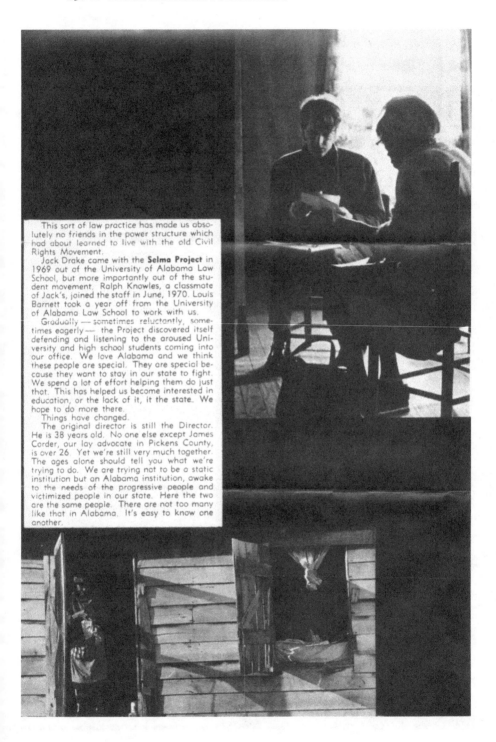

This sort of law practice has made us absolutely no friends in the power structure which had about learned to live with the old Civil Rights Movement.

Jack Drake came with the **Selma Project** in 1969 out of the University of Alabama Law School, but more importantly out of the student movement. Ralph Knowles, a classmate of Jack's, joined the staff in June, 1970. Louis Barnett took a year off from the University of Alabama Law School to work with us.

Gradually — sometimes reluctantly, sometimes eagerly — the Project discovered itself defending and listening to the aroused University and high school students coming into our office. We love Alabama and we think these people are special. They are special because they want to stay in our state to fight. We spend a lot of effort helping them do just that. This has helped us become interested in education, or the lack of it, it the state. We hope to do more there.

Things have changed.

The original director is still the Director. He is 38 years old. No one else except James Corder, our lay advocate in Pickens County, is over 26. Yet we're still very much together. The ages alone should tell you what we're trying to do. We are trying not to be a static institution but an Alabama institution, awake to the needs of the progressive people and victimized people in our state. Here the two are the same people. There are not too many like that in Alabama. It's easy to know one another.

SIP staff members, 1970–1971: Seated, Pat Page. Standing from left, Louise Moody, James Corder, Ralph Knowles, Louis Barnett, Francis Walter, Jack Drake. Not pictured: Steve Suitts, Minnie McMillan Williams, Steve Martin, Lucy Strode, Marie Daniels, Martha Jane Patton.

NEWSLETTER

For use the Newsletter is a live link with you, our supporters. We use it to tell about Alabama, not as a bizarre appendage to the USA, but as a place whose sins, though bolder, are all American. We share our problems, victories, and ways of looking at things with you. We want you to come back at us with better ideas, criticism or new thoughts. Surprisingly, a lot of you do. We have one over 80 grandmother in Berwick, Maine, who comments regularly. She told us once she usually gathers in 3rd class mail only to start the fire in her wood stove—but not our Newsletter. That sort of loyalty helps to keep us going.

Sending out the Newsletter is our way of assuming a responsibility toward those of you who make it possible for us to stay in business.

Each year the Selma Project depends more heavily on contributions from individuals. A contribution from you will help us continue our work. For tax exemption checks should be made out

"ACHR—
SELMA INTER-RELIGIOUS PROJECT"
P. O. BOX 2628
TUSCALOOSA, AL. 35401

Photographs / Nancy Redpath / William Albert Allard

"cross-cultural conference." My interest in this was that it would confront young people of different class, cultural, and racial backgrounds with—each other! Still a necessary step for us.

Jack Drake was SIP's first in-house lawyer. Again from my diaries, his activities included:

a) argued appeal before U. S. Circuit Court in Fort Worth, Texas, one of our Alabama Black Liberating Front cases.

b) represented about 250 black military people arrested at Fort McClellan in Anniston, Alabama, during a demonstration for more black-oriented entertainment on base, and a lot of other complaints. At one point during the protest the order went out to arrest everybody black on base. Charges finally were only brought against 17. The other 233 must have learned something about the Army when they were herded and penned up, then released.

c) defended a GI leader in a courts martial case at Fort McClellan. He was charged with ten things but found guilty of one.

d) continued a strategy over legal assistance to the Gulf Coast Pulpwood Association. In general, Jack was trying to see what legal remedies poor woodcutters had to help them make a decent living.

e) worked on the Forbush appeal. Jack represented Wendy Forbush, who wanted to use her own name on her Alabama driver's license, not her husband's. We lost the case in the federal district court before a three-judge panel [*Forbush v. Wallace*, 341 F. Supp. 217, 1971]. The ACLU and SIP appealed the decision. Wendy was also doing organizing among WACs and GIs at Fort McClellan.

f) spoke to students at the University of Alabama Law School orientation.

Ralph Knowles joined Jack Drake to become SIP's second in-house lawyer in 1970. Soon after, they opened their own law firm, which SIP retained. Ralph graduated fourth in his class from the University of Alabama School of Law. He was at that time serving as chairman of the Alabama Civil Liberties Union and with the ACLU's National Development Conference. At SIP Ralph worked, with no trumpets blown, to get misuse of the law overturned in cases such as the following paraphrased from the March 13, 1970, SIP newsletter:

The parents of a nineteen-year-old white girl went to the friendly probate judge of Dallas County, to report that their daughter had left their home in Mississippi and was living in Resurrection City, a commune outside Selma, Alabama. At nineteen, the girl was legally an adult in Alabama, but that was ignored. The judge ordered Sheriff Jim Clark to arrest her. Jack Drake received a letter from the commune asking for legal help for the girl.

After two days and a night in jail in Selma she was transferred to Bryce Hospital for the insane for "one month of observation," which was considered to be a legal limbo. She could not be committed, nor could she be released for one month, no matter when a diagnosis was made. Back then Bryce Hospital accepted and held a small but unknown number of young whites, whose affliction was not observing the Color Line. Resurrection City was a commune of black and white members that ignored that Color Line.

After an inconclusive diagnosis (or perhaps a political diagnosis), Ralph investigated and found that to be committed to Bryce or a mental hospital in Mississippi violated her constitutional rights. He started the wheels of the law, with its creaks and groans, turning. With short warning, Ralph learned that she was to be released at 3 p.m. on a certain day after the thirty-day examination period at Bryce ended. Her parents would drive from Mississippi at an agreed day and time to pick her up. She told Ralph that she objected to being "released" to her parents.

After discussing the situation with one of her doctors, I took these notes in my personal diary. "[He] told me that my interest in that girl's 'legal rights' was significantly like her own obsession with 'legal rights' which he saw as a mark of her own 'immaturity.' 'Immaturity' was the only diagnosis Bryce ended up giving her. Not however, a mental affliction. This meant she could not be committed for treatment, which meant Bryce could not institutionalize her. The doctor told me that 'working out her emotional relationship with her parents was much more important, more mature, than obsessing over her legal rights.' "

In the March 3, 1970, newsletter, I wrote:

I asked him if he had ever been arrested by two squad cars full of Sheriff Clark's boys. What is the "relationship" with her parents, save, at their doing a legal one? Her parents have put the states of Alabama and Mississippi, a sheriff, a probate judge, and two hospitals on their side. I am too old. I cannot imagine

Francis Walter, left, with Ralph Knowles, 1977.

the terror of feeling one's right to exist taken away by one's own mother and father. How fundamental an attack on personhood. May some of us live to be part of a new society that will acknowledge racism to be a severe psychic derangement. Then Judge Reynolds of Selma, Alabama, now a member of the Alabama Mental Health Board, can begin at Bryce Hospital his own struggle for maturity.

As a volunteer off-campus chaplain at Bryce, I was known there, and it was not unusual for me to be in the parking lot. Ralph told her that when she walked out of Bryce, she was free to do as she pleased. He added that I'd be waiting for her in the parking lot. I arrived at the designated parking lot early, to learn that her parents had already picked her up. They had been tipped off that she would be discharged an hour earlier than officially announced. Her parents brought along a policeman or sheriff's deputy for backup.

Her parents had her committed to Whitfield Hospital in Mississippi, for another evaluation period. Ralph contacted Mississippi ACLU lawyers, who agreed to follow up. We learned that Whitfield, aping Bryce, after an inconclusive evaluation, offered her a job at the hospital as an alternative to being handed over to her parents. It was something like leading discussion groups. Thinking this was preferable to being turned over to her parents, once more, and again having little choice, she accepted.

I telephoned her and asked if she would like me to come over and meet with her. She said no need. She had a "cool" plan for when she did get out to hitch rides to California. That was my first time to hear "cool" used in that way.

I telephoned again after she had accepted the job at Whitfield. The woman who answered the phone told me that she had failed to show up on her first day on the job, and nobody knew where she was.

Neither Ralph, the Mississippi ACLU lawyers, nor I had any regrets about what we had done to help her. She was out exercising her civil rights as a free adult.

Ralph became our man for mass arrests. He's been associated loosely with about 700 "clients" lately. This has been expensive. The work in Butler, Choctaw County, is about over. This is where Margaret Knott was slain. Blacks got Sheriff's deputies, clerks in some stores, an assistant school superintendent, the introduction of a little more due process in school disciplinary matters, and the dropping of most arrests for marching. Ralph has spent six days so far in Wilcox County where 429 people from 9 years of age to 85 were arrested for "illegal marching." Two of us were arrested there, Martha Jane, our Administrator, and Louise, plus many of the Freedom Quilting Bee ladies, including Mrs. Witherspoon and Mrs. McMillan, the Director and Assistant Director. Ralph is also being used in Clarke County where so far 120 students have been arrested. In Selma in November over 250 black students boycotted classes. One hopes there is some preview of the future going on here. Among the various reeling institutions in our society, public education is a walking dead man. If you are in agreement with that remark you will join us in wonder and hope as we watch black kids by the thousands in remote parts of Alabama coordinate massive, spontaneous protests. Not just protests against racism per se, but against lousy, inadequate, boring authoritarian educational systems.

Our rape case in Hale County is over. The three black defendants accused of raping a white woman got 15 years, 3 years, and no years. The black people in Hale County seem to feel that this almost represents a victory, so we can take some satisfaction from the outcome.

Pat Page was the first to join the SIP staff, recommended to me by the Reverend T. Y. Rogers, an SCLC leader in Tuscaloosa. She walked into the former hearse garage of the Druid City Funeral Home which was about to become the offices of the Selma Inter-Religious Project. The space adjoined Hiawatha Turner's barber shop, where I imagine I was the first white man to ever ease into the dignified owner's barber's chair.

Pat and I got a typewriter, plywood tables, two chairs, a Thermofax copier (later a mimeograph machine), and a street address. So here she was, efficient, uncomplaining, eager to welcome other staff as we grew. Pat stayed on after she married. We worked well together until our orbits spun apart.

Steve Martin came on our staff in September to work with poor whites and blacks who were in situations which required them to work together. His job was to help break down racism among poor people—to bring blacks and whites together who have been split and thus weakened by racism. He felt this was possible only by becoming involved in organizing work where blacks and whites had been forced together by economic necessity. He assisted poor whites and blacks during the pulpwood cutters' strike against the Masonite Corporation in Laurel, Mississippi. When the strike was over a substantial victory could be claimed. Steve said that a vital part of the strike victory was the strikers' realization that old racial myths had been used to keep them poor and dependent on big corporations for a subsistence living. It was reported that Masonite returned to the older, more fair method of computing wood and gave a raise. This represented a 40 percent increase over the prices offered before the strike. Steve accompanied James Simmons, a white woodcutter from Butler County, Alabama, and member of the Gulf Coast Pulpwood Association, to Washington, not to lobby for legislation, but to raise money for food and medicine for the strikers. James also gave a character witness for Charles Evers before an FCC hearing. Evers and other black and white people in Mississippi had been trying for years to acquire a television presence in Mississippi. The hearing was Evers's chance to defend himself against the charge that a man who would confess in an autobiography to having once been a pimp and a gambler should not own a television station.

Steve Suitts joined our staff, and it was a surprise to us all. Steve was a conscientious objector. In an unexpected turn of events, his Florence, Alabama, draft board allowed him to do his alternate service with the Selma Project.

While a student at the University of Alabama, Steve became a plaintiff in a suit against the Alabama Educational Television network. Steve and other students felt AETV was not representing the interests of poor people or minorities. The suit was only one area in which the media fell short that Steve brought to us. Because of that concern the Selma Project asked Steve to design a two-year program to establish media which would serve the community . . . for the promotion of free-thinking and free-living in its broadest area; to develop the full use of talents and abilities (of all citizens) which can be applied to media; and to make the media more fair and more responsive to the needs, interests, and problems of the local community.

Steve's lawsuit resulted in the stripping of the George Wallace-controlled AETV license by the FCC and awarding it to what is now Alabama Public Television. Steve's efforts and those of people in Birmingham also resulted in a $10,000 grant from a West Coast foundation toward developing a public radio station. Like other SIP staff members, Steve went on to a life of meritorious public service.

The Reverend James Corder was the oldest member of our staff. A Primitive Baptist preacher, he was the black civil rights leader in Pickens County, Alabama.

The federal government had created the term "lay advocate" to allow a citizen to sit with a person being interviewed by county, state, or federal operatives. This was very helpful for prosecuting violations of law. Reverend Corder recounted an interview in his role as advocate for a woman who had applied for food stamps. Asked why he was present, he responded, "I have been appointed the lay advocate for Pickens County. I'm here to represent this claimant." When he began taking notes of the interview, the clerk asked what he was doing to which he replied, "I'm making notes. I know you believe what you say is true but I have a way of checking on the rules to satisfy Mrs. ___ and myself that you are right." Corder said the official disappeared into the back of the building. After a long time she came back and said that Mrs. ____ was on the food stamp program.

Reverend Corder's evidence as a lay advocate for SIP could generate legal action via our attorneys. He began work for one year thanks to a specific foundation grant. His stipend of $3,000 enabled him to pay gas bills, make phone calls, keep his car going, and take off a little more time from farming than he could otherwise.

Reverend Corder chaired twelve evening "mass meetings" in small communities across Pickens County, requiring him to travel 474 miles. Topics at mass meetings were NAACP membership, water and sewer inequities in the city of Aliceville, availability of Selma Project free legal aid, public support of a black candidate for the Pickensville police force, the benefits of the proposed day care center, pulpwood cutters' problems, and food stamp problems. He called meetings to discuss and form a welfare rights program.

There was nothing like a rural mass meeting in white experience. A rural mass meeting was a town meeting, a counter-government, a school for courage, a forum for the silenced minority, and, perhaps best of all, a public dimension for the pursuit of mutual respect and love. Here are summaries of some mass meetings in 1971:

November 3, one member (of the Pickens County Rural Farm and Development Council, a movement group started by Reverend Corder) lost their home because of being a poll watcher. Name ____ of Rt ____ Box____ of Reform. Ordered to move by Mr. Billie McCool, Reform, Route 2.

November 4, discussed with the mother of ____ about her being forced to move because of being a poll watcher in Reform. (Later Corder helped her move.)

November 5, visited the superintendent's office of the schools of Pickens County on charging fees in elementary schools. The Selma Project subsequently sued to stop the fees, which was illegal under Alabama law. The school board asked to settle out of court and capitulated.

November 12, discussed with a group of people that the problem of paying entrance fees in elementary school is over. An important function of such victories: a legal victory over the all-white school board meant little until the community people were convinced they had won the victory. The system normally papers over the fact that it has been forced to change and mystifies the people by the patronizing device of announcing a new largesse.

It was Corder's job to help people see the truth that they won the victory on behalf of the community.

November 17, called a group meeting to discuss welfare rights and to form a Welfare Rights Program. (Right on! It is not socially productive to wheedle one welfare check on the 16th of November. That is just doing the work of the State of Alabama to make it do right.)

December 11, went to a meeting in Tuscaloosa in the Alabama Power Company auditorium, giving information to the State Advisory Committee of the U.S. Civil Rights Commission that was holding a public hearing on school desegregation in Tuscaloosa and Pickens counties. Among other things, Corder alleged that his own children attended a re-segregated school: black kids in an older building out back, white kids in the main building. Key witnesses, black

Reverend James Corder, c. 1970.

teachers in that school, failed to appear. (State Advisory Committees lacked the power to subpoena, which limited their effectiveness. The U.S. Civil Rights Commission did have the power of subpoena.)

Marie Daniels did organizing work with women in the Gulf Coast Pulpwood Association, particularly when the women—black and white—took their husbands' places on the picket line when the men were arrested. Unbelievable!

Louise Moody worked at SIP until she resigned to go back to the University of Alabama to complete an undergraduate degree. Many people in day care centers for poor people were indebted to her for dropping out of school in

1969. She and I knew each other only slightly then, and we talked about her going to New York or maybe helping out at the Selma Project. What a deal! Twenty-five dollars a week to put order into our newsletter mailing list, bundle the newsletter, and raise money through mass mailings. She had to take an evening job in a bookstore to be able to afford to accept my offer.

Association with the Selma Project was based on the egalitarian principle that staff members could put forth new growth—that is, analyze a need and develop a program. If a new program was accepted, the originator could run with it.

Louise went from stuffing envelopes to helping black people license, fund, and operate day care centers for children on welfare. She helped three centers into operation. She brought four more to the verge of opening. She drew up a "how to" manual on poor peoples' day care centers and promoted and politicked into existence the Federation of Community Controlled Centers of Alabama for Child Care.

Louise was able to remain at home to join the movement. Hers was a vigorous and well-established white family living in and around the university town. She joined in the student anti-war movement at the university, joined an early women's liberation group, and although she lost, she ran as an independent delegate to the Democratic National Convention.

In another case she worked on, black parents requested that the Wilcox County school superintendent meet with them and students to address their grievances. The superintendent rebuffed their request, so the parents followed up with a protest demanding to meet. Among other matters, they demanded that the superintendent address the egregious and illegal misuse of Title I education funds coming from the federal government. Across the South in the 1960s and '70s, this was grand theft by white-dominated school boards of funds intended only to enhance the educational opportunities for disadvantaged children. The National Education Association at that time issued a booklet exposing the then all-white Wilcox County school board as the most litigated against school board in the United States.

Thanks to Reverend Corder, Louise helped develop an application to the Alabama Department of Pensions and Security (welfare) for the operation of a day care center in Pickens County. This agency showed no interest in day care centers in Aliceville, or anywhere else, to be controlled by a black-majority board. The feds demanded that whites and blacks be on the boards, meaning at least one white face. I served on several. But on the state level, because of federal dollars coming to it, the agency was forced to pretend an interest and fake support.

While working on that, Louise became friends with Glenda Brown, a young girl helping out in our office. Glenda had been "permanently expelled" from the Tuscaloosa school system. SIP lawyer Ralph Knowles successfully represented Glenda and wrote the following:

> SIP lawyers, in furtherance of our involvement in high school student prob-
> lems, took the case of an expelled 15-year-old black student to Federal Court.
> The student, Glenda Brown, lives near our office, and just walked in one day
> having heard about us. While newly appointed Federal Judge Sam Pointer did
> not rule as broadly as hoped, he did set some valuable precedent by declaring, as
> a matter of law, that a school board cannot constitutionally expel a student for
> over one semester beyond the one in session unless there is substantial evidence
> that the student will be disruptive or violent in the future. To our knowledge,
> this is the first time a judge has found a penalty unconstitutionally severe even
> though no lack of procedural due process was found. Originally the Board
> expelled the student permanently. Because of the zone plan of desegregation in
> Tuscaloosa, she could not have gone to school anywhere in the county.

What Ralph got overturned was a vindictive ruling by the school board. Glenda had been assigned to a white high school, one of only a few students of color sent there. She did not take the physical abuse from white boys lightly. To protect herself (before metal detectors and school cops) she began taking a pocketknife to school. She once used the knife in her defense without serious consequences, and when it was discovered, she was permanently expelled from all Tuscaloosa schools. For Judge Pointer, the refusal to ever give Glenda an education was too harsh.

One day, during the time Glenda was barred from attending school, and helping out in our office, Louise and I were going to Aliceville in Pickens County to scout out some suggested locations for the proposed day care center.

SIP staff, 1970s, meeting around their conference table. Clockwise from left, unidentified woman, Jack Drake, James Corder, Francis Walter, and Steve Suitts.

Louise asked Glenda if she'd like to go along with us. We felt no unease during the drive to Aliceville most likely because Louise sat on the front seat to talk about the day care center with me, and Glenda in the back. Even a Klan member scoping us out would think Glenda was an underage maid being taken to work by a white couple.

In the small town of Aliceville we had more than one site to look at. Walking from place to place, it would have been no problem if Glenda had stayed ten paces behind us, shuffling along like a good colored person. However, Glenda was bouncing around us, joking, asking questions, having a good time, learning about day care.

As I sit writing today, it occurs to me that on that day Glenda was for the first time in her life experiencing relaxed camaraderie in public with new friends who were white. No wonder she was bouncing around.

On the other hand, that could have been threatening to many of the white folks of Aliceville. Three strangers, two white, one black: what the hell are they planning to do? Not that Aliceville was teeming with pedestrians, but we did stand out. Louise and I knew that but would never have suggested that we take precautions by asking Glenda to lag behind us.

However, a young white man began following us, making no effort to hide, but suddenly stepping behind a building when we looked back. And brassy Glenda did look back in a way that let him know she knew he was back there, but of no importance to her.

Nothing happened. We made it without incident.

How strong the wall between black and white seemed back then. But all of a sudden the wall seemed to be tumbling down. The feel of white control, white contempt and abuse with impunity, was giving way. Back then, to so many of us, it was glorious to see. Today, we know that the wall was far from gone.

Time passed. It seemed that Glenda would never be allowed back in school. And if she was, how would she be received back into the Tuscaloosa system?

One day Louise announced that she had gotten a full scholarship for Glenda to attend Verde Valley School in Sedona, Arizona. Glenda went there and graduated, but did not keep in touch. My second Faye and I, some years back, traveled out West and visited Verde Valley School. They sure remembered Glenda at Verde Valley as we did at SIP. Her loud entrance through our office door became a byword for us: "Where's them lawyers?" Glenda's going to that excellent school in that stunning locale lives in my memory, as I'm sure it does in Louise's, and makes us happy.

Sadly, after Louise left SIP, the Alabama Welfare's Aid to Dependent Children funds were cut to exclude support of day care centers for poor children. The Freedom Quilting Bee building had an approved kitchen and all the necessary space and equipment for the licensed day care center it was operating. It hung on for some weeks serving kids whose mothers worked in the quilting center but finally closed. Some parents had reverted to the old days, bringing eggs or sweet potatoes to the staff to keep their kids in day care.

Louis Barnett joined SIP in November 1970. At the time, he was a second-year University of Alabama law student. He took off a year to assist our lawyers and direct a project in which black law students at the UA law school would contribute research for significant cases being handled by the then twenty-five black lawyers in the entire state. Louis is himself black; he's from Mobile and graduated from Alabama State University in Montgomery.

At SIP Louis was supported by a designated grant. Among his many activities was trying to attract industry into Greene County while evaluating the effect that particular businesses would have on the lives of the people living there. Our criteria were how much control and profit could be wrangled for the laborers in these potential industries. Industry was not swarming to poor counties filled with unskilled labor. What often did attract them was the chance to become "minority employers." If at least 51 percent of the stockholders were black, these businesses could become eligible for federal loan guarantees. This was tricky, and sometimes the business would give or sell 51 percent of its stock to blacks. County officials entered into the bargaining. A company would use devices at its disposal to keep this 51 percent from exercising any control for a number of years. This factor could just as well attract a collapsing business as a healthy one. We suspected that it tended to attract more failing businesses which had nothing to lose. One of Louis's continuing struggles was over a business that wanted into Greene County and that would come with high recommendation from certain agencies. After long examination and thought, Louis opposed its coming to Greene. Months of negotiation were wasted. This was an unpopular position. Poor people hungry for any kind of work found it hard to understand why a firm with potential county and federal support should not be welcome. Just for starters, the company had never made a profit in its nine years of operation. Its parent company seemed to be bankrupt, and it manufactured an unusual and uncommon article that had yet to achieve the mass appeal it needed for success. Louis also helped create a MESBIC (Minority Enterprise Small Business Investment Company). This was a federal/private hybrid difficult to understand, but somehow it multiplied and guaranteed loan money. Greene was working toward getting one. Louis also assisted the probate judge on other details. He helped the county apply for the emergency employment funds made available by the federal government. He helped apply for federal funding of a county water and sewer project. He hoped to develop a trade mission between Greene County and Africa. He helped apply for a new OEO grant such as to put a black doctor in the county two days a week. He also took trips for the county commissioners to interview firms interested in locating in Greene County.

Minnie McMillan received a stipend and worked with the Freedom Quilting

Bee. Like Louis Barnett and others, she knew what to do and did it. If she needed guidance, Mrs. Witherspoon, the co-op manager, handled it. Minnie provided transportation using the FQB van, managed packaging, shipping, and other jobs that required reading and figuring skills. She was close kin to Mrs. Witherspoon.

Minnie carried off perfectly one unusual job she was given. SIP had friends in the University of Alabama psychology department, especially Dr. Raymond Fowler, chair of the department. During his tenure at the university, Dr. Fowler was active in the civil rights movement, joining the Alabama Council on Human Relations and serving as its vice president. He and his wife were part of a large contingent of white Alabamians who marched in Selma. In the 1960s he was doing research into the Minnesota Multiphasic Personality Inventory (MMPI), the mainstay of psychological testing at the time. One project was to test for bias across African American and Caucasian test takers, and he needed test results from a group of rural blacks to use in comparison. Dr. Fowler was also at the time developing how the computer could be used to grade MMPI answer sheets. His success in computer grading of the 567 questions on the MMPI proved to be quite a time-saver.

Minnie's part in this research included learning how to administer the lengthy, time-consuming test to poor, rural, and functionally illiterate subjects in the community. She lined up twenty or so subjects, arranging with each an individual time and place of testing. She gave each subject a small gratuity from the psychology department. Minnie's natural gifts of patience and sensitivity allowed her to familiarize subjects with the complicated process of test taking. She read each of the 567 questions to each subject individually, marking each answer on the answer sheet as they went along. Her excellent reading skills facilitated the subjects' comprehension of the questions. She was responsible for the security of answer sheets and getting them to the correct person for grading.

I was curious after all the data were processed, and asked one of Dr. Fowler's students what they learned from this subset of test takers. The student gave an impertinent answer: "We learned that all the haints and devilish spirits we don't hear much about anymore have congregated around Boykin, Rehoboth, and Alberta." But, thanks to Minnie, the MMPI researchers learned a whole lot more.

Martha Jane Patton was our office administrator. She kept up with the field staff, seeing that they got paid, producing the newsletter, and her formal job descriptions included "Other duties as assigned," of which there were many. She said that sometimes she wished she got out of the office more but recognized she was good at doing what someone had to do.

There were times that women in the office—Carol Self, Louise Moody, and Martha Jane—became aware of male privilege in the office, and insisted that the men help get the newsletter out, mimeographing, folding, bundling, etc. Jack in particular fumbled, miscounted, slowed down, in the hope that an exasperated woman would say, "OK, Jack, enough! I'll do it." But none ever did.

Martha Jane and Louise did do leg work visiting community day care centers. This took them one day to the Freedom Quilting Bee day care center in Wilcox County. Martha Jane, whom I telephoned in the recent years, remembered setting out wearing red vinyl high-top boots. When they arrived at the county seat, Camden was bustling with black kids and grown-ups from all over Wilcox County. The kids were yelling, "Bring your own toothbrush!" They were gathering again to address the indignities, ineptitudes, and inequalities of the just-integrated schools. "Bring your toothbrush" was the kids' way of rejoicing at being arrested, some not for the first time. And so, 427 adults and children were arrested for "demonstrating without a permit."

Martha Jane and Louise dropped day care business to go with the crowd. The leaders pled with them to add their white faces to the march. During our recent telephone call, Martha Jane told me that she expected the two of them, after a decent protest somewhere near the back of the procession, would head home. Not at all. The two were bustled to the front of the line between the two black leaders leading the march.

I don't for a minute suggest that Martha Jane and Louise were resistant or angry about this turn. It just happened.

Everyone was arrested. The vast majority were taken to an empty work camp used to house prisoners doing highway work. Martha Jane, Louise, Mrs. Estelle Witherspoon, manager of the FQB, and a few kids were put in the small county jail.

At the time, being unable to trace the confusion from a distance, I decided to call the county jail. When I reached Mrs. Witherspoon by phone at the jail, she was capably getting all the kids settled and fed.

The late Martha Jane retired as director of the Legal Aid Society of Birmingham. She was making watermelon-rind pickles when I called her a few months after her retirement.

47. Lois Deslond's Surprise Birthday Party

Lois Deslond came to the Freedom Quilting Bee as a live-in advisor recommended by one of the Sisters stationed at the Edmundites' Mission in Selma. The Sisters helped out in the FQB office doing bookkeeping.

Lois belonged to a Roman Catholic "Secular Institute" she had joined in Louisiana. Members took temporary vows of poverty, chastity, and obedience—sort of a religious Peace Corps.

Lois came with lots of ideas, realistic goals, bags and satchels of needles, thread, cloth samples, none ever exhausted, nor was she. She was closely attached to the FQB, living in Wilcox County with one of the quilters. Near the end of her work with the quilters Mrs. Witherspoon gave Lois a surprise birthday party, and here it is directly from my journal:

> Wednesday, August, 1966 —I cannot do justice to this touching expression of love. It was a deeply moving experience. About 30 people came, almost all after a full 11 or so hours picking cotton, not to mention—for the women—fixing supper and getting cleaned up. For her birthday Lois got:
>
> 1. About $11.00 in one dollar bills inside paper envelopes saying "Happy Birthday" in pencil.
> 2. Three or four cakes
> 3. A sack of raw peanuts
> 4. 2 pairs of stockings

Above, the Witherspoons' dogtrot house in Wilcox County; right, looking through the open dogtrot, a view of their outhouse.

5. A pair of pillow slips each with "His" or "Hers" on it. Lois, who was unmarried, laughed at that or rather, smiled.

6. A jar of home-preserved peaches

7. A jar of home-preserved tomatoes

8. A paper sack of muscadines [wild grapes]

9. A shoe box with half a fried chicken, a one-serving size box of "N" corn cereal, a patty of mashed lye hominy

10. A lemon meringue pie

We drank Kool-aid, ate cake, sang "Happy Birthday," "I've got that Joy, Joy, Joy down in my heart," and "This Little Light of Mine." We made the Witherspoon cabin shake.

Lois also gave parties. Her parties were occasions of teaching. Again at night after all chores were done. At one party, she asked everyone to draw something. An old woman said her drawing was of a "Hoot Owl." Lois stitched a copy of the Hoot Owl onto a quilted potholder, turning it into a popular, inexpensive, useful work of art that the FQB wholesaled hundreds of to gift shops. The Hoot Owl potholder provided people who would not, or could not, afford a quilt to have something from the FQB.

In the SIP newsletter, Leslie DeMane, a young woman from Connecticut, just out of high school, reported on her volunteer work at the Freedom Quilting Bee the previous summer.

Our first stop was going to be at the Eugene Witherspoon's where Lois DesLond the Co-op manager, was staying. The roads were in good condition and the green hills were dotted with cattle and farm houses looking very tranquil. Alberta contained two general stores, a gas station and a post office. The big moment was approaching . . . we turned into Mr. Witherspoon's dirt driveway passing cotton fields and encountering a few ruts . . . here was a wooden shack and a middle-aged Negro man sitting on the porch.

There was a green jeep parked in the yard which soon became a constant companion for me. We beeped the horn and out came a young woman that I immediately knew must be Lois. After a friendly greeting we all went into the house and met the Witherspoons. Mr. Witherspoon was a great outdoorsman and was known as a good hunter and fisherman. His personality was charming. Mrs. Witherspoon also was warm and hospitable welcoming me to her home and the community and hoping my stay would be happy.

Next a small child with bright, expressive eyes looked me over and introduced herself as Louise. She was going to be in second grade in September and I never met a more bright, alert, attentive child. Her pet name was "the company keeper" which well suited her personality. We said goodbye for now and went on our way to meet my new family, the Youngs. Callie Young was chair of the FQB Board.

The Youngs' home was about four miles away but off the highway considerably. It was thought to be a safe and happy residence for me. The first words out of Mrs. Young were, "Come on in" and they soon became a daily phrase in her vocabulary! I was greeted with open hearts, minds and loving affection which grew steadily for both the Youngs and myself as the weeks passed. Immediately I was taken to my room and there on the bed was a welcome sign in bright magic marker lettering ... Lois had thought of everything! I was shown my night pot and wash pan. There were two chests for my clothes and two windows in the room and the big double bed was covered with a gay quilt that Mrs. Young had made.

Fr. Walter spent two nights and days before leaving for Tuscaloosa. I was left to act as an assistant to Lois and help her in any small way possible. We became constant companions and I daily could feel deep love grow out of our relationship. She continually amazed and delighted me! Lois is a nun without a habit and is associated with the Order of Caritas. Her mission here was to help the ladies in the community achieve better quality in their quilts, to give assistance and criticism when needed. Her speculating eye could pick out the best quilt made by the women and she would then explain to them why it was the best. Lois introduced new stitches, taught them how to embroider, made potholders and various other items. Mainly she was their friend! She would listen to people's problems and console them. By the end of the summer when it came time for her to leave she had fulfilled her mission and much, much more.

The Freedom Quilting Bee is a cooperative formed to help the people help themselves. As days passed I realized how very important this help was to them.

I found myself in more and more wooden shacks and eating more and more cornbread and watermelon. I was learning something every day and getting to understand the way the people lived. When I first looked at those wooden shacks off the road surrounded by cotton fields I felt great pity and sorrow for all the poor people. How could they live under such primitive conditions? What will help them? I soon found the many winding roads leading to the wooden shacks taking on new meaning.

The father, usually a laborer, usually earns less than 500 dollars annually under the modern slavery of the tenant farmer. The mother might be bearing another child while her other children run ragged and the family is hungry. Why, I asked, does she have another baby? Why does she bring another into the world knowing he or she will be hungry? There isn't money to give the other children the necessary things. Things such as a medical checkup or a college education, or more important, the proper food to grow healthy and strong. Some women had nine or ten children and how they all slept in those small homes is incredible.

Until recently no one ever thought about selling a quilt to raise a bit of money. The women made quilts, many of them, but they were used to keep themselves warm. In winter they might use four or five on a bed to keep out the cold.

Children were everywhere! Surprising at first not to see many teens. The older ones, I found, move away to work in a larger city in the north, or perhaps California. The Negro population decreased 20 percent over the last ten years because there is nothing for them to do. But are they any better off living in a ghetto in Chicago, New York, or Los Angeles? Over one and a half million Negroes have left the South since 1950 and I wonder if they are better off in their new homes than in a wooden shack here? The job situation is sad here. The women can always hold the family together by taking a job as a domestic. Many of them work for six months at a time away from home doing this type of work. Some men do likewise by working in factories up north.

The children particularly touched my heart. They were so eager to learn and so starved for outside culture. I, too, was an equal attraction for them. They had probably never thought a white girl would want to come and work among them. I had their complete attention when I read a story or just talked with them. I would look into their eyes and study their faces and all the time smile while I cried inside. My thoughts were torn every time I realized how difficult a life they faced. I find myself running from this mad civilization we live in and yet the road ahead for them will be a hundred times rougher and rockier.

Hospitality never ceased to amaze me. Everything these people had they offered. Their homes became yours and I think they would have gone hungry to offer me their food. They had so little to offer yet they offered all they had. If they were poor in material wealth they were rich in love. Their kindness and generosity to be good neighbors was fantastic! I couldn't have stayed with a nicer family than the Youngs. I can picture Mrs. Young mixing up a batch of biscuits for me now. She certainly fed me well; all those good preserves and the peach cobblers did their duty! I left a few pounds heavier than when I arrived! Like all poor communities there is a basic, stable item. Here cornbread is traditional and served at all meals. There isn't a balanced diet because money is not available for them to buy the proper foods. They either grow or kill most of their food supplies and the diet is high in starch. When I saw the naked children with their fat tummies I knew what caused it.

What outside culture was open to this community? The church is their main diversion and religion is an important part of their lives. Many are Baptists and I grew accustomed to Mrs. Young's spiritual singing. Revivals and meetings of some sort or other were held at the church practically every night. Many children and grown ups have never seen a movie. Selma has two integrated theaters [not truly integrated, but having a separate section for blacks] but apparently the forty-mile distance is a bit inconvenient and they cannot afford it.

The question that needs to be answered is what will help these people? It is unfortunate and sad for me to but I feel it shall take a long time to make their lives any better. Things change so slowly and the South still moves much slower than the North. The pace is completely different and the need to step things up and move a little faster will not come overnight. They need a factory or some such thing to creates new jobs. I feel they are willing and have a desire to work. Everyone can use a steady income and this would bring some security and peace of mind as well. Many whites do not want to hire Negroes for fear of themselves or their business. There are so many complications and many minds must be improved before things can progress.

Better living conditions are needed. Better education, a broader outlook on life is a definite requirement for them all. These people must learn to overcome their fears which they all rightfully have against their neighbors, the white citizens in the community. They have been afraid in the past but they don't want to say "yes suh" to the white man anymore. . . .

I ask myself what I can do about this situation? If only there was a key made to unlock the minds of all people and free their minds of prejudices. The whole world is a mass jumble of problems and I wonder if peace of any kind shall ever come. I wonder what I have or can yet accomplish that might help?

The color of a person's skin should not matter, whether he be black, white, or yellow, he is still a human being. We all have one things in common, we are all loved by God. I thank you, Lord, and all the people of Alberta, Fr. Walter, the Youngs and Lois for all the gifts of friendship and love I received this summer.

Johnny Greene was born in Demopolis, Alabama, where my great-great-grandparents had settled, as described earlier. VISTA was founded in 1965 under the OEO as a U.S. domestic version of the Peace Corps. Johnny got to know VISTA workers in the Demopolis area, and invited black and white VISTA friends to a party at his father's hunting lodge. A hunting lodge down South is a white male gun totin', whiskey drinkin', poker playin' getaway, hunting also included.

Johnny's friends did not fit that bill. Nor did Johnny tell his father, who had pull at the courthouse, about the party beforehand. Johnny was arrested and committed to Bryce Hospital for thirty days of "observation." One outcome could have been committal for treatment of whatever was decided was his mental disease.

The staff at Bryce was impressed with Johnny's intelligence, writing, and typing skills, especially in writing grant proposals, he told us. They asked him to stay on at Bryce a while and not worry about a diagnosis.

How this happened I do not exactly recall but a Bryce official came up with a way to get Johnny out of Bryce and out of his family's hair. Johnny had a natural appeal; he was intelligent, independent, and witty, my goodness! A staff member urged Johnny to apply to Vocational Rehabilitation in Tuscaloosa. He did, became their grant writer, and was released from Bryce. After working for Voc Rehab a while, he became secretary to Ezekiel Harrison, a close relative of Margaret Knott, a black woman killed by police in a demonstration in Choctaw County, Alabama. Harrison was director of SPEAC, a project for which SIP had secured a federal grant, and Johnny came into the orbit of the Selma Project and landed in our office.

Vocational Rehab suggested that he apply for a full scholarship to Columbia University's School of Writing in New York by including an example of his writing, which he did. Columbia informed him in effect that he was a journalist and suggested that he send his application to Columbia School of Journalism, which he did. Johnny's application was accepted—full scholarship, New York City. This began an outstanding career in journalism that took him around the world until his early death.

Ave et vale, Johnny. Hail and farewell.

Below is Johnny's personal account of Margaret Knott's funeral from SIP's newsletter. He submitted it with his acceptance-winning application to Columbia.

Yesterday we left Tuscaloosa early in the morning and drove south. We crossed the river at Epes rather than Demopolis, which disappointed me in a way, and we stopped for gas. Since Martha Jane and I had not eaten we roamed through the gas station/grocery store and bought two bananas and a box of vanilla pudding and ate it whole so that we could be forming banana pudding along the way. We wondered if we should buy small things like mints and candy which we would have on us in case we were jailed.

When we crossed the Choctaw County line and headed into the "big woods" of that area, winding around the steep curves beneath the overhanging trees, we were passed by whites in pickup trucks who looked back through their rear windows at us. Some of them had guns hanging across the back windows of their trucks.

Butler seemed deserted until we found the church. Around 150–200 blacks were clustered about outside it, mostly the men, and their quiet talking from the distance of our parked car resembled a steady hum, as if a plane were about to dip down out of the beautiful sky. Across the road from the church several state troopers and national guardsmen watched from parked cars; each held a camera or a pair of binoculars, one held a walkie-talkie.

Newsmen scurried around the wide, red-dirt church yard and their camera crews followed, rapidly and seemingly in desperation.

"Are you the hippie?" a reporter asked

"I don't understand."

He laughed. "I was in the sheriff's office a while ago," he said, "and the radio in there came on and said, 'A white priest and a hippie have just crossed the county line.'"

"I guess I am then," I answered.

We waited outside the church, near the two mules, and looked at the wagon which was to hold the box. Not very many flies were around, as I had briefly imagined, because the sky was so clear, the sun so vicious, or perhaps I don't remember them now, thinking back.

Inside the church the pews were filled with older black women, dressed in their dark colors, some wearing towels over their heads or wrapped around their necks. They periodically wiped off their sweat with the towels, almost in unison. At the pulpit area the box was open and people filed past. We had to go outside the church and around to another door to walk past the box.

I did not want, initially, to look at the girl; only to close my eyes and pretend that I had seen her. I'm not exactly sure today which I did, but the vision I have is of an ordinary young woman, rather plump, with large breasts and tightly closed eyes.

Then we waited in the sun again, moving our legs once every now and then, leaning from side to side, the stereotypes of waiters: unsure and yet certain, impatient and yet hesitant to move, secure against a cement post and in the blistering sunlight, alone and together.

They signaled and we formed two lines, the women in one, the men beside them. Francis and I tried to be near Martha Jane, but our line moved up too quickly and we lost her. I looked back once and saw her wide-brimmed hat with the black velvet ribbon, and then she disappeared behind the sea of twisting heads and solemn faces. I took another hand now, a rough black one, and I looked at the old black woman with her towel wrapped about her neck and shoulders, her coin purse removed from her handbag. She held the coin purse in her free hand and let the bag hang from her arm.

It could have been Bernice or Bessie, Eloise or Elsie. It was the same hand which had cooked for me and bathed me, maybe when I was an infant it even loved me, from a distance. I wanted to squeeze it, dramatically, but I knew that it would not do any good, that it would be misunderstood or considered excessive, that holding it was enough. We began to move. Ahead of us a black girl walked on a crutch. She had only one leg. One of the marshals shouted in our direction, "They're singing 'We Shall Overcome.'" When we began to sing another marshal came towards Francis and me and asked for Rev. Walter. She told Francis that he was wanted up front, so we left our places and followed the marshal. As we moved out of the line I looked behind me, up the hill, at the long line which extended the length of the hill to the church steps. Francis and I had to run most of the way to get to the front. The line ahead of us was longer than the one behind and as we ran and walked fast, the voices rose and fell in chants of "We Shall Overcome Some Day."

Dr. Abernathy was in the mule-drawn wagon at the head of the line. Ezekiel was in the first line of five or six black men behind the wagon. He motioned Francis to walk beside him, put me on the line behind them, beside a black minister, the Rev. Rembert, who carried his certificate of ordination under his arm. As we walked and sang together, I felt that our voices, at least, atoned for some of the Black Belt's guilt.

The wagon stopped at the intersection where the girl was killed. Abernathy read from the Bible and another black minister prayed a long, sing-song prayer filled with love and compassion, understanding and devotion. The intersection was surrounded by whites who stood on the sidewalks in front of their stores and stared at us. Cameras clicked everywhere and the television crews jogged to keep up with one another, the sound men and camera men going in different directions at the same time so that the umbilical cord connecting them wrapped around them both and sent them spinning again into opposite directions. Abernathy read more scripture and then he talked, his rich, deep voice filled the square and seemed to penetrate the beautiful sky over us. No birds were flying. Everything was quiet and still beside his voice. ". . . Butler, Alabama, is darker than a thousand midnights . . ." And then he left the wagon and moved to the spot and kissed the ground where the girl was killed. We sang again, as the wagon moved away, down the final miles of the march. Now we sang the old songs of the early civil rights movement: "Ain't gonna let nobody turn me 'round, marchin' down to freedom land" and "Come by here my Lord, come by here."

At the end of the march we got into our cars and drove the twenty miles to the church. It was strange when we approached a line of cars along the highway and there was nothing but a line of houses along the road.

"This isn't it, they've just stopped to rest," I said.

"No, look," Martha Jane said, and she pointed to her right.

Through the trees and over-growth along the highway, a large building was visible on a hillside. It was surrounded by a mass of people and it seemed to pulsate, simmering in the fantastic heat and light.

It was impossible to get inside the church, but I did manage to squeeze into the rear for a few seconds. The choir sang as I slipped back outside. There were no breezes anywhere. A lighted match was no problem, the flame did not even bend. The giant black man who helped me get back outside announced in a loud voice, "Please clear the center aisle so we can get the corpse inside."

The CBS newsman and I sat on the grass, shadowed from the sun by a florist truck, and listened to the funeral on the loudspeaker in the window above our heads. Francis and Martha Jane sat down with us, and periodically one of us would go to the back of the church, to the water hydrant, for a drink. The newsman asked questions and I watched the SCLC men, all young and fresh and hand-some—black men from the early movement searching for rejuvenation of their agency, dressed in their jeans and denim jackets or overalls. "Sunshine" Owens moved around on his crutches, his wizened head and white beard glistened as often as his teeth, his staunch expression embodying the entire history of the movement and too many other hot, dusty marches behind the boxes of martyrs.

Selma Project people who had missed the march began to arrive. The whites now grew in number from the six in the march to around ten or twelve. They grouped with us, beneath the florist truck, and listened. Abernathy began his sermon.

Very few exact phrases from his speech remain with me. Perhaps it was the intensity that made each word, each pause of his voice, explode with me, compel me not to remember. His words were pained and painful, strong and sad, and his rising voice echoed the cadence of a movement many of us had thought was dead. He carried us back to the first days of the struggle and suddenly a nervous, brave girl on a counter stool in Woolworth's did not seem so very far away, so distant from the child in the box inside, who also suffered because of the color of her skin. He spoke of others who had died in the movement and as he called their names the sounds of the bullets ripping into their young bodies throbbed against my forehead and into my heart, as if each blast was the toll of a bell marking a sunset, or a sunrise, as if each blast was nail hammered into the heart of each one of us who sat on that parched earth and listened with our heads lowered and our prayers still unanswered. For me each blast was the dull strike of a clock as it rang out the end of another hour in my already too short life.

Abernathy quit speaking and no one moved. Others spoke then and there was singing. Francis was requested to come inside at some point, perhaps it was during the sermon, I can't remember anymore. But toward the end of the funeral we all somehow got inside the church and we were standing together when the piano began to play and everyone rose and took hands. We sang "We Shall Overcome" again, at the tops of our voices, and even if we had wanted to, we could not have cried. We swayed together as we sang, holding hands and trying to remember and forget at the same time . . . but the open box and the child inside would not relent. We could not forget.

After the funeral we were invited to eat in a cement-block building behind the church. Various black women rushed about dipping from aluminum tubs, putting peas on one plate, chicken or beef or bread on another. We sat around and talked with them while we ate. Francis tried to give me some of his bread but I asked one of the ladies for more and got peas and chicken again too. It was the first time that day that Martha Jane and I had eaten. She picked over her food, as always, which made me even more impatient to eat faster. And then she smiled, which is all she ever has to do.

Albert Turner, a black leader from Perry County, came in to eat. He sat with us and we asked him how he had liked being in jail. He was jailed the day before over a school incident in his county. He laughed and said, "I told them that if they couldn't find anything else to arrest me for, just to arrest me 'cause I'm black."

The food was good but occasionally the vision of a girl in a box would float before my eyes and I would want to rush for the door, gasping for air. I'm glad I didn't see them close the box, I wouldn't have been able to eat at all. Francis told me not to worry about it, that people had been eating after funerals for thousands of years, that the two things are connected. It seemed repulsive to me.

We left the church eventually and walked down the road toward the car. As we crossed the churchyard it suddenly seemed tiny, dwarfed by the line of giant trees across the road. Earlier it had seemed so huge, so encompassing, as if the entire world that I knew and loved had momentarily collected on that side, which now alone and stark on its precipice, seemed so small. The grass was bent from all the feet and cars, and paper cups and napkins were scattered about with no wind to pick them up. It was not quite sunset but a mild haze seemed to erase the fierce glints of the earlier sun. Ralph and Cheryl and Martha Jane and I paused in the road, surrounded by the still-settling dust, and looked back up to the church. Francis was coming toward us again, trying to catch up with us, and the black shape made by his clerical uniform as he jumped over the ditch, his arms outstretched, almost took him into flight. We reached our car and Francis caught up with us by coming through the woods and tall grass.

We went by Ezekiel's house and then on to another. At the second house, where the family of Margaret, the girl, lived, the young SCLC men sat around in the now coming twilight and talked. Inside I found Abernathy surrounded by a group of his lieutenants and workers. I sat on the floor. His voice was different now. It was deliberate, and the rhythm of his cadences was gone, exhausted perhaps by the intensity of his sermon. He spoke of realities of technicalities, of finances and county structure. The young men surrounding him drilled questions to the people surrounding them. Their own voices now assumed the cadence of their leader and their intensity was eager, impatient. Abernathy would clear his throat and everyone would hush. Then he might ask a question or calm one of the younger men. But every word was spoken with respect for his listener, his audience. His presence of mind, his consciousness of the total situation, and his command in the midst of the drama were thrilling to watch. I wondered again, as I had years ago during some of Dr. King's dark hours, if Abernathy had not really been one of the driving forces, perhaps the real power, behind SCLC's determination.

It was odd when we returned last night. I got out of the car and saw a white man coming along the sidewalk. I felt my muscles grow tight as I tried to shrink within my frame, away from his fury. I had done that, all day, when I had faced the glares and angry faces of the whites of Choctaw County. Then I caught myself. "This is what happens to blacks every day," I told myself. And then I was sad, actually it was then that I really felt I might cry after all, because I realized how very different two worlds can—two geographical worlds separated by one river and some trees and sixty or seventy miles. And I was mad because I was no longer in Butler. And I was anxious to march again.

---

48. Day Care

The SIP newsletter of April 1971 reported on day care centers:

The Jon Daniels Center across the Pettus Bridge in what is called East Selma. Alice West, Jon's Selma foster mother, was the primary organizer.

The new Freedom Quilting Bee Center in Alberta. The FQB stainless-steel kitchen equipment met day care licensing standards.

The Gees Bend Center, also licensed.

The King Memorial Center in Orrville, not far from Selma, not yet licensed. All of these had majority-black boards.

The newsletter continued in a hopeful vein as shown in this reprint:

The Probate Judge of Greene County has requested our help to open five centers in Greene County. County owned buildings are available. These operating and projected centers number ten. We are now hearing of other communities who want centers.

Centers in rural Alabama can operate on the $50 per month available for Aid to Dependent Children. This sum coupled with the $.75 a day food subsidy and the kitchen equipment subsidy will pay salaries and even provide transportation if licensable structures can be provided through other sources.

Licensing is extremely difficult; a morass of overlapping bureaucracies control the process. Some state officials still lie and create delays that turn each licensing process into a hostile proceeding directed against adversaries rather than a helpful dealing with public servants. We have experienced state social workers interviewing mothers, singly attempting to discourage them from indicating interest in day care centers.

Congress and the President are going to do something about day care, pressure is too great to avoid some sort of federal support. The availability of even the smallest amounts of capital will make the operation and control of day care centers possible in Black and white poor communities. It is just there that the newly abandoned public school buildings are standing ready for use. Who will control these institutions? We now see that we must:

A. Create a league of poor peoples' day care centers for mutual support and bargaining power.

B. Provide curriculum assistance by compelling the universities to assist these groups rather than operating irrelevant university-located centers for the benefit of graduate students bound for a life of teaching teachers to teach.

C. Provide curriculum training ourselves.

D. Locate a person skilled in pre-school education. Money would have to come with this person from elsewhere. This person would coordinate our day care work.

E. Operate a center ourselves to serve as a model for the poor peoples' centers we work with.

F. Continue to open new centers operating on the present shoestring budgets. The more people who are into operating centers before legislation provides new funds, the more real needs will be met as business and professional education follow the money in. We may be unable to realize but a fraction of these goals but that is where we want to go in day care.

If only 10 percent of that had been done! The newsletter that month also reported this:

Correction! Someone in the Alabama State Department of Pensions and Securities read our last (#38) Newsletter and asked us to retract what, indeed, was an error. We said that the Jon Daniels Day Care Center in Selma received $32 a month for each child on Aid to Dependent Children welfare payments. Jon Daniels Center really gets $40 a month from the welfare per ADC child. We apologize to the Department of Pensions and Securities for this careless mistake. The maximum payment in Alabama is $50. Since we have opened up this dialogue with the welfare department we'd like to invite our readers there to submit an article to the Newsletter explaining why Jon Daniels Center and the center in Boykin only receive $40 instead of the allowed $50. The new center at the FQB got $50 after the staff rejected an offer of $40, and indicated it possessed some pirated leaves out of the guidelines manual used by Alabama Welfare Department.

And then, and then it all came crashing down. Not thirty-two, forty, or fifty dollars. No dollars at all. Those day care centers for poor kids closed. The butter melted from President Johnson's "GUNS AND BUTTER" promise. The guns were further augmented by our federal government as the butter disappeared.

Today, even well-off parents cannot afford day care.

---

49. Comparing the Small to the Great

With the reader's indulgence, I will compare the small to the great—the Selma Inter-Religious Project and what we did, with the acts of King Abijam, in the First Book of Kings 15:7, and all that he did. "The rest of the acts of Abijam, . . . are they not written in the Book of the Annals of the Kings of Israel?"

This formula appears each time the biblical writer of the First Book of Kings rounds off all he wishes to say of a King of Israel. This both amuses and saddens me.

How circumscribed we are by our time and space. The writer penned these words on fragile papyrus or vellum although he wanted us to know that the Annals of the Kings of Israel were secure, permanent, locked in the royal library. He felt we could check whenever we wanted to. The Annals of the Kings of Israel have been dust for 2,500 years. Yet, his words, which seemed to him perishable, live for having been copied over and over.

Similarly, the Selma Project lives on in its fifty-odd newsletters, Nancy Callahan's *The Freedom Quilting Bee*, Charles Eagles's *Outside Agitator*, the documentary *With Fingers of Love* about the Freedom Quilting Bee, Vaughn Barry's *Bishops, Bourbons and Big Mules*, William Schneider's *The Jon Daniels Story with His Letters and Papers*, and Paul Good's *The American Serfs*.

I wrote a goodbye to SIP newsletter readers in December 1972. It was wordy, took up all of the last-ever newsletter. Today, I am pleased with parts of it:

> "There is a zeal of love and a zeal of bitterness . . ." A co-religionist, Benedict, wrote that 1,400 years ago . . . There is plenty of bitterness available, easy to find in Alabama. For starters, when one deals with people of one's own class, race, and station, only to see them allowing opportunities, money, and resources draining away out of cowardice and the preservation petty privilege—that is a source of bitterness. Bitterness is used as a substitute for Love. Either will fuel the soul's engine . . . But there is Benedict's terrible warning. "There is the zeal of bitterness which leads to perdition, the zeal of Love which leads to God . . ."

Then there is the remark that Stokely Carmichael made to me in 1966, "Hate is just as effective a tool for social justice as Love."

I cannot agree with Stokely. An intuition deep inside, to which I am now obedient, says "Love is primal. Without Love, in the end nothing."

A reunion of Southern Inter-Religious Project staffers and board members, Sewanee Inn, Sewanee, Tennessee, June 25, 2015: Front row, from left, Martha Jane Patton, Faye Walter, Francis Walter, Cheryl Knowles (SIP board member), Ralph Knowles, Millie McNeil (Martin's spouse); back row, Steve Martin, Steve Suitts, James Jackson (Cheryl Knowles's spouse), Allen Tullos (SIP volunteer), Candace Waid (SIP volunteer). Not pictured, Sandra Lawle and Duna Norton. (Photo by Leslie Lytle, Sewanee Mountain Messenger*)*

Acknowledgments

I wrote this book over many years, and I just wrote it out in longhand because I don't type. Kathy Hammond typed some of it; Faye Walter did the rest and supported me and the process throughout. Steve Suitts contributed the foreword, for which I am grateful. He also proofread the manuscript and made suggestions to improve it, as did Joel Sanders. Susan Ashmore helped procure and identify the included photographs. I also appreciate that NewSouth Books took on this project and worked hard on it over the course of several years. Thanks to the NewSouth staff, including Suzanne La Rosa and Randall Williams, Lisa Harrison, Lisa Emerson, Matthew Byrne, Beth Marino, Kelly Snyder, and Samantha Stanley. And Memoria, imp though she is, played the greatest hand.

— F. X. W.

Appendix 1: Letters

March 15, 1957, Bishop Charles C. J. Carpenter to Francis Walter:

Dear Francis:

I am very proud of you and of the fine record that you are making up there at the Seminary, and I am particularly proud that you have been recommended by the Dean and Faculty of the Sewanee Seminary to be a Fellow and Tutor at General Seminary next year.

I feel that this is an unusual opportunity for you, and want you to know that if you want to take advantage of it you will have my complete approval, and backing.

While we need men very badly in the work in the Diocese, we also want our men to be as well prepared as possible, and I feel that this offers you a splendid opportunity for preparation which will enable you to be more effective when your active ministry begins.

Let me know what you decide to do about this, and know that I am standing by to help.

May God bless and guide you always.

Sincerely,

C C J Carpenter

February 19, 1958, Bobbin to Francis Walter (sent after my ordination to the diaconate and my return to New York)

My precious Boy,

Your good letter gave me somewhat of a lift. I know you are right in all you say but I seem not to be able to [stop] worry[ing] about how things are going to shape up. My biggest worry is about David, as you well know. We will let it rest there now, until something more definite shapes up.

I went to town yesterday as I had to see Dr. Miller about my feet, which have been needing his care for some time. The weather was hot so I did not think I would be able to take more cold. While there I went on a hunt for some shoes like I wear at home. These I wear now have both my big toes out through the holes. Well, I walked miles going into several stores, even to Sears and looked through the new catalogue but shoes with heels are not made any more—everything has those flat heels. Having a tendency to fall backwards all the time they throw me worse. So I shall just wear my air conditioned ones longer.

Now this a.m. it is cold and we are promised a drop to 34°–28° tonight with freezes. I was looking at the big crop of loquats that are on the tree and thinking that I would be able to give lots of them to Edna, who once told me she was so fond of them. I hope a freeze is not going to ruin them.

As I went to town I saw several bushes of azaleas in full bloom. The big bush in Mrs. Pearce's yard is lovely. Do you have even a crocus?

I do hope your one day visit to us will materialize. That I can look forward to.

I am going to be extravagant and use another 10¢ stamp. I got David to get me stamps. He got ten cent stamps thinking they were what I used, and he refused to go to the P.O. for me yesterday to exchange them, so I will have to use another one this morning.

When I found out about D's bad report card I said then that he needed to be coached and he said he would not have a coach. That was his position about it. He says that his English work that he failed in is not in the book, but while he had his arm broken and could not write, The teacher would put the work on the blackboard and the pupils would write the answers. I don't understand it but he says he has now learned about past participles, etc. and is bringing his F up. I hope he is right.

I love you my darling

Your Bobbin

February 19, 1958, Bobbin to Francis Walter:

My precious Boy,

Your good letter gave me somewhat of a lift. I know you are right in all you say but I seem not to be able to [stop] worry[ing] about how things are going to shape up. My biggest worry is about David, as you well know. We will let it rest there now, until something more definite shapes up.

I went to town yesterday as I had to see Dr. Miller about my feet, which have been needing his care for some time. The weather was hot so I did not think I would be able to take more cold. While there I went on a hunt for some shoes like I wear at home. These I wear now have both my big toes out through the holes. Well, I walked miles going into several stores, even to Sears and looked through the new catalogue but shoes with heels are not made any more—everything has those flat heels. Having a tendency to fall backwards all the time they throw me worse. So I shall just wear my air conditioned ones longer.

Now this a.m. it is cold and we are promised a drop to 34°—28° tonight with freezes. I was looking at the big crop of loquats that are on the tree and thinking that I would be able to give lots of them to Edna, who once told me she was so fond of them. I hope a freeze is not going to ruin them.

As I went to town I saw several bushes of azaleas in full bloom. The big bush in

Mrs. Pearce's yard is lovely. Do you have even a crocus?

I do hope your one day visit to us will materialize. That I can look forward to.

I am going to be extravagant and use another 10¢ stamp. I got David to get me ten cent stamps thinking they were what I used, and he refused to go to the P.O. for me yesterday to exchange them, so I will have to use another one this morning.

When I found out about D's bad report card I said then that he needed to be coached and he said he would not have a coach. That was his position about it. He says that his English work that he failed in is not in the book, but while he had his arm broken and could not write the teacher would put the work on the blackboard and the pupils would write the answers. I don't understand it but he says he has now learned about past participles, etc. and is bringing his F up. I hope he is right.

I love you my darling

Your Bobbin

September 23, 1958, Bobbin to Francis Walter

My precious Boy,

Barring missing you, I had such a happy day Sunday. I called David in time for S.S. [Sunday School], and he got up, dressed, ate breakfast without any argument. While at breakfast, he said, "I'm glad we decided to go to Biloxi today, as we could not go out on the water on such a rainy, cloudy day! That is the first I knew that he was going with F & G. [Francis was my father, and Gretchen the woman he dated and married after my mother died.] They got off for their Sunday together about 10:30 in good humor. Had such a nice day and were very happy together when they got home about 9:00. F. did not bring G. out so he would have the excuse to take her home later and leave D. [David] alone.

Monday was another day and I was expecting the usual in the evening when F. came home, but was pleasantly relieved as everyone was in good humor which lasted all evening. I am sure you reached David's better nature with your gentle, brotherly talk with him. I gave him a dollar for spending money (F. said there were amusement parks there), but he used it for firecrackers. G. gave him a dollar's worth of firecrackers also, so he had a good time yesterday evening making noise with some of them.

Mrs. Freeman [a neighbor and friend] came over Sunday a.m. about 6:30 to ask if I would like to go to Christ Church as Lucille was going to take her, as L. wanted to see you before you went away.

In announcing the weather over the nation on Sunday, Miss Monitor said, "New York 62°, raining." So you don't get away from the rain even there. Mrs. [Warren] Field said it was cold up there, and they had to wear coats, so be careful and keep well. I am not going to tell you how much I miss you, only to say I love you so very much.

Your Bobbin

September 26, 1958, Bobbin to Francis Walter

My precious Boy,

I was happy to have news from you yesterday. Things were in a mess when you got to school but I know you were glad that your rooms had been refurbished. By now you are down to work I suppose. Will look for the longer letter today or tomorrow. A letter came from Miss Patsy also yesterday. I am going to send it on to you so you may [see] how the two of them are pulling along together.

Willie is a surprise to me and I hope he will always be as good and helpful to our girl as he is starting out to be.

David seems to be getting along in harmony with the world though struggling sometimes with his schoolwork. I was so aggravated at F. [Francis] Wednesday night.# He rushed off after dinner, 2:30 to be exact, to be with Gretchen and did not get home until 9:30. I went several times and sat with David who was struggling over his English. Trying to find in various encyclopedias a solution to his problems. How I wished that I had eyes to help the little fellow, but I could only try to give moral support by being with him. He finally had to give up and did not complete his homework. F. walked in about 9:30. David should have

Mobile once gave a half off Wednesday and a half on Saturday.(This footnote is in the wrong place) been ready for bed by then but he yet had to get a bath, etc. Of course he was in no mood to have to get up before. . .the next morning.

I just don't understand F. [Francis, my father] never have and never will.

I passed the news of you on to Minnie and Ida B. both so glad to hear from you. Ida B. said she had a long talk with Jo Dix this week [Jo was the Christ Church secretary.] She rang her to thank Ida B. for the nice dinner and pleasant time at her house. Said she has missed you so much that she has written you two letters since you left. I know you have left a big hole in things at Christ Church as they all miss you greatly. And why not! I know what it means.

Lenie started this week coming on Tuesdays, and I am leaving all the washing for her to do as I promised to do. It was a little difficult on Monday not to have the starching done but it all worked out. Yesterday was the first day, for some time, that we got off without rain.

I love you my darling and there is no need for me to tell you. I miss you, so I won't do it.

Your Bobbin

February 8, 1959, George Crenshaw, Mobile, to Francis Walter (Crenshaw was then a vestryman at Good Shepherd; he and Walter became good friends):

Dear Father Walter,

I received your letter and also heard from the rector of Christ Church.

We talked with the Bishop at the convention about our situation and our decision to call a Priest regardless of Race. His thoughts on the subject were conservative as expected; however he stated that he would not stand in our way in case we went through with our plans.

The parishioners and the Vestry have agreed that we must have a priest and your letter was a God send.

Now there is only one thing in our way from offering you a call to Good Shepherd; before your letter arrived, the Vestry had sent a letter to Father Jones in Knoxville, Tenn. offering him a call as request[ed] by canon 15 and we are awaiting an answer from him. As soon as we hear from Father James I will let you hear from me. In the meantime please bear with us.

Since you will not be going to Christ Church, and in the event that Father James' letter is in the negative, how would you be interested in coming to Good Shepherd? That is as a resident rector under canon 15 or for a specified length of time? Let me know as much as possible about this so that I can inform the Vestry.

With all good wishes,

George E. Crenshaw Jr.

February 25, 1959, Bishop Charles C. J. Carpenter to F. L. Perry, senior warden of Church of the Good Shepherd, Mobile, Alabama:

Dear Mr. Perry:

When I talked with you and other representatives of the Church of the God Shepherd, at the time of the Convention in Montgomery, and told you that I did not think it would be good for us to try to get a white priest to take charge of the work at the Church of the Good Shepherd, I had in mind what had often happened in times past when not too able white clergymen were sometimes put in charge of Negro parishes.

I had no idea that it would be possible for us to get a man of the caliber of the Reverend Francis X. Walter to take charge of this work.

I talked with Mr. Walter recently when I was in New York and found that he was most interested in the Church of the Good Shepherd and had talked with one or two of you gentlemen about this.

This is to tell you that a call from the Church of the Good Shepherd to Mr. Walter would have my enthusiastic and complete approval. His deep interest in this work is wonderful news to me, and I presume it will be to you. He is eminently fitted for this, and has a real vocation therefor, and if the Wardens and Vestry of the Good Shepherd desire to call Mr. Walter, this is my statement in accordance with the directions of the Canons that he is a Priest in good standing in the Protestant Episcopal Church and eligible for this call.

Upon hearing of his interest, I am more encouraged about the future of the work of the Good Shepherd than I have been in many years.

Please keep me posted and let me have a copy of your call to Mr. Walter if you desire to issue this call.

With all good wishes,

Sincerely,

C C J Carpenter]

copy to Mr. Walter

March 1, 1959, George E. Crenshaw Jr. to Francis Walter

Dear Father Walter,

I talked to the Senior Warden yesterday and was pleased to learn he had received two letters. One was from Father Jones, who indicated that he was still undecided about coming to Good Shepherd, so he is out of the picture now. The other letter was from Bishop Carpenter. I haven't read either letter but the Senior Warden tells me that the Bishop is emphatically in favor of your coming to Good Shepherd. So it appears that two obstacles have been removed.

It appears from talking with different members of the Vestry that a call will be on its way to you soon. Vestry meeting is tomorrow night and the letter may be drafted then.

We have been moving forward slowly but surely here and all the good news shall surely give us a boost forward: There are some great plans afoot here. The Sunday School is doing fine, a renovation program is under way both at the Rectory and the Church. We are having Thursday evening services during Lent; and Father Wilson from Fairhope is giving us Holy Communion on the second and fourth Sundays; and of course our Lay Services.

Knowing what is about to happen to our Church is quite a thrill to me and I am eagerly looking to your arrival; there is so much that a Priest can do to lead and guide a church and its people to greatness. I believe that if Good Shepherd ever gets anywhere in community service and world service you will be the person to guide us there.

Yours in Christ

Geo Ed. Crenshaw

March 10, 1959, Good Shepherd Vestry to Francis Walter, New York

Dear Rev. Walter;

The Vestry voted unanimously to call you to be the Rector of The Church of The Good Shepherd Mobile, Alabama.

The following is what can be offered at this time subject to changes according to times and conditions.

Salary thirty six hundred dollars ($3,600.00) per year, the Rectory will be provided with current expenses, such as lights water, gas and telephone bill being payed by the vestry.

Hoping through the grace of God and our prayers you will find it possible to except this call.

With all good wishes,

The Vestry, Frank Fields, Clerk; F.L. Perry, Senior Warden

March 12, 1959, Francis Walter to Good Shepherd Vestry

Dear Sirs:

I was pleased to receive your call for me to be rector of The Church of The Good Shepherd. As Bishop Carpenter indicated in his letter to you of February 25th, I am most interested in what I feel are the many exciting potentialities of your parish. More than that, I am certainly aware of the real devotion of many of your communicants as I was able to see this on my visit with you this past Christmas. These things make me want very much to accept this call to be your rector.

However, before I formally accept your call I would like to ask that you allow me to come to Mobile to talk with you in person about my ideas of the parish's future, my acceptance of the call and our relations as rector and vestry were I to become your rector.

I feel this to be quite necessary; in fact, I think it would be unfair to both of us if we did not have this opportunity for a sincere discussion of the things I mentioned above. In most calls, the vestry, or a committee, has an opportunity to talk to the prospect face to face before the matter is finally decided. You have never had an opportunity to talk to me as a group about any of the important things that will concern us both if we agree to work together in the years to come. Should I become your rector I would want my vestry behind me in all the hopes I had for the future of the parish, not perhaps in any detail, but I would want at least the assurance of its faith & confidence in me as a person. Accordingly, you, as a vestry, would want me, as your rector, to be ready to work with you constructively.

In other words, I feel I owe you gentlemen a personal talk with me. I would try to state my feelings about The Church of the Good Shepherd and let you know what I would expect of the vestry and congregation were I to accept your call. Your call to me put you out on a limb, in a sense; I feel a talk like this with me would give you the opportunity you deserve either to accept me and my ideas or decline to accept me. In case of the latter decision this would free you to elect someone else. Please understand me; there is no doubt in my mind that I want to accept your call, however, in fairness, to you I do ask to meet with you before formally accepting.

Because of the goodness of a friend of Grace Church, Jersey City, where I assist on weekends, my expenses for the trip will be paid. Because of Easter holidays at the seminary I would be able to leave New York by plane Easter Monday March 30th arriving in Mobile early Tuesday morning, and returning Sunday night the 5th of April.

I would be ready to meet with you Tuesday night or any time thereafter till Sunday.

I would be happy to celebrate the Holy Eucharist for you Sunday. This would also give me time to visit with my family. I can stay with my family while in Mobile. Their address is 3804 Austill Lane, Spring Hill, Mobile G4 62923.

Let me say again how happy I was to receive your call. I look forward eagerly to meeting with you. Please let me know is my suggestion about us meeting is agreeable to you.

Yours in Christ
Francis Walter

March 13, 1959, Francis Walter to Bishop C. C. J. Carpenter
Dear Bishop,

I received my call from The Church of Good Shepherd yesterday. The letter did not state whether you received a copy as you requested, so I will quote part of it to you.

This is the only part of the letter having anything to do with the conditions of the contract.

I have written them saying that I wanted to accept the call but would not do so formally until, in fairness to both me and the vestry, I come to Mobile for a personal talk with them. I stressed how important I felt this to be. And to you Bishop, I would add, especially in this case where a Southern white man is to be working in what must be a deep spiritual fellowship with Southern Negroes. I told them I wanted to speak to them of my ideas about the parish, my feelings about the relations I would have to them as rector to vestry. I want very much to forestall anyone saying, "We never knew that Walter would want to do that, or be, such and such." I told them that this was the only fair thing to do since they had never had an opportunity as a vestry to talk with me as a prospective rector for the parish. I concluded by assuring them of my real desire to accept the call and my hope that after hearing me they would want me and be ready to work with me as a person with certain ideas & characteristics and not just as a rather abstract unit with the potential of filling their vacant cure.

Happily for them and me an anonymous friend of Grace Church, Jersey City, has volunteered to pay my expenses to Mobile. I can leave N.Y. Easter Monday as the seminary is on vacation.

I need to know from you if the letter I have from them, more exactly the portion I quoted to you, is a sufficient representation of the intent of Section 2 of Canon 15 for me to accept it without change. Need any other matters of a financial or canonical nature be brought up? I need not tell you how pleased I am at the way things have turned out.

As to the money for the Volkswagen I am buying: the total cost is $1599.95. I have made a deposit of $100.00 already. Banks require a third down on automobile loans. This amounts to $533.32. I can afford the deposit, so I need $433.32 to negoti-ate a loan. Since I am now sure to be living in Mobile, I will borrow the money from the Merchant's Nat'l Bank, where I've had accounts before. I would like to make the arrangement for the loan while there the week after Easter Day.

Sincerely yours,

Francis X. Walter

March 16, 1959, Bobbin to Francis Walter

My precious Boy,

I had a hard time trying to sleep last night as I was composing letters to you in answer to yours we received on Saturday.

Well, I did not get anywhere with my composing but in this one I shall just be blunt and s [illegible] are all very unhappy about [illegible] decision to [illegible] The Good Shepherd parish.

That [you will] be here in Mobile gives us great joy but it is tempered [illegible]. Priest of parish [illegible] more than [illegible] you did when you [illegible] services [illegible] you would have to visit [illegible] your parishioners enter into [illegible] social life, etc, etc. [Illegible] of the old school [illegible] feel it will ruin your future [illegible]. The Bishop did [illegible] and that is why he was so long answering your request.

I asked Minnie and Ida B. not to say anything to anyone what you are planning to do, [illegible] wait until you come down for the week to let it be known what your final decision is. I know you are disappointed in me but I had to tell you what is in my heart.

Don't do it.

I have been counting off the weeks till you will be through there and not in just a week more and you will be with us for a few days. That is good news.

I am wrong about that, as it figures up 2 weeks from today when you will be here.

Willie and Miss P. come this week-end. They haven't been home for 6 weeks and I have missed her so much. I enclose David's write up.

I do love you so dearly my precious boy.

Your Bobbin

March 17, 1959, Bobbin to Francis Walter

My precious Boy,

Since hearing your wonderful letter to Minnie this morning I am more ashamed than I can tell you I wrote to you as I did.

Every day I fall on the way side but now I realize what a [illegible] poor Christian I am. On Sundays (which is the only [illegible] I get to church) I ask God's forgive-ness for my transgressions and pray to him to guide me thro the week to be more

Christlike but fail to do my part. When you are home I want you to sit down with me in [illegible] and make me see how wrong I have been, [illegible], [illegible] this work that you are to do.

One of my troubles is that I do not realize that you have reached the age of maturity and wisdom.

Your grandmother wants the best always for you and if you feel that this is the best for you, you must be right, so I ask tolerance of you until you talk to me. Wish I could say what I want to in a letter, but I just don't know how to express it on paper.

Suffice to say that I love you my darling with all my heart and most happy that you are to be in Mobile.

Your Bobbin

March 18, 1959, Francis Walter, Church of the Good Shepherd, to Bobbin

My dearest Bobbin,

You must get a refill for your ballpoint pen for, though you couldn't notice, much of your letter was missing words and phrases. However, enough was there for me to piece the meaning together.

I don't believe that I could write to you of my feelings about the call I am to accept if I did not know that I would be home in 12 days. Though I can say nothing I couldn't write, I will be able to assure you again and again of my conviction in this choice and let you know, not at all that you disappointed me, but how much you and your sisters amaze me by your lovely and gentile attitudes toward Negro people. If this is what you call "the old school," then I am for it.

How could I expect you to feel any other way? You and your sisters and your brother and your parents are not to be judged outside of your age but in it. It has been your part to raise a child and grandchildren, not to be a student of political and sociological history. How lovely your ways are to me, and the way of all those in your generation who can truly be called gentlefolk. There is so much of the gospel in your thoughts and ways. It is people like you who are to be praised, who have done what they could in the little chicken runs that southern society give us to operate in. So you must never feel that I am disappointed in you or any member of the family who may disagree with me. I comfort myself in believing and want to help you realize that I intend to do in my generation what you have done in yours to be gentle and right for the sake of my neighbors and for Christ's sake. I am convinced that my generation is profoundly different from yours. I am not content to go on acting in the old ways as if I were a young man born in the year of the centennial, as if I lived in a society that had to cling to certain traditions based on an agricultural economic heritage of a peculiar kind.

(By the way, I know some of this may be over your head, but I may as well write for the whole family in this one letter.) I am doing what my conscience tells me I ought to do and so much more than that, I know you would agree with me, wouldn't my mother want me to be doing as I am? You believe in us, your child and grandchildren. I only want you to believe in what we do.

I want now to answer the objections you raised in your letter:

First, you are unhappy because you know that being a priest to Negroes means visiting in their homes, and entering into normal social relations with them. You are quite right because I do intend to minister to them like any normal priest would to any normal people. But here I have a wonderful advantage over you. To me, Negroes are just normal people. There's nothing very astounding about that. Imagine a man of the 1800s who had been told all his life that tomatoes are not a normal vegetable but are rather poisonous. Suddenly the news comes to his town that tomatoes are not at all poisonous. Upon examination and trial they have been found to be just like any other of God's tasty vegetables, which he has set aside for us to eat. The man's parents don't believe this, but he does and starts having tomatoes with his salads: after a few months he realizes what an unnatural waste had occurred before people accepted tomatoes as an ordinary vegetable. What a waste. What a waste of human, personal relationships to cut ourselves off from whole areas of humanity containing persons just as capable of all the warm relations we feel for each other, just as capable too of mediating and receiving the grace that God is accustomed to pour out through human relations.

But of course it took me two years at Grace Church to learn that. I was as wary as a bantam hen around a black snake when I was first thrust into direct man to man relations with different people, not only black different people but people richer, poorer, blacker, dumber, smarter, more educated, less educated, more neurotic, less neurotic than myself. You couldn't imagine yourself entering into such relations with Negroes. Of course you couldn't, my dearest, but that's not the point. The point is I can imagine it for myself—and not imagination only. I do it every day of the week in N.Y.C. though I admit it's something you learn or better you have to unlearn a lot if you're a southerner. I hope that does in your first objection.

Your second point is easier to refute because it is based on a misunderstanding. The Bishop did not delay answering my letter because he wanted to dissuade me. The first the Bishop knew of my idea was in a personal talk with him in NYC Ash Wednesday. He knows the situation full well. He asked me if it was something for which I felt a call. I said yes. He said somewhat cautiously, "People may think you're a trifle odd, do you mind?" I said no. We talked about a half hour and parted company in great spirits; he because he felt he had a priest who knew what he wanted for a vacant parish and I because I hadn't been sure he would be so receptive and was therefore vastly relieved.

You only mentioned those two, but I can imagine other objections. I'll bet you think I'll be lonely. Let me assure you with my ideas my real loneliness would have been in ministering to some lily white, conservative, middle to upper class bigoted set of "ordinary" Episcopalians. Please understand, I'm not categorizing this sort in an ugly way. It takes real saints to minister to them; they, too, are to be loved even more than black southerners for many reasons.

I was terrified when I lost my place at Christ Church. It was the one place where I felt there was a ministry. I could handle doing that. The vision of ministering, say, to the people of Greensboro did terrify me. Another objection of yours could well be that mine will be an unfruitful ministry, butting my head against a stone wall. For me, Bobbin, the stone walls are the hearts of the thin-lipped white men who can shed respectability instantly to snarl the word "nigger" in tones signifying such a burden of fearful, blind evil that I am terrified and can only say, "Lord, I can't face it. I am sick. I can't cope with it, help me." He has helped me, for he has given me a chance to serve my people in my own county; he has given me a chance to do a job I want to do. To use my youth in one of the most pleasant ways it can be used—in service to Him with excitement and confidence.

I don't plan to force any of my ideas or my social relations on my family. I foresaw and have accepted the possibility of a rift between me and some of you. From my side I love you all and will continue to do so as a member of the family no matter how much we disagree. I hope for the same from all of you. I am not going into this blind. I am willing to give up a great deal to gain a great deal. The trouble with you all is that your eyes can see the great deal I may have to give up. You look at that and are unhappy. Your eyes are quite blinded to the great deal I stand to gain. I don't blame you for this at all, but I will blame you (for you've all got heads on your shoulders) if you don't at least admit that the "great deal" of gain you can't see may exist.

Your boy

March 19, 1959, Good Shepherd Vestry to Francis Walter, New York
Dear Rev. Walter:

Your letter of the 12th. received with great joy. We are very happy to know that you have tentative accepted our call to be Rector of our church.

It seem to be a coincidence that you are suggesting the very thing that we had discussed. We were going to ask you to come here for a conference with the Vestry during your Easter Vacation even if it were at our expense, for we felt that it is very important that we understand each other if we are to accomplish the task before us. Therefore you can be assured that we are heartily in favor of your suggestion, and we are looking forward to seeing you and meeting with you on the 31th. of March at 7:30 P.M. in the Parish House if it meets your approval.

Many good wishes and a Happy Easter

Yours in Christ,

The Vestry,Frank Fields, Clerk; F.L. Perry, S.W.

March 20, 1959, Francis Walter at All Saints in Birmingham to Good Shepherd Vestry
Dear Sirs:

I have your letter of the 19th. I am glad we already give evidence of thinking alike. This makes the future look very happy.

It meets with my approval perfectly for us to have our first meeting at the Parish House, March 31, at 7:30 P.M.

God bless you all this Easter.

Yours in Christ,

Francis Walter

Thursday, March 19, 1959, Louis _____ to Francis Walter
Dear Francis,

Thanks for your interesting letter and I rejoice that your anxious watching of the mailbox has resulted in the receipt of the letter for the Church of the Good Shepherd. I am glad that you will have the chance now to decide what would be best for you and the Church of the Good Shepherd and most in conformity to the purpose of God.

I am sure that you are aware that this will be a "hard row to hoe." This will not be a sermon nor advice, but I am sure that you have thought seriously that 'a prophet is not without honor except in his own country'—where he is most likely to be misunderstood and—in this instance—to be considered a "traitor." I met a "former' Baptist (high church Baptist) clergyman on the faculty of "Ole Miss" University in Nashville, a friend of Bill Dimmick's. This man was asked "to leave," for his views. His job at the time that I met him was to be "an observer" and "objective viewer" at spots of racial tensions for the National Council of Churches. I commented to him that I thought that I always wanted to stay in the South—to speak to and to "lead" my "own" people in this challenging time, for I thought that there would be a "rapport" there. He told me that he once thought too, by now he finds himself considered a traitor—even by his family now (a Mississippi delta family). His family constantly chides him—"We don't know what happened to Bill. He didn't learn all that at home."

Good luck and a plentitude of grace and assistance in making your decision. It would be very useful, I am sure, for the Good Shepherd to have, through the people of that parish—to give to "its" community the leadership as desperately needed.

The baby is fine. Hope you'll have [a] chance to be with us soon. If you are going to & through Birmingham and can "stop off" or can "call," please be sure to do so.

Faithfully your friend,

Louis

March 22, 1959, Mamie to Francis Walter

My dear Francis

Ever since I was told that you had asked to be sent to Good Shepard Church, I have thought of nothing else. And Bobbin, Arminnie and I are deeply hurt that you should have done this, and I feel you have certainly let your family down, especially Bobbin. Why in the world do you want to come here where you will create trouble instead of good. I think its fine if you want to work with negroes, but not here, get a church somewhere else. Have you thought one time about your family? What this will do to David, and your Daddy's business. Think this over, and think more of us, and not yourself.

Love

Mamie

March 23, 1959, Francis Walter, New York, to Louis

Dear Louis,

You were kind to reply quickly. And you are much appreciated for your thoughts. I did not take your letter at all as a sermon, rather, since it parallels my own thoughts so aptly, I take it as an indication we are still thinking alike as friends.

I do take the matter seriously & do try to discover God's will for me. I must know my conscience as it is illuminated by God's grace & then of course I must act on it.

Thus occupied in my decision the Bible takes on added relevance, "being wise as a serpent and innocent as a dove" is one good example.

It would kill me to be a traitor to the land & people I love. The South has so much to offer the United States and I so much want to do my part to save that heritage & pass it on.

As long as I can have a ministry, I don't put too much worry in being considered a traitor, as you say. I would be dismayed, & feel that I have denied my conscience were I really a traitor to my people. I have found insight and comfort in the prophet Jeremiah, who is the example par excellence of a minister who identified with his people (with his complete acceptance of them—good and bad elements), led them, & exhibited real and deep "rapport."

From conversations just recently with a Church Army worker from Galveston, I see more and more that lack of clergy (since there are no Negro clergy) for Southern Negro churches is the main problem. Following the advice of the Bishop's Committee on Negro postulants for more consideration of the importance of ministry to Negroes, I feel truly called to this work as far a God gives me to know my own will. Francis

March 23, 1959, Bobbin to Francis Walter, New York

My precious Boy,

We received your letter Saturday—lots of it I did not understand, but from it all we gather that you are determined to carry out your plan.

I had a nice long visit from Miss Patsie this weekend which I needed. Willie blew in for a few minutes then went on to his home. They were all leaving for Pascagoula for a fishing trip until Sat. evening. He came down with a friend, leaving the car for Miss P., who came Friday, spent the night and Sat. with us. It has been such a long time since she was here (4 or 5 weeks) and it was just wonderful to have her.

I do miss my children selfish old woman that I am.

They tell me that Mobile is a beauty spot now with the azaleas in their prime. Francis [my father] wanted to take me to see them, but there is no satisfaction for me to ride around that there is color [only] as I look out, so I refused and just enjoyed walking down our drive looking at ours at close range. Ours don't last too long as they have that blight and soon lose their beauty, but now they are lovely, and you are going to enjoy seeing them in their glory.

Mrs. Field told me yesterday that she has been so busy this past week getting her house in order and has put it on the market for sale. She has been thinking on this for some time, so has finally done it.

I hope she will not live too far away as I will be deprived from getting to church on Sundays.

Did I tell you that our $15 cat has disappeared? [They had just spent $15 on the cat that Bobbin hated at the vet.] She was here last Wed. morning and we haven't seen her since then.

Yes, she was "a cute little kitty," a la Francis [my father], but I don't miss her. It makes one less thing to do, feeding her fell to me.

Miss Monitor said yesterday that the tem in N.Y. City was 29° and here ours were up in the 60's, having to have the doors open. March is almost over, and maybe by next month you will be able to shed your overcoat.

I do love you so dearly my darling boy.

Your Bobbin

March 23, 1959, Arminnie to Francis Walter:

My dear Boy

Some weeks ago I promised myself and you that no more clippings about the racial situation would go your way, that you had a surfeit of it [from me this year]?

No doubt you've seen the proposal of the Methodist Laymen, but I enclose the clipping anyway, which you may read or destroy if it has already come your way.

I passed the contents of yours to me of the 14th to Mamie and your grandmother, in which you appeared so satisfied with the prospect ahead of you. We will talk about it when you are here next week.

I love you—
as always
Arminnie

P.S. The television across the room is in full blast. I can't think or concentrate. My roommates seem well. It is a cold morning—the furnace is percolating for the first time today—10 am 3/23/59

First page of Arminnie's above letter.

March 23, 1959, Francis Walter, New York, to his father

Dear Daddy,

I received this morning the letter Patsy tells me you all wanted her to write me. I honestly appreciate all your frankness. I hope the other letter you have from me will help you to understand somewhat of my feelings.

I am arriving a day earlier than I expected at first. I will come in March 30th at 3:33 in the morning. I ask you again wouldn't you rather leave the car in the parking lot for me to pick up?

I find the next part of this note awkward to phrase, but I must say it honestly: As I said, I don't want to involve my family in any of my affairs that they may find unpleasant. Of course, this is impossible since just thinking about me on your part can cause suffering and separation. As I said, though, I feel this is what our Lord meant about taking up our crosses and leaving father, mother, and family.

If I stayed at home while in Mobile, I would plan to have no member of the Church of the Good Shepherd pick me up at home or come to see me there. I don't want to involve you.

From the tenor of Patsy's letter, though, it may be better, and I am quite willing to stay with Leigh Arsnault. Undoubtedly it is your house. This is for you to decide. We can settle it when I get home so as not to involve ourselves in phone and telegram messages.

Of course, it hurts a bit to put that on paper, but I think it only fair. From here I really can't estimate your feelings & you don't write.

Believe me, I will not take it as a mark that you don't love me if you feel it would be better for me not to stay at home during the next week.

Ever your son

March 23, 1959, Francis Walter, New York, to his father

Dear Daddy,

I received this morning the letter Patsy tells me you all wanted her to write me. I honestly appreciate all your frankness. I hope the other letter you have from me will help you to understand somewhat of my feelings.

I am arriving a day earlier than I expected at first. I will come in March 30th at 3:33 in the morning. I ask you again wouldn't you rather leave the car in the parking lot for me to pick up?

I find the next part of this note awkward to phrase, but I must say it honestly: As I said, I don't want to involve my family in any of my affairs that they may find unpleasant. Of course, this is impossible since just thinking about me on your part can cause suffering and separation. As I said, though, I feel this is what our Lord meant about taking up our crosses and leaving father, mother, and family.

If I stayed at home while in Mobile, I would plan to have no member of the Church of the Good Shepherd pick me up at home or come to see me there. I don't want to involve you.

From the tenor of Patsy's letter, though, it may be better, and I am quite willing to stay with Leigh Arsnault. Undoubtedly it is your house. This is for you to decide. We can settle it when I get home so as not to involve ourselves in phone and telegram messages.

Of course, it hurts a bit to put that on paper, but I think it only fair. From here I really can't estimate your feelings & you don't write.

Believe me, I will not take it as a mark that you don't love me if you feel it would be better for me not to stay at home during the next week.

Ever your son

March 24, 1959, Francis Walter, New York, to Mamie
Dear Mamie,

I appreciated the frankness of your letter. What I have to say to it I will consider [as] an addition to a long letter I sent Bobbin last week. I asked her to share it with you and you may send it to Margaret [Wells] if you like.

How can I assure you that I have thought deeply about the possible consequences this will have on my family? And on my relations with it? As to the latter, I am ready, if necessary to fall out of my family's favor to follow my own conscience.

I pray however that the love we bear each other will survive those great differences of opinion. I know you must follow your conscience in your social relations. I accept that, and I ask you to do the same in my case.

However, you are right in making the distinction that it is one thing for me to do this in Mobile and quite another to do it elsewhere. Let me give you my thoughts on those points. I hope it helps you see that I have thought them over carefully.

In the first place, I am bound to return to Alabama to work in the diocese, more than that, I want to. Secondly, I don't want to go to the Good Shepherd because it is a Negro parish, not primarily or secondarily, it is as an unproductive urban parish that could be a witness to Christ right in the neighborhood. This should sound familiar, for it is just the sort of place Christ Church is.

An interest even in ministry, plus my experiences in New York make me feel called to this sort of work. I know of no other parishes in Alabama needing a priest who fit this situation. There are no Negro parishes open in Alabama anyway, save the Good Shepherd, but I don't want to go to any Negro parish just because it is a Negro parish.

But I am interested in Christ's ministry to Negroes in the South. There are no Negro priests to fill already established missions. The churches are just dwindling away. White priests do not go or are not allowed to go to these places. The Negro people are on the move in the South—to get the social justice they have been so long denied. Would you prefer them to look to communists or pagan leadership or leadership inspired by our Lord? You are right then in that sense—I do feel Negro work to be important. In that sense, God is calling for men "Who will go for us." I've waited some time for someone else to go. No one has, so I decided.

Your next point is its effect on David. I feel that to be the least of my worries. David's generation as it matures will espouse views I will probably consider radical. If David is affected by it at all, it will be if he thinks about it, and if he does it can do nothing worse than help him see past the horizons of Mobile County and Alabama. Quite seriously, I am not at all worried about him. If people think his brother is a nut, well he can either beat them, ignore them, or agree with them. Other folks' brothers and fathers are worse than nuts, and little seems to come from it.

Next you mention Daddy's business: first I am convinced that you overestimate the danger. I have thought of economic reprisals but put them out of my mind as too farfetched. I don't intend to crusade. I want to lay low. I want only to be the best priest I can be to my people. I have decided then that the probability of an angry public visiting economic reprisal on Daddy's business if too farfetched to consider.

Let me close with this. Daddy or anyone else can disassociate themselves from my ideas by merely saying so. Indeed, they must if their consciences tell them I'm wrong and they are right. More than that I am prepared to disassociate myself from you all physically if you want me to do so. I would not cease to love you, and I trust that you all could still love me if we did that.

Goodness, you have got me into a pretty pessimistic strain. I don't look forward to any of these dreary things happening. Of course, don't misunderstand me. I know you are hurt by this; it hurts me to hurt you. This must happen in families at times.

Your letter is not complete enough to reveal your full feelings about the matter. Because of that I am asking you to let Bobbin know if you care to see me the week I am at home.

I want very much to see you if only by my presence to let you know the sorrow I feel at having hurt you. But if this would be too much for you, I will understand. As I say, I can't tell by the tenor of your letter just how deeply you feel.

It hurts me to say [all] the above but you were frank with me, and I feel it best to continue in that vein.

You are welcome to let anyone read this letter.

I hope I can see you soon and am sorry to have been the cause of hurting you.

With my love,

Your Boy

March 25, 1959, Bobbin to Francis Walter, New York

My precious, precious Boy—

Of course we want you to stay with us this next week, though what you are planning to do does not meet with my approval. I still love you so dearly, need you, and want you here.

Lenie* is "polishing up the big front door" and it would be a great disappointment not to have you with us.

I rang Bishop Carpenter yesterday. I felt that I just had to have a talk with him. He was out of town so I talked a long time with Bishop Murray who was most kind, patient and understanding. He was writing to the Bishop [Carpenter] that day and in his letter he would tell him how deeply I felt about this.

There seem to be so many angles to this thing. Most of all I am afraid for your future in the Church, and for your safety from the K.K.K.'s, who may move in and harm you. I am very miserable so you see I need you here to talk with you.

Mr. Mann* had just [heard] Tuesday morning at Christ Church of your plan, and came yesterday in the afternoon and had a long talk with me. Wallace was here today. He wants very much to see you when you come, so you must make a point of seeing him. He is so gentle and before leaving said the sweetest prayer for me which brought the tears which are near the surface anyway. Should I write all this to you? Well it is all from the depths of my heart my heart my darling.

Francis of course will meet you at the airport Monday morning at 3 am and of course I will be up and ready to see you.

All my love to you, my precious one,

Your Bobbin

*Volena—Lenie—was the daughter of Evergreen, who was Bobbin's maid long before this. Evergreen would bring Volena, when she was a baby, to work and keep her in the kitchen. Volena grew up to become my mother and grandmother's maid in Mobile. Volena and Bobbin acted like an old married couple, bickering, working together, and though the idea is questioned today, loving one another. She was friend and counsellor to my mother, and attended my mother's, sister's, and grandmother's funerals, sitting with the family. Bill Mann was the rector of our parish, St. Paul's. In my opinion, for him there was no problem about race. Things had evened out just fine for him around 1900, when all the old Confederate states were given back the power to govern. Wallace was a seminary classmate. He was at this time an assistant at Mamie's church in downtown Mobile. As Bobbin said, he was gentle and had an uncanny ability to connect with people. He was later killed in a senseless murder at his church in Louisiana. Bobbin was in bed by 7 p.m. and up at 3 am, drinking coffee and playing solitaire. Her homemade pine lap board, glossy from slapped-down cards, is used by us today.

April 9, 1959, Mamie to Francis Walter

Dearest Francis,

I was sorry not to see you again and I hope you had a satisfactory talk with the Bishop.

We are certainly all distressed over the thought of losing Wallace. I guess he is going on for higher things. I hope he won't leave this diocese for always, everyone is so fond of him, and he has helped Trinity [Church] and is splendid with young people. I was so glad Dr. Maury didn't find Bobbin's eye any worse, he did find an inbedded [sic] eyelash under the lid. She says her eye felt all right today.

Ann [my cousin, Mamie's grandchild] was so sorry you didn't drop in to see her, she is giving up her job next week she feels that the baby needs her. She will move here so we will all be together again.

I haven't seen Minnie but she's all right. I have lots of magazines [The transport of magazines from Mamie to Arminnie was a big deal. It needed to be done timely!] for her, guess I will get Francis to come for them.

qThis is a stupid letter but what I want to say most is that I love you just the same, and that nothing could make it different with me.

Lots of love from just same old Mamie

April 13, 1959, Francis Walter in New York to F. L. Perry

Dear Mr. Perry,

I am somewhat heartened by the headway I've made in our search for a priest. Dean Rose, of this seminary, has already sent one person to me, and I have written to one recent graduate now in Baltimore. The staff at my own parish in Jersey City have suggested two men, one of whom sounds very good. I am going to ask Father Laughlin of Grace Church to write him when I hear from Baltimore. This Thursday I will have lunch with Father Kilmer Myers# of St. Augustine's Chapel, New York City. Father Myers is one of the founders of the urban missions [and the author of the 1957 *Light the Dark Streets*].

I have been told that if anyone would know of a priest he would. Besides this, he is quite interested in the problem of the Negro southern churches. I understand he has recently returned from Florida, where he discussed the problem there.

Good Shepherd is too good for just any priest, nor should we let the long vacancy panic anyone into taking the first man who comes along, so I am being choosy. If nothing comes of these leads, a friend of mind knows Dean Coburn of the Episcopal Theological Seminary in Cambridge, Mass. He has volunteered to write the Dean and drive me up there for an interview to see if he has anyone in mind.

God bless you all,

Francis Walter

Appendix 2: FQB Member Statements

Our friend Jeri Richardson did her doctoral thesis in Art Education on the Freedom Quilting Bee (See Chapter __). Jeri asked members to write their life stories, including why they were members of FQB. She offered a small honorarium for their participation. To me it is the most gripping and historically valuable part of the thesis.

Jeri Richardson wrote:

> In the interest of preserving the character and charm of these reports, the investigator has used as much care as possible in transferring them into typed manuscript. The original essays were hand-written by the informers. In the instances where punctuation was lacking the investigator has not added punctuation, but has utilized spacing to facilitate easier reading.
>
> These essays are presented in their entirety because the investigator views them as a means of communicating a "feeling" of the people that would be lost in an attempt to relate what the essays are "about." These reports reflect many of the people's feelings—sorrow, weariness, hope, bitterness, humor, tragedy, and despair. In many instances, the stories are deeply touching. They reflect their authors in a way that could never be done by means of scholarly writing and for this reason they are presented as their authors put them down.

Four essays selected from the appendix are reprinted below. Richardson preserved the spelling and punctuation of the originals.

> A. [I] was born in November and did not have a daddy and my mother had light childrens.# The time was hard then sometime we had something to eat, sometime we did not. Sometime we had to eat just dry bread and we did not have shoes to put on our feet. I was cold and our feet was burest open. Now the time has change with the help of the Lord.
>
> he Blessed us. With a Welfare, Help. I was. Born Nov. 9th in 1897. Which makes me 70 years old but I have Worked hard all my life sometime I Worked

far as little as 20¢ a-day & 40¢ a day. & 75¢ & $1.00 but after all I am Thankful to be a live today Which is Feb. 11, 1968 there has been a time when I Would have to wait far my cow to come home to milk her [almost all cows belonging to poor blacks were free range]. Before I could feed my 5 little children I would have the ash.Cake already done. & oh. Boy thay would have a time.

I read this essay several times before realizing the "and did not have a daddy and my mother had light childrens" meant that a white man, or men, had fathered all her mother's children. Given the poverty the writer describes, we can assume that the father(s) provided no support to her mother. So here we consider sexual gratification as another way white people extracted value from black people. Her mother's extreme poverty meant no support came from the male, white side of the family.

Another essay was on poverty, though I suspect the writer would not frame it that way. She dwells on the last paragraphs in which she reflects how much better life is today and how she wishes to help others work in the Co-op.

B. This is the story of my life. My name is ____. I was born in 1888, May 22 in Wilcox Co. in a one-room log cabin, with a dirt chimney. There was three childrens, three girls. ____, ____, and myself. The house was made of log. We slept on a bed called, (sonmagone) nailed up beside the house and the mattress was made up of hay grass. We didn't have any Clothes. We wore one dress, that was all we had. We oses to go to old friends houses to get some old clothes to make dress, and we also got cold bread from friends to eat. We went to school, but didn't have time to get lesson, we had to go in woods to get wood to make fire. So, we didn't have time to get lesson. The schoolhouse was made out of log seal up with board with a dirt chimney. We did all our cooking in a fireplace. We had a one room school house with one school teacher. We didn't have any lunchroom, we took our lunch to school in a bucket (lassy and bread) jar with buttermilk. All the while going to school we didn't see andy money. We didn't have any buses we walk about four miles to school. We didn't have any shoes until I was twelve years old. (with brass toes) the shoes. There was no freezer, stoves, Refrigrator in those days. My mother didn't have any body to help her so, I had to help plow. I plowed an old mule. My father left us when we were young. We didn't eat flour unstil on Sunday monring. On Sunday we go to Church. Unstead of paying money in church we took an egg to church.

Today: It is so much different. I am living in my own home. With comfort living-rooms, bedroom, and kitchen. I eat and drink what I want. I go places, and wear what I want. I like the idea of being a member of the Quiting bee. I enjoy it. I will try and help the other who want to be a member of the Quilting Bee. This life is so much different that we're living today.

The author of Essay C writes how her life was expanded by a trip made to participate in the first Smithsonian Folk Life Festival held in 1967 on the Washington Mall.

ESSAY C. Boykin Ala. 2/5/1968. I am _____. I am a citizen of Gees Bend Boykin Ala. I have live here all of my life nearly about. in my life I have had it hard and good in spots. I was taught in my growing up as to be Kind hearted loving and so far I love All peoples and try to be nice to every Body. I am now marriog the second time and enJoy married life. I have done some traveling. I have made servel trips to Birmingham Mobile Montgomery Selma and as far as I have ever Been was to Columbia Ga. o I thought I Had enjoy going on trips but when we went to washington through all those Different states I had long heard of O it just Thrill me throu or throu. I have work hard in my times I have raise up a number of childrens we has put serverl throu high school Also collage I have been the sectuary for the p. t. a. I have been the treasure for the p. t. a. I have been a workman for the school for a nomber of years also I am Sunday School Teacher for the no. 3 Class I have been president for the Choir. I have taught Bible Class on sunday evening. I use to do Some cutting and sewing some time ago. I use to make my husbon and Boys work shirts. I have had to bring water from a long ways Our houses has not been suffishion to live in. I was raise up in a Christian home I have had nice trips tut I never had such a Comemendous trip O it was so wounderfull and so enjoyable. I never enjoy such a Bussing and a great trip before And Since the Freedom Quilt Bee been in our community also in our country I found where smart women can get their own money and can do some emproving in their Homes more than ever. can get some of their Heart desire Rev Francis Walter has done a comemendos

job in our country. since He brought this Freedom Quilting bee in rotation
we never had a thought of selling quilts we always make quilts But never sold
not to many he really has help poor peoples he saw all peoples as Brothers.
now let me tell you all about that wounderfull trip to washington was giving
to us as members of the quilting bee O it is more Than tongue can exsplain we
stop by to a Holliday Inn and we was treated so nice I just enjoyed seen states
and citys I have Long heard of. And when we got to washington Around 4 .o.
Clock in the after noon I saw more cars than ever look like all the cars was in
washington. the next day There stood 2 buses taken the peoples Around sight
seen for a coupler of hours we saw that great wide pool we saw the place where
president Kennedy was burried we went alround the White house O let me
tell you now we live in the Willard Hotell a very fine place to live in and was
Treated so nice. O I had such a good Time untill I pat myself after a while I
pinch myself. is this me so after While I call my self to see if I was in a dream
and behold _____ was realy in washington having a good time we had a trip
up in the washington monument. And you can amagine just How I felt I really
did not feel like myself. And Freedom Quilting bee is the Cause of it all And
Rev. Francis Walter is the obigation of it all and O. how we thank him and the
Lord for such a wounderfull progress has Bend made in our lives we thank the
peoples who standing at his back helping to help us enjoyed reviewing those
old status old houses sitting in the smithsonnaies Builsing O I saw more than
tongue can exsplain if it had not been For the Freedom Quilting bee I to day
never would had seen the part of the world I have seen so give the credit to Rev.
Walter Do thank him would love very much as to get another tripe in this life
so I have so much to be Thankfull for so I do hope the Freedom Quilding will
continion on and on it has made a great light in places I pray god blessing on
Every one who are standing up for Quilting Bee so long
     p.s. well I have work so hard and so long in the cotton patch and Bills
take all at the end I dont Have no more than I did when I start untill I
rather work at quilts now.

Martin Luther King and Ghandi would be humbled by the privilege of
meeting this next essayist. The crisis of being in a demonstration and not
knowing whether she or the march leader would live or die—she describes

this way: "I was [underlining mine] afraid of white peoples but never no more a white man look just like a color man to me now. I learn to love white peoples as my self…"

ESSAY D: A story of my life and what it like today I was born In wilcox County live here In wilcox all of my days on a farm when I was 6 years old my mother taught me to say my a. B. D. she also taught to me the lord prayer every morning when I get out of bed and every night when she put me to bed. then she taught me to rite my A.B.C. and my name. she say now you are old enough to start to school you will be leave me from 7 o clock until 3.30 p.m. also you will be leaveing your other young sister and brother I seem so hard to do I start to cry she told me you have to go to school to learn to read and rite spell and count because one day you going to need it Very bad so today I rally need it. since that day I have learn to love my friend to make friend with other people I came from a mighty long ways she learn me to love my teacher I came from the family of 14 kids 7 Boys 7 Girls father and mother we didn't have but 3 chairs father mother and my oldest sister I had to sit on the floor by the fire light or by a lamp light to get my lesson I didn't know what a Electric light was then I hand 2 dress 2slips 2 pair of panties everday mother had to wash my dress and keep me neat for school every the time was Very hard then I had to walk 1–1/2 mile to school every five days a week some days it be raining but I had to go it be snowing it be cold to Mother told me child you have to go rain or shine sneek or snow cold or hot. You have to go. I was so glade when father got 1 mule and a 1 horse wagon when it be raining cold bad wheather father will take us to school every day I sure was glade to because some morning I get to school I had to go into the woods and get Rennedy trash wold to make a fire the ground be frozen hard to. I be so cold I cry when I get my hand and feet warm. when the teaher come to school we be made a fire she walk In the room she say its sure is warm in here to I say to my self if you had to walk as far I had to you would be so warm……I like my marriage life ok we work together in peace and love. our kids have a better time I had they have light to study typewritter to type learn to short hand on it.….Now I learn to love my neighour as thyself I goin to fright for freedom in 19,6 4 we march in the cold we stood in the rain they throw tis gas on me smoke bumbs I was dso afraid until I didn't know what to do one day_____ lead the march from Sontafrance church to the Alabama National gard comeing to Camden so the police stop us their we sit in the street it was so cold until then my mine went back to when I was a child and had to walk a mile 1/2 every morning to school so we set there together_____lad flat of his back in the street after and the police drove his car about half way of him and _____didn't move he gave me some nerves I was afraid of white peoples but never no more a white man look Just like a color man to me now. I learn to love white peoples as my self every time I pray I say lord please rember my white brother to please.

How I like the freedom quilt Bee; and what it mean to me. I am Very entering in the quilt Bee I have met many of difference faces both white and color and made friend with both. Many of peoples that I have never seen before I learn to love them because they have learn me a lots that I didn't Know about sewing I have learn to make pot holes I have learn to make nices of quilt most of all I have learn to coporate with peoples more better I peace and love I have learn to enjoy my self Very much the freedom quilt Bee is a pritvage as well as a pledge. I also have learn to understand that we have to overcome eveil with good. I enjoy being a member of the quilt Bee Very good I know that together w stand and alliod we fall. but I will like very mush for us to stand together for ever in the quilt Bee we know that peoples are watch this quilt Bee to see what it is during but we going to try to make it the best of all. we are emproveing seem like in every thing we go to do I use to say I couldn't make a baby bed quilt but please beliver me I have made babys bed quilts, for the quilt bee to. and I like my sweet manger Very much to. she help me to do a better gob.

Sources

• Indicates sources with particular relevance to Jonathan Daniels

Bob Adelman, edited by Susan Hall, *Down Home Camden Alabama*, A Prairie House Book, Quadrangle Press, The New York Times Book Company, 10 East 53rd Street, New York, NY 10022.

Donald S. Armentrout, "A Documentary History of the Integration Crisis at The School of Theology of The University of the South," *Sewanee Theological Review* (Easter 2003).

Susan Youngblood Ashmore, *Carry It On: The War on Poverty and the Civil Rights Movement in Alabama 1964*–1972 (Athens, GA: The University of Georgia Press, 2008).

Helen Bannerman, *The Story of Little Black Sambo* (London: Grant Richards, 1899).

S. Jonathan Bass, "Bishop CCJ Carpenter: From Segregation to Integration," *Alabama Review*, Vol. 45, July 1992, Number 3, published by the University of Alabama Press, Tuscaloosa, Alabama.)

• Larry Benaquist and Bill Sullivan, producers; narrated by Sam Waterston. *Here Am I, Send Me: The Story of Jonathan Daniels*. A preview is available at http://episcopalmarket-place.org/Featured_Video/Here-am-I-Send-Me-The-Story-of-Jonathan-Daniels.

John Beecher, "To Live and Die in Dixie," in *One More River to Cross: The Selected Poetry of John Beecher* (Montgomery: NewSouth Books, 2003)

Carl and Anne Braden, *The Wall Between*, Monthly Review Press, New York, 1958.

Roark Bradford, *Ol' Man Adam an' His Chillun* (New York: Harper and Brothers Publishers, 1928).

Director Katrina Browne, co-directors Alla Korgan and Jude Ray, co-producers Elizabeth Delude Dix and Juanita Brown. 2008, *Traces of the Trade: A Story of the Deep North*.

Nancy Callahan's *The Freedom Quilting Bee*, University of Alabama Press, Tuscaloosa and London, 1987. A paperback version from the University Press is also available.

Will D. Campbell, *And Also with You: Duncan Gray and the American Dilemma* (Franklin, TN: Providence House Publishers, June 1997). Christine Jacobson Carter,

Southern Single Blessedness: Unmarried Women in the Urban South 1800–1865 (Champaign, IL: University of Illinois Press, 2009).

Victoria V. Clayton. *White and Black Under the Old Regime* (Whitefish, MT: Kessinger Legacy Reprints), 1899.

Margaret Collins Denny Dixon and Elizabeth Chapman Denny Mann, *Denny Genealogy* (New York: The National Historical Society, 1944).

• Charles W. Eagles, *Outside Agitator: Jon Daniels and the Civil Rights Movement in Alabama* (Chapel Hill: University of North Carolina Press), 1993

The First Book of Kings, chapter 15: verse 7a., The Harper Collins Study Bible, Harper San Francisco, New Revised Standard Version Bible, © 2001.

• Frady, Marshall. *Southerners, A Journalist's Odyssey.* New York: The New American Library, 1980. See "A Death in Lowndes County," page 138.

David Frost, Jr., Witness to Injustice, edited by Louise Westling (Jackson, MS: University Press of Mississippi), 1995.

Good, Paul, The American Serfs: A Report on Poverty In the Rural South, Ballantine Books, New York, 1969.

Peter J. Hamilton, *Colonial Mobile: An historical study, largely from original sources, of the Alabama-Tombigbee basin from the discovery of Mobile bay in 1519 until the demolition of Fort Charlotte in 1821* (New York: Houghton Mifflin, 1897; revised and enlarged edition by R. D. Hamilton, Mobile: The First National Bank of Mobile, 1952).

The birth of the Black Panther Party in Lowndes County is captured in the documentary film *Lay My Burden Down.*

Jay Higginbotham, *Old Mobile, Fort Louis de la Louisiane, 1702–1711* (Mobile: Museum of the City of Mobile, 1977).

Highet, Gilbert. Poets in a Landscape. New York: Alfred A. Knopf., 1957.

Holy Women, Holy Men (Episcopal book of martyrs, saints)

Paul Good, The American Serfs: A Report on Poverty in the Rural South (New York: Ballantine Books,1968)

• *Lesser Feasts and Fasts.* 1991 (and later). New York: The Church Hymnal Corporation, 1991.

Diane McWhorter, *Carry Me Home, Birmingham, Alabama, The Climatic Battle of the Civil Rights Movement*, Simon and Schuster, New York, 2001.

Charles Morgan Jr., *A Time to Speak* (New York: Harper and Row, 1964).

Children of Pride by Robert Mason Myers.

Gunnar Myrdal, *An American Dilemma: The Negro Problem and American Democracy* (New York: Harper and Brothers, 1944).

C. Kilmer Myers, Light the Dark Streets (Greenwich, CT: Seabury Press), 1957.

Louise-Clarke Pyrnelle, *Diddie, Dumps and Tot: Or Plantation Child-Life* (New York: Harpers, 1882; Gretna, LA: Pelican Publishing Company, 1963, 1989).

Roy Osborne, *Telesio and Morato on the Meaning of Colours (Renaissance Color Symbolism II)*, 2nd ed. (Lulu.com: Thylesius Books 2016) footnote 345; see http://www.lulu.com/shop/roy-osborne/telesio-and-morato-on-the-meaning-of-colours-renaissance-colour-symbolism-ii/paperback/product-22782478.html.

Pickett, Albert James, History of Alabama, 1851. Republished by Birmingham Book and Magazine Company of Birmingham, Alabama, 1962. USE NSB EDITION

John Pym, Ed., *Time Out Film Guide*, 10th ed. (London: Penguin Group, 2002).

The Freedom Quilting Bee Cooperative of Alabama: An Art Education Institution by Jeri Pamela Richardson, © Jeri Pamela Richardson, 1969.Submitted in partial fulfillment of the requirements for the Doctor of Education degree in the School of Education, Indiana University, June 1969

J. Thomas Scharf, A.M., L.L.D., *History of the Confederate States Navy: From Its Organization to the Surrender of Its Last Vessel* (New York: Rogers & Sherwood; San Francisco: A. L. Bancroft and Company, 1887).

• William J. Schneider, ed. *The Jon Daniels Story With His Letters and Papers* (New York: Seabury Press, 1967).

Michael Scott, *A Time to Speak*, Doubleday and Company Inc., Garden City, New York, 1958.

Selma Project can be found on the Internet at Hathi Trust Digital Library, Selma Inter-Religious Project, Newsletter and SIP Newsletter?

Maurice Sendak, *Where the Wild Things Are* (New York: Harper & Row, 1963).

• Shattuck, Gardiner H., Jr. *Episcopalians and Race, Civil War to Civil Rights*, The University Press of Kentucky, 2000.

Robert Leslie Smith, *Gone to the Swamp: Raw Materials for the Good Life in the Mobile-Tensaw Delta*, (Tuscaloosa, AL: University of Alabama Press, 2008.)

William Benjamin Smith, *The Color Line: A Brief in Behalf of the Unborn* (New York: McClure, Phillips and Co., 1905)

Marie Stanley, *Gulf Stream* (New York: Coward-McCann, 1930).

Louis Tucker, *Clerical Errors* (New York and London: Harper and Brothers, 1943).

Vaughn, J. Barry, Bishops, Bourbons and Big Mules: A History of the Episcopal Church in Alabama, the University of Alabama Press, 2013

Francis Walter, "Integrating St. Luke's, 1954." *Keystone Newsletter of the Sewanee Trust* (Sept/Oct. 2005).

Gregory A. Waselkov, *A Conquering Spirit: Fort Mims and the Red Stick War of 1813–1814* (Tuscaloosa: The University of Alabama Press, 2006).

Julie Hedgepeth Williams. *Three Not-So-Ordinary Joes: A Plantation Newspaperman, a Printer's Devil, an English Wit, and the Founding of Southern Literature* (Montgomery: NewSouth Books, 2018).

• Willis, Jack. Documentary film, *Lay My Burden Down*. <jw33@mindspring.com> and <jwillis@linktv> (212) 877–1329, 1967. Shows the conditions Jon worked under in the Black Belt counties of Alabama.

With Fingers of Love, documentary DVD about the Freedom Quilting Bee, University of Alabama, Tuscaloosa, Alabama. Center for Public Television and Radio, University of Alabama, Box 870150, Tuscaloosa, AL 35487–0150.

Vaughn, J. Barry, *Bishops, Bourbons, and Big Mules, A History of the Episcopal Church in Alabama*, the University of Alabama Press, Tuscaloosa, Alabama, 2013.

Index

My Race to FREEDOM

"Complex portrait of a complex life ... exercised with dedication." — Bob Moses

Gwendolyn Patton's life centered around Detroit, Michigan, until she came to Montgomery in 1956 to visit relatives and found herself in the midst of the Montgomery Bus Boycott. That experience sparked a lifetime of civil rights activism, as Patton became a member of the Montgomery Improvement Association, supported the Freedom Riders, organized in Tuskegee, and participated in the Selma to Montgomery March. *My Race to Freedom* is the story of how a young woman found her voice to help her community.

Powerful, rich in compelling detail, My Race to Freedom *illuminates this essential truth: a successful civil rights movement depends on the perpetual motion of the human heart and spirit.* — KEN WOODLEY, author of *The Road to Healing*

Paperback • 384 pages • $25.95
978-1-60306-450-7

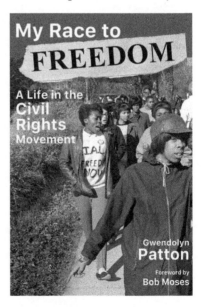

My Race to FREEDOM

A Life in the Civil Rights Movement

Gwendolyn Patton

Foreword by Bob Moses

Enjoy this book?
Follow NewSouth Books!

 facebook.com/newsouthbooks

 twitter.com/newsouthbooks

 instagram.com/newsouthbooksus

Sign up for our email newsletter to get news about our latest releases and events delivered straight to your inbox. Visit www.bit.ly/nsbinbox to sign up!